Power, Race, and Gender in Academe:
Strangers in the Tower?

Power, Race, and Gender in Academe

Strangers in the Tower?

Edited by
SHIRLEY GEOK-LIN LIM
and
MARIA HERRERA-SOBEK

Contributing Editor
GENARO PADILLA

With the assistance of Susan Y. Najita

THE MODERN LANGUAGE ASSOCIATION
NEW YORK   2000

For information about obtaining permission to reprint material from MLA
book publications, send your request by mail (see address below), e-mail
(permissions@mla.org), or fax (212 477-9863).

Library of Congress Cataloging-in-Publication Data

Power, race, and gender in academe : strangers in the tower? / edited by Shirley Geok-
lin Lim and María Herrera-Sobek ; contributing editor, Genaro Padilla, with the
assistance of Susan Y. Najita.
    p. cm.
Includes bibliographical references.
ISBN 0-87352-269-9 (cloth) — ISBN 0-87352-270-2 (paper)
    1. Minority college teachers—United States. 2. Women college teachers—United
States. 3. Minority college teachers—Selection and appointment—United States.
4. Women college teachers—Selection and appointment—United States.
5. Discrimination in higher education—United States. I. Lim, Shirley. II. Herrera-
Sobek, María. III. Padilla, Genaro M., 1949–

LC3727.P69 1999
378.1'2'089   99-044991

"Raising Standards While Lowering Anxieties: Rethinking the Promotion and Tenure
Process," by Annette Kolodny, was originally published as chapter 3 of *Failing the
Future: A Dean Looks at Higher Education in the Twenty-First Century,* copyright
1998 by Duke University Press, Box 90660, Durham, NC 27708.

Published by The Modern Language Association of America
10 Astor Place, New York, New York 10003-6981

For
Charles Bazerman
and
Erik Jason Sobek

CONTENTS

ACKNOWLEDGMENTS

We thank the members of the 1994–96 MLA Committee on the Literatures and Languages of America, especially Greg Sarris of the University of California, Los Angeles; Martha Evans and Phyllis Franklin of the MLA; and the contributors to the volume for their patience. We are also grateful to Martha Barajas, Pat Richardson, Jim Viegh, Ellen Gómez-López, Sheila Hwang, Jodi Johnson, Denise Segura, the Chicano Studies Department and the Center for Chicano Studies, the English Department, the Luis Leal Endowed Chair, and the Women's Studies Program of the University of California, Santa Barbara.

Introduction

SHIRLEY GEOK-LIN LIM AND
MARIA HERRERA-SOBEK

*P*ower, Race, and Gender in Academe: Strangers in the Tower?* began with discussions by members of the Modern Language Association's Committee on the Literatures and Languages of America at the committee's 1994 and 1995 annual meetings in the MLA's New York headquarters. Almost four decades after the civil rights movement began and two decades after the first affirmative action programs were implemented, what stories can be told about the entry of women, gays and lesbians, and people of color as faculty members and administrators into American institutions of higher education? Has there been a record of success in integrating departments of English and modern languages, as tracked through numbers and, more significantly, through the transformation of curriculum and pedagogy and administrative structures? What are the challenges, problems, proposed solutions, and transformations that face the university when faculty members from traditionally underrepresented groups enter academia? What kinds of things happen when traditional outsiders move or do not move into positions of tenure and/or administrative power? While much has been published concerning pedagogical and curricular matters in journals such as *Profession* and *College English*, relatively little attention has been paid to the social and professional pressures on women, gays and lesbians, and people of color, who are frequently assumed to accomplish the mission of multicultural education with their appointment as faculty members.

The subtitle of this volume, *Strangers in the Tower?,* plays on the ambivalences and transformations in the construction of such traditional outsiders in academe. The scholar and teacher who has been socialized through years in the profession can hardly be considered a stranger in the tower, yet the view of women and ethnic and gay minority faculty members as strangers persists even among liberal members of the Modern Language Association. The subtitle, for example, was initially suggested by a member of the MLA Publications Committee. The question mark, that interrogatory note, however, is our ironic insertion of disclaimer into this notion of the university's subaltern. The volume's weight falls on the mark of the question: Who is calling whom a stranger? Who *is* the stranger as we enter the twenty-first century? What is to be gained or lost by such processes of otherization or self-identification? What tower are we speaking of? If there are strangers, who are the tower guards and what are they doing about this presence? How do we understand strangeness or alterity in the context of pedagogy, departmental collegiality, and university administration?

The essays gathered in this collection aim to serve as a resource and teaching guide for junior faculty members as they enter the profession and for administrators and colleagues who evaluate classroom performance and service and make hiring and tenuring decisions. While many of the essays testify to individual struggles, together they offer critical analyses and historically relevant reflections on the complex ways in which institutions have responded to the challenge posed by nontraditional faculty members. When race and gender become dynamic categories that affect business as usual in the business of higher education, it is the personal voices of the nontraditional that frequently get elided but need most to be given a hearing. Many of the essays address not separate issues but the ways in which issues become entangled; thus, the three areas of institutional socialization —the classroom, the department, and university administration— can seldom be read as separate arenas and forces affecting individuals and the profession as a whole. Collectively, as a reviewer said, the essays in the volume offer "timely, important analysis" at a moment— looking back at the end of the twentieth century and forward toward the beginning of the twenty-first—of "utter importance to rethinking academic culture in response to significant demographic shifts in the teacher class."

Experience for ethnic, gay and lesbian, and women faculty members provides significant moments for theorizing structures of power. The volume opens with Johnnella E. Butler's memorable analysis of the status of contemporary higher education, "Reflections on Borderlands and the Color Line." Butler explores the concept of double consciousness, as first expounded by W. E. B. Du Bois and later developed by Gloria Anzaldúa, and offers concrete proposals for establishing a more equitable, less discriminatory university. She argues that African Americans and Chicanos/Chicanas and Latinos/Latinas have developed a double consciousness, a unique bifocal perspective on the world, acquired at the cost of the pain of racism and oppression. Even as these groups have learned to survive and to balance their distinct double identities as American and as ethnic, the end of the twentieth century has brought a backlash against affirmative action programs, anti-immigrant legislation, cuts in welfare for women and children, and so forth. To train students to think critically in a prejudice-free manner, Butler provides a set of guidelines for integrating ethnic studies and status quo programs into a restructured university curriculum.

This broad mapping is given particular conviction in four essays that address representative groups through the use of personal and autobiographical voices. The essays by John A. Williams, Cheng Lok Chua, William Penn, and Robyn Wiegman speak about and for African American, Asian American, Native American, and lesbian and gay perspectives and experiences without being limited or reduced to those representations. Williams, an author noted since the 1960s for his edgy fiction and sharp social commentary, wryly expounds in "Through the Glass Looking" on his twenty-six years of teaching creative writing in the academy. Ranging across some three decades of experiences in English departments in community colleges, colleges, and universities, his essay bears tough witness to the academy's witless, although always willful, discriminatory practices against African Americans and other minorities even after the civil rights movement's reforms initiated in the 1960s had taken place.

Cheng Lok Chua's essay, "A Stranger in the Department," traces his career as a Chinese immigrant in American higher education. In his vitae, prejudice and discriminatory practices in academia came from the Anglo Saxon establishment and also from Asian American writers and faculty members. Chua's narrative points to strategies that minority faculty members can deploy, strategies of personal excellence and collegiality, to advance professionally and to acquire a voice in the university.

William Penn's contribution, "Feathering Custer," expounds on the foundations of identity and examines the way "real" and fanta-sized identities function in political environments, both historically and as practiced in some academic departments. A creative writer, like Williams, Penn uses close readings of the images and actions of George Armstrong Custer and his opponent across the Little Big Horn, Sitting Bull, to raise questions about assimilation and resis-tance and the uses of authority. This history provides a narrative frame for recent events at Penn's home university and suggests ways that faculty members can refuse to play out fantasies of power or identity. According to Penn, his essay, different in style and method from the other essays in the volume, proceeds from his interest in what he calls "narrative essay — telling the story of ideas in ways that are imaginative and linguistically interesting . . . as good fiction or creative nonfiction" (letter to the editors).

Finally, in this grouping, Robyn Wiegman's essay offers a critical rereading of the "family" as the dominant social structure through which English departments regularize their relationships with faculty members. Her unpacking of such departmental rhetoric forcefully in-dicts the collapse of public and private spheres and the heterosexism implicit in such socialization, and it inserts a queer perspective to in-terrogate the narratives that produce and perpetuate "historical priv-ileges." A powerful critique of the normative heterosexuality that she argues goes to the heart of departmental practices and the everyday protocols of institutional life, her essay compels us to examine the asymmetry that structures power to the disadvantage of the queer faculty member whose position in the university is always already constrained by the marriage trope.

The second half of the volume focuses on the institutional rami-fications for the entry of nontraditional and diverse teaching pro-fessionals into the university. Annette Kolodny's essay, "Raising Standards While Lowering Anxieties: Rethinking the Promotion and Tenure Process," zeros in on the obstacles women and minorities face in climbing the tenure and promotion ladder at United States colleges and universities. Providing statistical information regarding the hir-ing of women PhD candidates at universities—the figures in the 1990s are consistently low—Kolodny addresses the issues that keep women from being hired and advancing in the professorial ranks. She points to such factors as unfamiliar research areas, hidden workloads, lack of access to informal male networks, differential standards, and inappropriate statements by external referees. An influential senior faculty member at the University of Arizona, Tucson, Kolodny demonstrates how a university can both raise standards and make its structures congruent with social justice. These changes are offered in the appendix, "College of Humanities Promotion and Tenure Procedures."

In "Minority Hiring in the Age of Downsizing" Carrie Tirado Bramen uses statistics and empirical studies to refute the perception that some white male academics have about minority hiring. Fear that white men are not being hired because the jobs are granted to minorities is clearly not warranted, as demonstrated by the very small number of African Americans, Chicanos/Chicanas and Latinos/Latinas, Native Americans, and Asian Americans hired in most departments. Bramen points out that the real culprit in the loss of jobs is not the scapegoated minority PhD but the general downsizing of campuses across the nation.

Such institutional stresses also appear in that first site of debate and controversy, the classroom. Two essays narrate the specific struggles of women of color, as faculty members and graduate teaching assistants, to have their professional status legitimated. Turning to the classroom as a central location for struggle, Susana Chávez Silverman risks the autobiographical voice to anchor her essay, "Tropicalizing the Liberal Arts College Classroom." She describes her experience as an untenured, biracial, female faculty member at Pomona College, a prestigious West Coast liberal arts college. Interweaving the personal and the theoretical—and taking her cue from such theorists as Henry Giroux and Nancy K. Miller—she addresses the vexed issues of power, gender, sexuality, and race in the classroom. Engaging current discourses of feminist, queer, and "multiculti" pedagogy, she critiques the elisions and essentialisms and the spaces for positive change that postmodern, radical pedagogical praxes suggest in order to carve out her own space for a hybrid "tropical pedagogy" in today's academy.

Sheila Minn Hwang centers her essay, "At the Limits of My Feminism: Race, Gender, Class, and the Execution of a Feminist Pedagogy," on the problems minority teaching assistants face when students and other faculty members typecast and stereotype them vis-à-vis discipline and teaching proficiency. The female teaching assistant of color lacks the raced and gendered identity that confers authority and knowledge on white male professors. The female person of color continually has to prove her authority to teach a particular topic. Hwang recounts the challenges to her position as a teaching assistant and a woman of color in the classroom. These challenges place constraints on her ambition to implement a more radical style of teaching — a feminist pedagogy — and force her to fall back on more traditional styles to retain a modicum of authority.

The last two essays offer case studies in which new teaching professionals actively negotiate through a maze of historically embedded institutional structures that challenge and frustrate even as they appear to welcome new contributions. In "Now That They Have Us, What's the Point? The Challenge of Hiring to Create Diversity," Sandra Gunning explores the working relationships and problems that follow once women and minority professors are hired. Gunning underlines issues related to sexual harassment, work overload, mentoring of students, and other areas not addressed by departments eager to hire women and persons of color. Marginalization and alienation of junior faculty members are two possible outcomes of hiring a diversified faculty without thinking through and developing policies that effectively incorporate the new faculty members.

Drawing from an analysis of colonial educational structures still visible at the University of Hawai'i, Manoa, Ruth Y. Hsu offers a vision for a more equitable distribution of resources. In " 'Where's Oz, Toto?': Idealism and the Politics of Gender and Race in Academe," Hsu argues that all knowledge has a political dimension, and she debunks as myth the concept of liberal idealism often thought to characterize the operations of the university. While Hsu notes the scarcity of women and minorities in academia at large, and at the University of Hawai'i in particular, she argues that numbers alone will not radically change a hierarchical structure that promotes and nurtures the colonial status quo institutionalized a century ago. Rates of tenure and promotion are low for women and minorities, and scholarship and theoretical paradigms used and conceptualized by women and minorities are devalued by evaluators. Her economics-based analysis of academe illuminates and critiques many of the operations that have often been obscured as business as usual.

Together these eleven essays, reflecting on individual African

American, Chicano/Chicana, Asian American, Native American, gay and lesbian, and white female histories in academe, cover diverse tracks in the profession, from creative writing and journalism to ethnic American, Caribbean postcolonial, and eighteenth-century literary studies; diverse levels of professionalization, from graduate student teaching assistant to junior faculty members, to tenured senior professors, and distinguished professor; and diverse activities in the profession, from beginning teacher to curriculum coordinator, department chair, and division dean. Despite such diversity, the struggles of underrepresented faculty members in the post–civil rights era —their hopes, fears, successes, failures—can be said to augur a shape for the transformed twenty-first-century university in the United States. Arguably, the achievement of such faculty members is to contribute to the rise of the American university, an academe that has abandoned the ipso facto segregated contours of the male and white dominant German model for the democratic vistas of the multicultural university.

Reflections
on Borderlands
and the Color Line

JOHNNELLA E. BUTLER

> Racism in America is much more complex than either the con-
> scious conspiracy of a power elite or the simple delusion of a
> few ignorant bigots. It is part of our culture. It arises from the
> assumptions we have learned to make about the world, our-
> selves, and others as well as from the patterns of our fundamen-
> tal social activities.
>
> — Charles Lawrence

The problem of the twenty-first century will not be the problem of the color line but, rather, the problem of the persistence of the color line in the borderlands.[1] We have evolved in our social dynam-ics to transnational, transcultural, transracial, and transethnic spaces—spaces that some of us naively welcome, many of us find threatening, others resist and deny, and a few find challenging. In the United States, at the end of the twentieth century, we acknowledge the massive demographic shifts that will make our nation visibly mixed race, multiethnic, and multiracial. Simultaneously, we ques-tion the racial designations and identities that have driven and shaped our legal system, our folkways, our educational content and structure, our economy, and our social and cultural mores. The courts and a silently supportive public reinforce demands and legal argu-ments for gender *equity* while distorting affirmative action—which provided the precedents for gender equity— to racial *preference*.

Higher education has had and still has the opportunity to influence elementary, secondary, and postsecondary education, public policy, and inter- and intraracial relations toward the goal of an equitable and just society. But being *of* the national culture, it reflects much the same historical ambivalence toward democracy and equity that the nation has exhibited. The "culture wars"; the emergence of battles within ethnic studies and efforts to support or destroy racial- or ethnic-specific and comparative ethnic studies; the success of and conflicts within women's studies; efforts toward multicultural American studies; debates over interdisciplinary studies; and the ambivalent support of the humanities, an area of study that holds the potential for our greater understanding of and identification with one another—all evidence the possibility of crossing "fixed" boundaries in higher education. Such border crossings and conflicts have vast societal implications.

The boundaries of such borderlands simultaneously shift, become entrenched, disappear, are newly constituted, become fragmented, are reenvisioned. Borderlands are contested areas, contested not just by the larger population that controls the boundaries but also by those who have been restricted by the borders and who, themselves, often reinforce and even reproduce those boundaries within the restrictive borders with, for example, anti-equity legislation and color, class, and gender hierarchies. The boundaries of the color line in the United States have shifted. Yet racism remains, and binaries that reinforce difference negatively regenerate modernity's fragmentation with the postmodern's replicative solution of the both-and binary. We do not know how *not* to reproduce boundaries; we do not know how we can, in the borderlands of our diversities, both negotiate and recognize differences to reveal samenesses and studied cooperation. Moreover, a certain moral bankruptcy clouds — and even renders unnecessary — the democratic goal of social equity and justice. In a recent *San Diego Union-Tribune* syndicated opinion column, the African American conservative Glenn C. Loury laments that when he "suggested to a gathering of conservatives that their seeming hostility to every social program smacked of indifference to the poor, [he] was told that a surgeon could not properly be said to have no concern for a terminally ill patient simply because [the surgeon] had moved on to the next case." As Loury points out, "The analogy alone speaks volumes."

I have conducted over seventy-five faculty development work-shops and have either directed or codirected ten major grant-funded faculty development projects during the past seventeen years. These curriculum transformation projects, based on the content of ethnic studies and women's studies, focused on incorporating into core cur-ricula and humanities and social science curricula material on men and women of color. These workshops, projects, and related consul-tancies are part of the work of a number of scholars, largely from the field of women's studies, who have actively related our scholarship in the humanities and social sciences to curricular, pedagogical, and in-stitutional change.[2] This essay distills the praxis behind my experi-ences and work in curriculum transformation, as a woman of color, and reflects on the location of such work in higher education and in our national move to a borderlands mentality. I intend to provide in-sight into contexts and dynamics that men and women of color must engage when they decide to intervene in the structure and content of the academy. In addition, I hope to provide for readers who are in decision-making positions a sense of the urgency with which they must make viable that which is possible. My approach is personal, practical, and theoretical, for I have always either intuitively or deliberately un-derstood the interaction of these three aspects of our professional lives as teachers, scholars, and administrators in higher education.

"As If" the West and the Academy Are Mine and of Me Also

Although my life experiences and my studies have demonstrated to me time and time again the harsh truth of the epigraph to this essay, I have lived *as if* the repetitive and deeply rooted intractability of racism were not so. In fact, I think most African Americans live by this *as ifness* to lesser or greater degrees (Kent 53).[3] The source of persistence and stability, this as ifness is what propelled slaves to rebel and "fly back to Africa," and it is what haunted their betrayers; it prompted other slaves at the first hearing of emancipation to drop whatever they were doing and seek their lives in freedom. That same as ifness has allowed me, over the past twenty years, to work through faculty development and curriculum transformation, to help meet the closest approximation of the truth in our teaching and scholarship in higher education. The stakes are high: either the fulfillment of our nation's democratic ideals for equity and social justice or the institutionalization of an increasingly individualistic and materialistic nation, divided against itself by the cultural, political, and economic capital of racism, ethnocentrism, sexism, and classism.

The scholarship, teaching, and discourse of ethnic studies, women's studies, American studies, cultural studies, and what is sometimes called the multicultural movement have, over the past thirty years, given scholarly voice and room for debate and analysis of the results of our nation's "dream deferred," our continuous avoidance of addressing the conflict between our democratic ideals and our actions. This dilemma, for which the life of Thomas Jefferson stands as a trope, was presaged by Alexis de Tocqueville and defined by Gunnar Myrdal and many others of more or less radical perspective. These debates and analyses can be heartening, particularly if one views them with a certain as ifness. Nonetheless, the contradictions inherent in such a perspective are readily apparent. While many steadily continue to revise syllabi to transform the ways we conceptualize texts, traditions, theories, policies, histories, scientific research, legal study and practice and while we seek "service learning" opportunities, internships, and job opportunities for our students, the increasingly diverse population that many of us entered the profession to teach is dwindling. At the exact time we are preparing for the enormous demographic shifts in higher education and seeking ever better ways to help bring about ways of thinking and acting in the world with responsibility to one another, an understanding of the past and its legacies, and an optimistic, cooperative, and relational pluralism, the door of opportunity to higher education is narrowing by the dismantling of affirmative action.

Just when the humanities appeared to be revitalized by its extension beyond the imposed mainstream and its traditional Western, Anglo limits, Patrick Buchanan's call to "take back our culture" and the government's recommitment to "the tyranny of the majority" through its repudiation of Lani Guinier, among other actions, created an atmosphere in which scholars could declare that the past has no useful function to the present and equate deracination with a universal whiteness.[4] The homeless line the streets; young African American and Latino men fill our prisons; white militia members bomb public buildings; the government considers the possibility that a missing bomber that flew out of formation on a training mission might have been stolen; Native Americans, still on reservations, struggle against dire poverty with casinos; Asian Americans live the stereotyped spectrum from model minority to gang members. "Ethnicity" has become "postethnic" in its erasure of the recent past and the very much vibrant presence of racism and classism, a move reflected in the university classroom when we equate ethnocentric scholarship with a "lack of sensitivity" or teach scholarship by and about "minorities" as an addendum giving voice to the shrill and discontent. And I do not hear, in various voices and ways, that "the West is all of us" but, rather, "What's wrong with the West?!"—the same exasperated cry I heard from a faculty member in a workshop fifteen years ago when I was discussing ways to teach Kingston's *Woman Warrior* and reconceptualize our American literary tradition rather than simply add to it.

Western civilization and higher education are *mine* and *of me*. As a full professor at a large research university, as one of the first generation of African Americans to teach in overwhelmingly white colleges and universities, I and my other colleagues of color, despite our achievements, must still demand "to sing America."

My "Self"-Engagement with the "Other"

This academic year, 1998–99, is my twenty-ninth year teaching. How I have spent that time and how I intend to utilize the remainder of my time in academia have been shaped by ancestry, family, education, political events, and personal experiences that forced me to evaluate whether the choices I had made, or was about to make, could assist in lifting the burden of race from myself and those around me. A tall order, some might think. A tall order, I agree; it is one no child should either desire or have to shoulder and one with which no adult should have to contend all of her life. However, growing up as an African American child from an aspiring, lower-middle-class family, I observed my parents as they fought against the lie of "separate but equal" in the Virginia schools and as they sought to protect my sister and me from the inequities and brutalities of segregation. During the 1950s and 1960s, their example, combined with the hope of the civil rights movement, inspired in me an updated version of the late-nineteenth- and early-twentieth-century call to arms "for the uplift of the race." Responsibility for using my talents, opportunity, and position motivated me and others like me, as it had many before us.

My maternal grandparents and grandaunts and granduncles had demonstrated the kind of potential that dedication to education, family, and racial uplift could unleash for Negroes. My grandfather, Alfred Edward Spencer, Jr., graduated from Virginia State College for Negroes in 1899; his two sisters, Catherine and Justina, graduated a few years later. My grandmother, James Ella Spencer, graduated from normal school, the Piedmont Christian Institute. These brothers and sisters, children of slaves, owned businesses, worked for the railroad, distinguished themselves in World War I, worked as domestics and farmers. Grandpa Spencer taught school, served as a principal, helped establish a library for Negroes in Roanoke, and organized against the Klan. Aunts Justina and Catherine founded the first elementary school for Negroes in Henry County, Virginia, and Granny Spencer opened the first kindergarten in the state of Virginia. My paternal grandparents and grandaunts and granduncles struggled as farmers, sharecroppers, domestics, and taxi drivers to send their children to school. Life in the North and the possibility of education and better lives spurred them on from land around the Maryland plantations on which their slave parents had worked. Grandpa Thomas Nelson Butler owned his hack stand and frequently chauffeured Marcus Garvey. Granny Ethel Elizabeth Butler, cousins, and aunts scrubbed floors to send my father to parochial school and to college. On both sides, God, Lincoln, and race leaders like Booker T. Washington, W. E. B. Du Bois, Marcus Garvey, and Mary Bethune inspired the promise of democracy.

Stories from my family's past, along with a hopeful present, engendered in me similar determination and hope in the promise of democracy: my mother's stories of Hampton Institute, where she notated spirituals, accompanied the celebrated tenor Roland Hayes during a visit, and heeded Grandpa's advice to prepare for the limits of racism by preparing to teach although she was a gifted performance musician; her loving and fierce dedication to teaching young Negro pupils in one-room mountain schools, her struggles as the first black teacher hired to teach at a white school in Alexandria, Virginia; my father's joyous basketball coaching, his excelling at golf in a segregated America with no place to contend; his teaching of chemistry and physics because research companies offered him custodian positions despite his training; his becoming an assistant superintendent of the Alexandria City Public Schools and an architect and nurturer of Alexandria's desegregation and integration plans.

So I grew up knowing and loving my parents, my family, and their worlds. I also grew up in a city where a bronze Civil War soldier faced south at a major intersection and where Confederate flags blew in the breeze at the bus transfer stop where my white Catholic-school classmates and I changed buses to go home to their newly integrated neighborhood. I understood very early the ways histories silence and how these distorted histories serve the perpetuation of injustices that destroy bodies and threaten souls. I saw my "self" as strong and focused, but I was always experiencing situations and attitudes that sought to project an "other" onto me that was hardly like me or other young "colored" girls and boys. My black "self" confronted the white "other" in the segregated schools of my childhood and the integrated schools of my young adulthood; by being "the first Negro student," "the only Negro student"; by studying Latin, playing Mozart and Beethoven sonatas, and reciting Paul Lawrence Dunbar; by inviting to speak, when I was the student council president at Saint Mary's Academy, a lawyer from the United States legal team for the Nuremberg trials; by rallying to the inspiration of Marion Anderson, John Kennedy, Martin Luther King, Hubert Humphrey, Malcolm X, and liberation theology; by being the first Negro lead soprano in a Baltimore Gilbert and Sullivan company, developing my coloratura soprano in the beautiful and vicious world of professional classical music; by seeking a place that would allow, and finding mentors who would support, the study of African American literature. All these things developed in me, at an early age, an acute awareness of the fact that for United States culture to realize the dreams of my slave great-grandparents, my grandparents and parents who believed in the democratic ideal and struggled for the "uplift of the race," the white perception and dominance of blacks had to change. Much of that change, I later observed, pivoted first on making explicit the black perception of whites, with its inherent critique of the failure of the American dream, and second on re-visioning the story of America to include the beautiful and the ugly for the sake of accuracy, equity, and justice.

Seeing the White "Other" through the Black "Self"

My dissertation explored the relations among Paulo Freire's analyses of oppression and his goal of conscientization, the African American struggle for freedom and its literary expressions, and pedagogy and literary theory (Freire 19).[5] The ways in which miseducation, segregation, racism, and classism affected both African Americans and Euro-Americans continually surfaced as I taught African American literature and studies and examined African American history and intellectual thought. Involvement in the nascent women's studies movement spurred me to seek ways for African American women's experience to be defined in the context of both black women's and African American history. Inspired by the black arts movement, I sought to find ways in the academy for the African American experience to be defined through the eyes and lives of those who experienced it and for that history to become incorporated in the economic, social, literary, political, and historical discourse of the academy. Thus African American history, literature and other arts, sociology, politics and economics had to both stand alone as scholarly and teaching pursuits and work comparatively as significant parts of the comparative studies of the racial and ethnic diversity of the United States. The "mainstream" had to be seen for what it was: dominant Anglo-American ethnicity subscribed to and transformed by other white ethnicities who could and did assimilate to power and privilege.

The teacher, the student, and the classroom were obviously the primary entities in the academy where some change could be effected. But what kind of change, and to what end? And how could my talents help? It seemed to me then, twenty-some years ago, that the change needed was simple—and in hindsight deceptively so. Higher education should convey in teaching and scholarship, seek in learning, and encourage in environment *the closest approximation of the truth, a soul-liberating accuracy.* This truth is equated with the accuracy and perceptions gained from engaging consciously and actively the complexities and contradictions of our very finite and human selves and stories. Such a change, I thought, would not be easy but would certainly be welcomed by colleagues and students of all hues and backgrounds. Morality in race relations and fulfillment of the democratic ideal, I thought, would most certainly be embraced by most Americans, if they only knew all the stories, studied the ways their themes conflicted, overlapped, and paralleled. Furthermore, I expected that the academic world would eagerly want to pursue what was simply honest scholarship and better teaching for all its students.

Several colleagues in black studies, women's studies, and American studies shared with me a similar view. One colleague in particular,

Margo Culley of the University of Massachusetts, shared my sense of the importance of joining pedagogy and content and the humanities and social sciences when teaching about the intersections of race and gender in the evolution of cultures and societies and especially when studying and teaching about the experiences of black and white women. From our collaboration in the late 1970s came my first major grant-funded project, "Black Studies/Women's Studies: An Overdue Partnership." Sixteen faculty members from the five-college consortium in the Pioneer Valley of Massachusetts met for two years, examining the structure of knowledge about black women and the intersection of race and gender in black studies and women's studies. Through our codirecting and through the interdisciplinary and intercampus collaboration, Margo and I saw ourselves as modeling the coalescing and cooperation necessary to give an academic voice to discounted, distorted, or obscured stories that were the keys to a full understanding and living of America's promise. The project culminated in the institution of sixteen substantially revised courses at the five participating schools and a conference that facilitated discussion of pedagogy, content, and institutional change among five hundred faculty members from New England (Butler, "Complicating" 73).

In that project, black male and female faculty members took white women's studies seriously, and white women faculty members began to reevaluate their assumptions about bonding through gender. Black women faculty members challenged male-centered black studies methodology and interpretation. Black male and female faculty members articulated and struggled through differences over the importance of gender. White women began to move away from the insistence on the primacy of gender. All of us began to conceptualize the interconnectedness among race, class, gender, ethnicity, age, sexual identity, and religion. Our notions and formulations of women's studies and black studies changed fundamentally as we studied black women's history and listened to their voices. Faculty members accepted the challenge of rethinking the student-teacher relationship and the reliance solely on the lecture format and of relinquishing sole authority to the role of the informed facilitator who learns with her or his students. Most significant, faculty members struggled with perceptions of one another. And most difficult, I recall, was the white faculty members' acceptance of the black faculty members' perceptions of them and of the critiques of "mainstream" history, literature, politics, and economics that emerged when we interrogated interrelationships between black history and white history.

My childhood and young adulthood had prepared me well. My self-confidence and sense of history helped me to continue, through teaching and faculty development, the self-assertion characteristic of African Americans throughout our history, an assertion that challenged the imposition of "otherness." Now, many students, courses, and faculty development projects later, I reflect on the difficulty of what those of us took to be our major academic work—curriculum transformation. I also now know why my father often smiled at me, saying, "I'm glad that God takes care of babies and Johnnella."

Disrupting the "Self-Other" Dichotomy

In a recent review of *Thirteen Ways of Looking at a Black Man*, by Henry Louis Gates, Jr., the reviewer states the central theme as "a variation on the one that Ralph Ellison addressed in *Invisible Man*: how does race heighten the perennial American question of self-definition; how does it, in effect, color both white perceptions of blacks, and black perceptions of self?" (Kakutani). The statement struck me in its omission of black perceptions of whites as part of America's self-definition. That commonplace omission and the omission of the Asian American, the Native American, the Chicano/Chicana, and the Latino/Latina perceptions might be termed the *Europeanist presence*, an analogy to Toni Morrison's *Africanist presence* (6-7). This presence is apparent in *Invisible Man* and in all black literature, explicitly or implicitly. Because it is ostensibly politically powerless, scholars and other Americans dismiss this presence that was honed through experience and positionality. Moreover, there is, in our national and societal cultures, an excessive, distorting concern with the blacks' perception of self, to the exclusion of whites' self-perception and the role of blacks' perceptions of whites.[6] It is a curious concern that turns white perception of black history, psychology, and expression into cultural capital either as entertainment or deviance and allows little room for black-initiated assertions based on a positive sense of self. Thus, rarely have whites had to concern themselves with the perceptions blacks have of them, and blacks have understandably—and perhaps wisely—reserved their perceptions of whites for the privacy of their homes, in the humorous obscurity of cultural in-jokes, signifying toasts, and folktales, or in the banter of intraracial friendship.

White hegemony over the racial and postcolonial discourse manifests the privilege of definition enjoyed by whites. In the early 1970s, when scholars in critical pedagogy and early feminist critical thought spoke of the self-other dichotomy, the "self" was the subject struggling for agency that the dominant "other" sought to objectify. In Freirean terms, the self-other dichotomy might be represented as the "self" comprehending the significance of the difference between the "self's" casa and the "other's" hacienda. In Du Boisian terms, the African American's "twoness—an American, a Negro; two souls, two thoughts, two unreconciled strivings"—functioned as "two warring ideals in one dark body, whose dogged strength alone keeps it from being torn asunder." As Du Bois explains, "The history of the American Negro is the history of this strife—this longing to attain self-conscious manhood, to merge his double self into a better and truer self" (365).

Du Bois sought the disruption of the self-other dichotomy through *merging* of the two. Inherent to this merging is the goal of shared power and cultural exchange of the best of traditions. The Du Boisian struggle is for the "self," the Africa who has much to teach the world, to merge with the "other," the America who has much to teach Africa. The African American self-other discourse, closely related to the Freirean discourse of conscientization, has been lost in postcolonial discourses in which the self and other are differently positioned, given different histories and historical moments of analysis, with focus on the colonial and former colonial in relation to the colonialist. Thus the other becomes the objectified colonial self, and the self becomes the agentive, objectifying colonialist.[7] From the African American situation of quasi-domestic colonialism, this inversion suggests the complete internalization of the dominant other. The self, once struggling for agency against a dominant other, accepts the position of other to the now dominant, colonialist self, and disruption becomes highly improbable. The interaction of the Du Boisian merging process is disallowed by the stated paradigmatic binary of self as the definer and other as the defined. Thus the term *hybridity* assumes currency in describing a dichotomous existence, suggestive of ambiguity and ambivalence rather than a productive, generative contradiction. Assertion against the defining self becomes extremely difficult as the other sees himself or herself first and foremost in terms of the now dominant self who defines that which constitutes the colonial or, in specifically United States terms, the African American, as inconsequential—the offspring of an irrelevant past and a misguided persistence for the importance of race.

In my work in curriculum transformation and faculty development over the past twenty-eight years, I have sought both to disrupt and to reveal and utilize the generative tensions of the Du Boisian–Freirean binary as it appears in scholarship, teaching, and institutional structure. Through the disruption and analysis, the limitations of the melting pot as well as the limitations of its ideological expression in much of our canonical scholarship and teaching become apparent. Conversations about representation and identity emerge as desired and necessary in understanding just who and what constitutes "America" and "American." In so doing, however, I assume the interrogation of the American white other as well as the African American, Asian American, Native American, Chicano/Chicana and Latino/Latina self as it is shaped by the cultural imperatives of assimilation, integration, and domestic colonialism. Thus my faculty development seminars increasingly engaged the Euro-American in its manifestations as self and as other. These manifestations include, but are not limited to, the development of Euro-American ethnic histories, arts, and identities, their definitions of whiteness based in Anglo-American perceptions, their embracing of whiteness (e.g., Irish), or their ambivalences toward whiteness (e.g., Jewish). The overarching question immediately surfaced: Who and what is an American? Accompanying that question were questions about the coerciveness of assimilation and the divisiveness of cultural pluralism as understood in the binary context. Most important, participants began to discuss ways of striving toward the realization of the democratic ideal of social justice and equity and to discuss the relationship of that goal to how we teach and what we teach, what we read and how we theorize. Then an even more encompassing question emerged: How do we disrupt the binaries that prevent racial or ethnic Americans from merging in a way that reflects their inclusion in a society that accepts change and difference as it evolves democratically rather than one that demands assimilation to rigid ways of being? Moreover, behind all this is the question of whether our sense of the "common good" and "civic culture" can expand to accommodate a constant and structurally encouraged exchange among classes, races, sexual identities, and religions.

Moving from the Color Line to Borderlands

Gloria Anzaldúa's *mestiza consciousness* for the Latina is analogous to the merger of consciousness that Du Bois proposed in 1903 to solve the contradictions of African American double consciousness. It is instructive that a Chicana feminist scholar, at the dawn of the twenty-first century, arrives at a construct from the Chicana-Latina experience in the United States that is strikingly similar to that of an African American male scholar at the turn of the twentieth century. Both derive from experiences with a racism and an ethnocentrism centered in the exaggerated individualism at the expense of community and the materialism of the worst of the American dream. Both Anzaldúa and Du Bois are of groups that, as pariahs, experience the worst of the American dream. Anzaldúa addresses in her concept of mestiza consciousness the mixed racial and cultural heritage of the Chicana; Du Bois's merging of the warring ideals addresses the mixed racial and cultural heritage of the African American, fraught with the ambiguities of the significances of the African heritage and the American heritages.

Du Bois

[T]he Negro is a sort of seventh son, born with a veil, and gifted with second-sight in this American world,—a world which yields him no true self-consciousness, but only lets him see himself through the revelation of the other world. It is a peculiar sensation, this double-consciousness, this sense of always looking at one's self through the eyes of others, of measuring one's soul by the tape of the world that looks on in amused contempt and pity. One ever feels his twoness—an American, a Negro; two souls, two thoughts, two unreconciled strivings; two warring ideals in one dark body, whose dogged strength alone keeps it from being torn asunder. (364–65)

Anzaldúa

[L]a mestiza is a product of the transfer of the cultural and spiritual values of one group to another. Being tricultural, monolingual, bilingual or multilingual, speaking a patois, and in a state of perpetual transition, the *mestiza* faces the dilemma of the mixed breed: which collectivity does the daughter of a darkskinned mother listen to?

*El choque de un alma atrapado entre el mundo del espíritu
y el mundo de la ténica a veces la deja entullada.* Cradled in
one culture, sandwiched between two cultures, straddling all
three cultures and their value systems, *la mestiza* undergoes a
struggle of flesh, a struggle of borders, an inner war. Like all people, we perceive the version of reality that our culture communi-
cates. Like others having or living in more than one culture, we
get multiple, often opposing messages. The coming together of
two self-consistent but habitually incompatible frames of reference causes *un choque*, a cultural collision. (78)

Du Bois

[T]he history of the American Negro is the history of this strife,
—this longing to attain self-consciousness manhood, *to merge
his double self into a better and truer self.* In this merging he
wishes neither of the older selves to be lost. He would not
Africanize America, for America has too much to teach the
world and Africa. He would not bleach his Negro soul in a flood
of White Americanism, for he knows that Negro blood has a message for the world. He simply wishes to make it possible for a
man to be both a Negro and an American, without being cursed
and spit upon by his fellows, without having the doors of Opportunity closed roughly in the face. (365; my emphasis)

Anzaldúa

The new *mestiza* copes by developing a tolerance for contradictions, a tolerance for ambiguity. She learns to be an Indian in
Mexican culture, to be Mexican from an Anglo point of view. She
learns to juggle cultures. She has a plural personality, she operates in a pluralistic mode—nothing is thrust out, the good, the
bad, the ugly, nothing rejected, nothing abandoned. Not only
does she sustain contradictions, she turns the ambivalence into
something else. (79)

Mestiza consciousness extended beyond the Chicana experience
becomes a consciousness that has as its goal the disruption and dis-
solution of the self-other oppressive binary, applied to both whites
and people of color in the United States. It becomes akin to Freire's
conscientizacaõ. Similarly, in 1971, Vernon Dixon and Badi Foster

argued for a diunital logic, one that allows a unity of opposites. Charles A. Frye proposed a philosophy of black studies based on a nonhierarchical, nondichotomous worldview that addressed the disruption of the self-other binary. In a related study, *Black Studies: Pedagogy and Revolution*, I examined the African American literary aesthetic in its context of the self-other dichotomy and proposed a pedagogy aimed at dissolving that dichotomy and its ambivalences. The both-and approach I describe in that work is not the binary replicating both-and of postmodernism, neither is it exclusive of the dialectical. Rather, it

> allows for both synthesis and unification for both the dialectical and diunital approaches, [and] corresponds to Freire's world view in that dialogue explores the opposite word and allows for generative themes to evolve and be explored, bounced off one another, and evolved into transformations of reality with the points of unity and diversity ever increasing and decreasing, expanding or diminishing at various points in time[. . .].
>
> Thus, the essential components for the decolonization of the Afro-American lie for the most part within Afro-American heritage in what is called the folk tradition, in the warring ideals, and in the both/and, dialectical and diunital world view in its transformations from the African to the Afro-American. The duality of the African American by virtue of the proposed pedagogy would not be dissolved but both synthesized and unified through the fusion of feeling and intellect (comprehension) in a whole consisting of distinct parts interacting simultaneously in a dialectical and diunital fashion to create generative themes. (101)

Codirecting three intense summer institutes from 1992 to 1995, I had the major responsibility for the faculty curriculum, the goal of which was to incorporate content on United States people of color into multidisciplinary core curricula. With an experienced faculty drawn from across the country, we had the opportunity to work together in defining the comparative themes and dimensions of African American, Asian American, Native American, Chicano/Chicana, Latino/Latina history, literature, and politics. Double consciousness and ambivalence emerged immediately as one of the key comparative themes, and we examined the different and similar ways that Americans of color and white Americans have experienced and responded to assimilation and Americanization; internalization of the "other" connected to race and ethnicity; and the development of personal and community identities, and historical (Du Bois's double consciousness) and contemporary (Anzaldúa's borderlands and mestiza consciousness) metaphors. The struggle with the dominating "other" within people of color and the function of skin privilege in disrupting the binary in assimilation for Euro-Americans led to the following questions: What is an American? What are new frameworks for community identity? How can the larger narrative for an inclusive civic culture and democracy be forged? Ronald Takaki's *A Different Mirror* provided a historiographical model for us the second year. It became clear to me and my colleagues over those three summers, as we juxtaposed the "stories" of American ethnic and racial groups, that rather than a "meat grinder" history, we had a history that allows for *African, Asian, Chicano/Chicana, Latino/Latina, Italian, Jewish,* and *Irish* to be adjectival modifers of *American,* descriptive rather than definitive of a past and an evolving present.

The question, then, that ethnic studies and women's studies foreground—perhaps subliminally and at times contradictorily—and that curriculum transformation also foregrounds is as follows: How do we encourage an American consciousness encompassing a cooperative, relational pluralism that connects, matrixlike, these merged entities with a mestiza consciousness to result in the American, the United States citizen, the America that Tocqueville projected, without the "tyranny of the majority" and binary individualism at the expense of community? This question challenges higher education to create curricula that expose students to ways of perceiving the relationships between and among people, our pasts, our pasts' legacies, our present lives and struggles, our environments, disciplines, and texts. It is a question that challenges us with further questions: How do we shape policies to encourage the best in human beings? How do we utilize scientific discovery and progress and technological advancement to the benefit of all human beings and our environment? How do we use our positions of learning and academic privilege to help the greatest number of students become human beings who care about one another and their environment? How can we reveal the unity in diversity, the sameness in difference, and how can we engage long-term intractable differences and conflicts in ways productive to humans and not necessarily with the goal of winning and defeating? How can we live together with different moral positions without hatred, violence, or imposition and without permissiveness and amorality? How can we begin to understand that my freedom ends where your denial of freedom begins? Can we reconcile individualism with community and individual needs and desires with community needs and desires?

Living in the Borderlands While the Color Line Persists

The problem of the twenty-first century will be the persistence of the problem of the color line in the borderlands. In 1970, when I eagerly inquired at Howard University about doctoral studies in African American literature and criticism, the chair very protectively (she knew my father) and simultaneously informed, advised, and admonished me that while I would be accepted to study there, she would not allow me to study black literature. "Do something useful," she urged me, "like Victorian literature." A few years later, faculty members at the University of Massachusetts gave me a similar message, making it clear that even studying exclusively American literature and criticism was not a welcome idea. While the two responses at the time did not seem much different from each other, in retrospect (and after meeting the Howard chair many years later when I presented a Mellon lecture at Howard on black women writers) they are miles apart. The Howard response I view as a pragmatic one institutionally and a protective one personally. The University of Massachusetts response simply echoed that of the literary field and of higher education: you are welcome if you do not bring your part of American culture with you. Thanks to the distinguished scholar Sidney Kaplan, I managed to study African American literature and the relations between theory and pedagogy at the University of Massachusetts through the school of education, the only place there I could pursue an interdisciplinary degree. I was ecstatic, for I could also develop my burgeoning interest in Asian American and Latino literatures. I am still inspired by the memory of Dr. Kaplan encouraging me that I could find my way, teaching at Smith and studying at the University of Massachusetts. I see now that I was moving into borderlands in a world that fiercely held to the color line.

Derrick Bell, in the prologue to *Gospel Choirs*, the last book of his trilogy, astutely recognizes that it is no accident that African American students often form gospel choirs on overwhelmingly white campuses. While I studied toward my doctorate, taught, and achieved tenure, I sang. I sang Mozart, Falla, Granados, Rodríguez, and lieder, but I felt most compelled to sing and speak about African American spirituals. So I developed two lecture-recitals that toured New England, "The African American Spiritual: The Divine Encounter with Historical Reality" (borrowing from James Cone) and "Black-Eyed Susans in Song: Music by Black Women Composers," cueing off Mary Helen Washington's anthology. Cone and others advanced the concept of black liberation theology that explained to me intellectually why the spirituals slaves sang throughout 250 years encouraged them to seize their freedom when emancipation came, despite the gross fears and uncertainties about the future. Washington's early anthologies (e.g., *Midnight Birds*) reminded me of the as ifness in black women's expressions—the way Zora Neale Hurston and Nella Larsen wrote as if their writing would be accepted and understood; the way Margaret Bond and Undine Moore composed music as if their works would be performed widely. The student gospel choirs energize, as my recitals did for me, the need to recognize simultaneously both the permanence of racism and the steady steps toward the eradication of its severe effects.

Bell's narrator, in a discussion with his spirit-guide, Geneva, spells out the power akin to as ifness in a world where borders collapse and are crossed while racism remains permanent:

> "But Geneva," I protested, "even if blacks achieve a new togetherness through gender equality, nothing in the annals of this country justifies a prediction that our efforts will alter the destructive course of a nation where, as W. E. B. Du Bois observed, the real allegiance is to reducing all the nation's resources to dusky dollars. In pursuit of that goal, native Americans were virtually wiped out, millions of Africans were enslaved, Asians and Mexicans were exploited, and millions of working-class whites have spent much of their lives in labor only a few steps less onerous than slavery."
>
> "True enough, friend. But surrender is not an option, and struggle may enable some of us to survive and maintain our

humanity. If we are never more than, as Harriet Tubman put it, 'strangers in a strange land,' with all that land's dangers, we still will have managed to salvage much of our strength as a people from facing those dangers while singing the songs of Zion."

"That's it, Geneva! Either in the music itself, or in the determination to keep going, sparked and nurtured by the music, we must learn to do what our enslaved ancestors did. We do have resources.[. . .]Our challenge is to identify and harness our 'everything' to meet the current crisis." (*Gospel Choirs* 15)

It's obvious enough that myriad coalitions are needed to meet the challenges of racism and to defeat it; yet it never seems obvious to human beings how to meet the challenge of maintaining our humanity. The two are linked, and not meeting the challenge of maintaining our humanity makes coalition building difficult and only fleetingly meaningful. The fullness of one's humanity is linked to that of others. Nathan Glazer's declamatory work *We Are All Multiculturalists Now* speaks to me of the white "self" recognizing to a greater degree than previously its social and cultural imposition on the many that are "othered." Nonetheless, it begs the questions of just what our nation and its institutions will look like and how we will define our civic culture and our common good. How will the self-other dichotomy in this nation, which affects us all but which is based on the black-white dichotomy legally, socially, and psychologically, move to a healthy assertion of "selves" that only "other" for the purpose of engaging distinctions?

The ultimate problem with issues of people of color in academe, of heterosexuals, homosexuals, and lesbians in academe, of the working class in academe, of affirmative action and our nation's future racially, is one of morality. Will we postpone the careerists goals, leave the fears of ridicule and discomfort aside to interrogate profoundly, for example, Barbara Christian's call for a literary theory that emanates from the literature? Will we then see the connection between her argument and Morrison's for recognizing the "Africanist presence" in white American literature? Will we admit the importance of Américo Paredes to our literary canon? Will we truly seek universal education as a national policy? Will we recognize that flaws in corrective policies should not negate the effort to correct? Or, recalling the conservative response to the black conservative Loury, are we so morally bankrupt that we will let the terminally ill patients grow in number because we think they are mostly, or all, black?

Living in borderlands, where we strive to recognize, accommodate, incorporate, embrace, and tolerate difference, is like darting through a minefield. The explosives, racism in its many subtle rather than legally sanctioned and structured forms, must be disarmed. Such a move demands first the dismantling of the social constructions of race, gender, ethnicity, and class and then their replacment with systemic constructions reflective of a cooperational, relational pluralism. This tedious process, vulnerable to backlash, ignorance, and human behaviors determined to maintain the illusory secure status quo, is the cultural work that leaders, groups, and individuals must undertake to reunite a United States torn apart by the denial of its past and the projection of a false consciousness.

Most of the people of color who joined the faculties of overwhelmingly white colleges and universities over the past thirty years had hopes that their presence and work would provide possibilities and structures for an academic, cultural, social, and political change in scholarship and pedagogy. That change, many of us hoped, would allow the different histories, the different perspectives, and the different experiences of the racial, ethnic, class, and gender groups to become part of an illuminating scholarship that would provide direction not only for better scholarship but also for bettering conditions for everyone.

I am poignantly aware of the complexity and difficulty of change of the sort I advocate. I am equally aware of the urgency of the need for such change. Not only are we, my generation of faculty members of color, the first to enter higher education in overwhelmingly white colleges and universities, but we are also the first generation of faculty members of color who are in a position to feel a keen responsibility to leave a legacy for those following us, the assistant professors and the associate professors of color. The ground has shifted tremendously. In 1969, when I began teaching as an instructor, the nation's atmosphere and the campus atmosphere were generally supportive. Pressure came from the black communities in cities and around colleges and universities to fulfill the dream of civil rights. That pressure was compounded by Asian American, Latino/Latina and Chicano/Chicana, and Native American communities and by white women tentatively aligned with women of color. It was unthinkable for a

Ward Connerly or a Shelby Steele to excuse the nation and the law from its responsibility on the backs of many thousands gone who struggled against its hypocrisy. It was unthinkable to take away the hope of self-sufficiency and the goal of responsibility—from students, the poor, those of us striving to succeed in the academy and to help it change to accommodate the worlds we brought to it—by blaming the victim. It was unthinkable that colleagues and administrators might openly contest scholarship, departments, and other institutional structures aimed at encouraging the universities and colleges to embrace our national complexities, our beautiful and ugly.

But now the environment of careerism and racist backlash and the specter of militias portend the academic shutdown of teaching and learning that explain our world and allow students time to think about how to live well with one another. We have no blueprints, no memoirs, no institutional stories to guide us now, for we all are in situations that we, as a nation, as people, have never experienced. We have crossed borders, and we don't know how to work with one another, how to speak with or listen to, really hear, one another honestly—and the color line persists. Stereotypes, ostensibly denied and cast away, have been reformulated to maintain the status quo. In addition to the lazy, laughing, and dangerous darky or the model minority Asian, we have a contrived master stereotype of the white liberal, a stereotype that many people of color are accused of employing when they attempt a critical assement of the race problem that remains.

There is an African American spiritual that says, "O, wasn't dat a wide river, dat river Jordan, Lord, wide river. Dere's one more river to cross" (Johnson 152–53). We've crossed the wide river of racial divide on many fronts. Yet we haven't reached the promised land. Harlem is a ghetto, about to be gentrified and become largely white again. Where will the poor, the homeless live? We've a huge river yet to cross. Our legacy, as faculty members of color and as white faculty members concerned about the future of higher education and of our nation, must be the forging of ways to feel, think, and teach together. It is our responsibility to continue the complex task of understanding our conflicting and painful stories, to help our nation value not only democracy but also the critical thinking and action that allow democracy to thrive.

Notes

I would like to thank Ruthann Allen and Michael Foote, my research assistants and graduate students; Vanessa Daniel, an undergraduate volunteer assistant; and John C. Walter for their several close readings of this work and for their very helpful suggestions. The epigraph is quoted in Derrick Bell's *And We Are Not Saved* (4).

1. W. E. B. Du Bois begins the essay "Of the Dawn of Freedom" as follows: "The problem of the twentieth century is the problem of the color line,—the relation of the darker to the lighter races of men in Asia and Africa, in America and the islands of the sea. It was a phase of this problem that caused the Civil War; and however much they who marched South and North in 1861 may have fixed on the technical points of union and local autonomy as a shibboleth, all nevertheless know, as we know, that the question of Negro slavery was the real cause of the conflict. Curious it was, too, how this deeper question ever forced itself to the surface despite effort and disclaimer" (372).

2. For an overview of the field of curriculum transformation, see Schmitz, Butler, Rosenfelt, and Guy-Sheftall; and Butler, "Difficult Dialogue."

3. The literary critic George Kent describes the character of African American folk humor and wisdom as springing from a certain "as ifness." In the chapter "Langston Hughes and the Afro-American Folk and Culture Tradition" he describes a "third major quality that folk tradition reflects in its less self-conscious form" as "an *as ifness*." "Whereas one feels behind self-conscious black literature the unarticulated knowledge that America for Blacks is neither a land of soul nor of bread, a good deal of folklore suggests a complete penetration of its universe, a possession of the land and self in a more thoroughgoing way than that expressed by white American literature. Spirituals, for example, suggest a complete mining of their universe. Many of the animal tales and general folk stories also suggest that a universe has been possessed and defined [. . .]" (55).

4. Walter Benn Michaels argues against race as a social concept, delegitimating race as a category of analysis and in effect denying the power of racial representation not only to deny individual and group rights but also to distort culture (*Our America*). Culture for Michaels is performed: therefore, he views concepts of ancestral or cultural heritage as limiting and essentialist (123–35). Depending on his interpretation of Melville Herskovits's conclusions in *The Myth of the Negro Past,* Michaels ignores the work of Lorenzo Turner, John Dillard, Geneva Smitherman, Portia Maultsby, Robert Ferris Thompson, and others, which demonstrate not static African retentions, as Michaels expects, but fluid African transformations, characteristic of cultural exchange, syncretism, and acculturation rather than total assimilation.

   In a similar vein, Ross Posnock equates deracination with deracialization (88) while demonstrating that "Du Bois's dialectic, in short, does not make culture a code word for Anglo-Saxonism" (94). He asserts that "against origins and starting from them, Fanon and Du Bois fashion a performative cosmopolitanism that anticipates the contemporary moment of post-identity" (88). Thus references to "blackness" are viewed as essentialist, emanating from a past with an artificial significance. Posnock sees opposition to Du Bois's call for the resolution of the "contradiction of double aims" that racism and ethnocentrism maintain in Sarah Lawrence-Lightfoot's interviewee's triumph over their ambivalent identities as African Americans in her book *I've Known Rivers*. Rather than accept their professed resolution of ambivalence, Posnock objects to their claims of success, largely because they credit embracing their blackness, their ancestral heritage (98).

In my estimation, both Michaels and Posnock signal scholarship that tends to deracinate the African American while maintaining a wholly racialized silent whiteness. Their interpretations of African American and African diasporic thinking are severely limited by dismissal of the very multiplicity of voices they purport to be recognizing, and their apparent postmodern disdain for history and reality demonstrates for readers the salience of Satya Mohanty's critique of postmodernism in *Literary Theory and the Claims of History*.

5. *Conscientizacaõ* is a Portugese word used by Freire and taken from the word *consciencia* meaning conscience, perception, consciousness. The corresponding form in English would be *conscientization*. The translator states, "Conscientization refers to learning to perceive social, political, and economic contradictions, and to take action against the oppressive elements of reality" (19).

6. See John Hoberman's and Walter Benn Michaels's works as examples of scholarly erasure of achievement and legacies of the past for African Americans; these works also imply that such achievement renders African Americans as victimized.

7. In postcolonial criticism, the self is the oppressor and the other is the oppressed. The resulting binary is not one in which the oppressed self must cast off the oppressive other for agency. Rather, it is one in which the other must achieve agency beginning with no self but only otherness. Thus hybridity is fraught with ambivalences, and there is no liberatory as ifness. I question whether the shift in United States cultural studies from the oppressed self that seeks agency to an other that seeks agency indeed reflects the self-perception of people of color in the United States. I do not think it reflects literary or artistic representation in literature by African Americans, Asian Americans, Native Americans, Chicanas/Chicanos, and Latinas/Latinos.

Works Cited

Anzaldúa, Gloria. *Borderlands / La frontera*. San Francisco: Spinsters–Aunt Lute, 1987.

Bell, Derrick. *And We Are Not Saved: The Elusive Quest for Justice*. New York: Basic, 1987.

———. *Faces at the Bottom of the Well: The Permanence of Racism*. New York: Basic, 1992.

———. *Gospel Choirs: Psalms of Survival in an Alien Land*. New York: Basic, 1996.

Butler, Johnnella E. *Black Studies: Pedagogy and Revolution: A Study of Afro-American Studies and the Liberal Arts Tradition through the Discipline of Afro-American Literature*. Washington: UP of America, 1981.

———. "Complicating the Question: Black Studies and Women's Studies." *Women's Place in the Academy: Transforming the Liberal Arts Curriculum*. Ed. Marilyn R. Schuster and Susan R. Van Dyne. Totowa: Rowman, 1985. 73–86.

————. "The Difficult Dialogue of Curriculum Transformation." *Transforming the Curriculum: Ethnic Studies and Women's Studies*. Ed. Butler and John C. Walter. New York: State U of New York P, 1991. 1–19.

Christian, Barbara. "The Race for Theory." *Within the Circle: An Anthology of African American Literary Criticism from the Harlem Renaissance to the Present*. Ed. Angelyn Mitchell. Durham: Duke UP, 1994. 348–59.

Cone, James. *The Spiritual and the Blues: An Interpretation*. New York: Seabury, 1972.

Dixon, Vernon J., and Foster, Badi G. *Beyond Black or White*. Boston: Little, 1971.

Du Bois, W. E. B. *Souls of Black Folk. Du Bois Writings*. Ed. Nathan Huggins. New York: Library of America, 1984.

Freire, Paulo. *Pedagogy of the Oppressed*. Trans. Myra Bergman Ramos. New York: Seabury, 1970.

Frye, Charles A. *Towards a Philosophy of Black Studies*. San Francisco: R and E Research, 1978.

Glazer, Nathan. *We Are All Multiculturalists Now*. Cambridge: Harvard UP, 1998.

Herskovits, Melville. *The Myth of the Negro Past*. Boston: Beacon, 1990.

Hoberman, John. *Darwin's Athletes: How Sport Has Damaged Black America and Preserved the Myth of Race*. New York: Houghton, 1997.

Johnson, James Weldon, ed. *The Book of Negro Spirituals*. New York: Viking, 1925.

Kakutani, Michiko. "Coping with the Idea of Representing One's Race." Rev. of *Thirteen Ways of Looking at a Black Man,* by Henry Louis Gates, Jr. *New York Times* 28 Jan. 1997, natl. ed.: C13.

Kent, George. *Blackness and the Adventure of Western Culture*. Chicago: Third World, 1972.

Lawrence-Lightfoot, Sarah. *I've Known Rivers*. Reading: Addison, 1994.

Loury, Glenn A. "Conservatives and the Issue of Race." *San Diego Union-Tribune* 2 Dec. 1997: B7.

Michaels, Walter Benn. *Our America: Nativism, Modernism, and Pluralism*. Durham: Duke UP, 1995.

————. "Race into Culture: A Critical Genealogy of Cultural Identity." *Critical Inquiry* 18 (1992): 655–85.

Mohanty, Satya. *Literary Theory and the Claims of History: Postmodernism, Objectivity, Multicultural Politics*. Ithaca: Cornell UP, 1997.

Morrison, Toni. *Playing in the Dark: Whiteness and the Literary Imagination*. Cambridge: Harvard UP, 1992.

Posnock, Ross. *The Color of Culture*. Cambridge: Harvard UP, 1998.

Schmitz, Betty, Johnnella E. Butler, Deborah Rosenfelt, and Beverly Guy-Sheftall. "Women's Studies and Curriculum Transformation." *Handbook of Research on Multicultural Education*. Ed. James A. Banks and Cherry A. Banks. New York: Macmillan, 1995. 708–28.

Takaki, Ronald. *A Different Mirror: A History of Multicultural America*. Boston: Little, 1993.

Washington, Mary Helen. *Black-Eyed Susans: Classic Stories by and about Black Women*. New York: Anchor-Doubleday, 1975.

————. *Midnight Birds: Stories of Contemporary Black Women Writers*. New York: Anchor-Doubleday, 1980.

Through the Glass Looking

JOHN A. WILLIAMS

> The control of the nation's cultural apparatus rests in the hands of English professors and critics [. . .].
>
> —Addison Gayle, Jr.

Over the twenty-six years that I was in the academy, I taught composition, African American literature, American literature (including extensive writings by African Americans and other usually excluded writers, a course I designed), a variety of undergraduate journalism courses (I'd kept my hand in it long after I had ceased to be an active reporter), and undergraduate and graduate creative writing. I held visiting writer-teacher posts at fifteen colleges and universities and two distinguished professorships, at the City University of New York and later at Rutgers University. As a tenured and visiting teacher, I was, invariably, the only black person in the department or, if not, one of two, perhaps three, black persons. When I joined the English faculty of Rutgers's Newark campus, for example, I replaced a black woman who had taught African American literature but had not secured promotion and tenure. Fifteen years later, I retired, leaving behind one African American full-timer and one African American half-time teacher with a joint appointment in African American and African studies. There had been two or three African American journalism adjuncts during that fifteen-year period, but overall not much had changed.

Black people did not place themselves in their past or present situation in this nation. They are in the academy today not only because it is right but also because of the civil rights movement of the 1960s attended by all the marches and insurrections and because of President Lyndon Baines Johnson's Great Society programs of 1964, including affirmative action, which seemed something like reparations for past racial inequalities. In fact, affirmative action was to be a vigorous attempt to improve educational and employment opportunities for African Americans. But opposition to the program has been building through the years. In California in 1996 it was strong enough to get Proposition 209 on the ballot, and a majority of its residents passed it the next year. The proposition forbids the use of race and gender as considerations in admissions to institutions, employment, and the securing of contracts. In opinion pieces by several observers, the arguments against affirmative action have been overstated or misleading. For example, the $5.4 trillion that Newt Gingrich and University of California Regent Ward Connerly claim was spent on the Great Society is not broken down so that we can see what precisely was spent on affirmative action; no doubt Medicare was the most costly item. But the obvious intent of the op-ed piece was to suggest that *all* of the $5.4 trillion was for affirmative action programs, or $1.1 trillion less than we spent during *fifty-odd* years of the cold war (Marzani 195). We aren't yet wise enough to have done that.

With misunderstandings of the program rampant, other minorities were quickly grafted on, and later, with Title 9, women were added to the list. Affirmative action was also expected to invest the beneficiaries with the powers believed to accompany gains in education and employment. Today, affirmative action has been voted out in California and Texas and continues to be under open attack everywhere else in the nation, from the Supreme Court down. Apparently, the Texas and California voters would rather not accept federal funding than give breaks to minorities. (Off nose, spite face.) For the process of establishing affirmative action was a stickup (carrot, stick): if the academy wanted federal money, it had to accept minority students and offer programs to help keep them in college. Most schools wanted, perhaps needed, the money, which could always be siphoned off for needs other than affirmative action if necessary. The result was the often hasty creation of powerless entities such as black studies, Asian American and Hispanic studies, and so on, and then women's studies. The people who ran and nurtured these orphans had to accept the compartments to which they were consigned.

And it is in these sections of academia that most ethnic faculty members are believed to be assigned. Over the years I've seen programs listing me as a member of "black studies" or "African American studies." Such assumptions were commonplace, if frighteningly indicative of built-in racist, programmed thinking (black teacher, black studies). People were surprised and confused when I corrected them, but I don't know that it ever gets better. Over two decades ago a neighbor discovered that I, too, worked in the City University of New York system. He had just been made an associate professor. I must easily have been fifteen years older than he, but he assumed, almost automatically, that I was an assistant professor. He was shocked when I told him I was a distinguished professor. I don't doubt that he plugged into his connections to verify my claim. We never spoke of it again.

While some black studies departments have weathered severe financial and academic storms and added graduate-level courses to their programs, it has been noted that there may be but one viable African American Studies *Dee-part-ment* (with the high-visibility faculty members drawing high-powered salaries and numbers of international scholars in attendance) in the country that is solidly funded, perhaps more by money outside its university than from it. Most others, it seems to me, are usually short of their tightly budgeted funds. To secure funds regularly enough to conduct programs, they must behave in ways considered appropriately academic by their administrators; they cannot always be what they wish; nor can they always hold the events, such as conferences, that they would prefer or invite the individuals that they may deem important for the status of their departments but whom the general faculty may find onerous. Speakers from the Nation of Islam represent a prime example. Indeed, studies on blacks and Islam remain a fertile but sensitive area of study still to be conducted in some black studies programs.

I usually suggest other writers when I'm unable to do readings or lectures for a black studies or an occasional English or creative writing department. When I've indicated replacements, among them a black writer considered to be one who rouses the rabble, there's an immediate silence on the phone and then ". . . anyone else?" Little chance these departments would upset their administrative superiors. If such an individual does slip through, there is little chance that he or she will be invited back. I've been the target of such treatment.

Hired to teach one summer, I was asked after the first week not to conduct classes but to visit other teachers' classes, if I wished. (I was later told that my lectures were "too strong.") This was in the late 1960s, and administrators were extremely nervous about what was going on—if anything—in their classrooms. Occasionally I did visit other classes, but I spent more time on the beach with my family. In addition, the hall where I was to give a major lecture suddenly was no longer available. A helluva way to treat an English teacher. The academy admires smoothness, abhors what it considers bumps, topics unfit for academia.

I did not teach African American literature at Rutgers; I knew that if I did, it would surely keep the door closed to new African American hires. And African American literature, for quite some time, was precisely what the other black teacher in my department taught, in addition to composition. Only occasionally did a white teacher take on black literature. There are, of course, great white teachers who are as expert as any black person on the literature (or more so) and who do or will teach or have taught in black studies slots, but basically the position seems reserved for black teachers, by administrators and faculty members alike. It may be the one area where many white teachers are perfectly willing to step aside, because they've not bothered with African American literature at all. On the other hand, ironically, black teachers of African American literature usually are specialists in European or European American literature in addition to African American literature. Increasingly, in case it has not been noticed, black students are no longer the only ones taking these courses. At most schools African American literature is considered more of a lower-level course than one demanding that full professors drift down to teach it.

When the several minorities stormed through the affirmative action door or got pushed through it, "people of color" became the operative phrase, but that was not the initial purpose of the program. Charles Krauthammer notes that

> America's sin was against Blacks. There is no wrong in American history to compare with slavery. Affirmative action distorts the issue [of reparations] by favoring equally all "disadvantaged groups." Black America was the only one that for generations was singled out for discrimination and worse.

Krauthammer suggested cash reparations in exchange for giving up affirmative action, but he failed to note that it was not the program that caused the distortion; it was the politicians who set ethnic and gender groups against each other as slices of the program's pie grew smaller with each new group admitted. At the same time some managers of the academy were espousing the myth of the model minority on the one hand while stunting the academic and political growth of other minorities on the other. How? By allowing academically unchallenging undergraduate courses to be run. It often seems more important to some administrators that minority students feel comfortable in the academy than be challenged by its academic demands.

I was vocally and in writings opposed to affirmative action programs being separated from disciplines already chiseled on the walls of the academy. I believed back then that our acceptance of these cubicles of learning would, in time, perpetuate the powerlessness designed in their foundations. It only took one generation for that to become obvious and for the nation to be manipulated into turning against affirmative action. Well, maybe there was a little progress—it lasted a decade longer than post–Civil War Reconstruction. The canons remain essentially the same, and that is the true measure of how little power we had. In addition, we and the programs we worked in became targets for conservative scholars (a few of whom once passed as liberals). Not a surprise, that, when one considers how hard much of the "traditional" faculty fought to prevent such programs from taking root at all.

Once we got inside the gates of the academy, we tended to become figureheads meant to suggest that racial harmony, if not progress, was in process. Some of us easily lent ourselves to this representation; if we behaved as though we truly held real authority, it was because we were playing the game we have always played: "Let's pretend it's going to be all right" or "I got mine, Jack; now you get yours." But we knew full well that there could be little genuine strength if in 1991 you were one of the nearly 25,000 tenured black persons compared with approximately 457,000 white persons or if you were one of the 3,572 full professors who was black compared with 132,000 whites in that rank (American Council 88–90). It is widely believed that, as irreducible as these numbers may have seemed in 1991, they are worse today if only because opposition to affirmative action renders them essentially static. There does remain in place, however, a cadre of black scholars holding chairs and full professorships in all disciplines who fought through the skirmishes of the past two and a half decades. What these numbers also mean for the future is the absence or diminishment of whatever input from minority teachers and students is permitted in the classrooms and faculties of the nation.

Our respective academies (like other American institutions) usually validated our selections by checking us out with other, already stamped and certified "okey-dokey" black academics. (White folks have always placed other white folks' Negroes' opinions into their own good/bad evaluations of black candidates.) On one visiting professorship I was asked my opinion of a young black professor from Yale who had applied for a position the school had advertised in the academic papers. The one other black member of the department, tenured, was on leave; that left me. I refused to be brought into that department's ham-handed process, knowing very well that it already had its quota of one black person, one or two black visiting profs like me, and Black History Month to handle any overflow. I suggested that, if theirs was to be a viable English department, its members really should be more familiar with African American literature, which was only *one* of the candidate's specialties. (That must have given them the hoots. From what I've learned of that department over the years there were no measurable changes in their personnel decisions, although they did briefly take on a poet of color and then let him go, allegedly for student tampering.)

The academy was never all that comfortable with the presence of most of us in it, whether as students or teachers. If we were teaching literatures with which white teachers did not want to be bothered, their discomfort became palpable enough for them to reject both those literatures and us. American education, for all the complaints about how much we have become "multiculturalists," has never and probably will never become intellectually, spiritually, and morally integrated. However bothersome all the history may be, we'd do well to remember that the College Language Association was formed in 1949 by black teachers who were excluded from membership in the Modern Language Association. CLA began issuing its own journal in 1957. Happily, there has been change in the MLA position. There has even been a black president, Houston Baker, Jr., whom I first met at an MLA-sponsored seminar on African American literature at Yale in

1975. Although I worked with some forward-looking MLA people years ago, there were always superiors, so the message went, who didn't want to move as fast as they did. Tired of "beating the donkey," I dropped out of the organization at about the same time I left the Conference on College Composition and Communication.

I accepted a distinguished professorship in the City University of New York's LaGuardia Community College in 1973, after previous stints at CUNY's City College, a western state university, and two private schools. (Of course, the salary was resplendent.) LaGuardia was a brand new unit of CUNY, designed to draw primarily minority students into a freshly designed work-study program. I knew I was to be a major draw: a black writer showcasing the triumph of democracy in the academy.

When I was not doing dog and pony on and off campus, I taught African American literature and then, wishing to be a real, blue-collar teacher, composition. I discovered that many of my students in that very multiracial institution, about forty percent, were not literate in their native languages, whether Spanish, Greek, English, or French. Nor were they readers. I often had them use class time to read. Far back down the line teachers had quit on these people, and here they were, poised on the edge of career moves they could not successfully make. Was the name of the game really to enroll students—whether they stayed students or not? (There was a whole borough, if not the city, to draw from.) Or was it to teach down the system that held them back? (No, most certainly not, I learned soon enough when advised not to flunk four students who'd done the same paper on Ernest Hemingway, if their attendance was average. This was not the only time an administrator questioned my grading.)

A distinguished professor in the CUNY system was not required to do much work; the rank was more for accomplishments outside that reflected well on the academy than for work done within it. But I worked hard. I believed, and still do, that good teaching rewards everyone—students, teachers, community, and nation. But after six years that proved to be more exhausting than I could have guessed in the beginning, I left, rested, and then moved on to another post.

Why another? Because teaching brought me (and I would think other writers) out of isolation into the real world inhabited mainly by the young, the future. Over a quarter of a century students became decreasingly active in public matters; their protestations went from being literally explosive to passive; their intellectual interests, it

seemed to me, were greatest when there was social and political fer-
ment. Attitudes shifted from "No nukes" to "Nukes, so what?" Business administration was in, the humanities out. Today business
administration and the humanities coexist uneasily, elements of the
former often supporting the latter (liquor, cigarette, and beer companies bolstering the arts and the humanities, for example).

Even as this transition was occurring, however, there were always
those few students who could be excited by the history in which literature lives and the figures who emerged from it. A simple comparison
between the jazz ages and works of Langston Hughes and F. Scott
Fitzgerald could electrify them—and gratify a teacher immensely. A
lecture to journalism students on Gustavus Myers's *History of the
Great American Fortunes* could still produce cataclysms in the eyes
of some of them. But, generally speaking, if students had concerns
about living in a world where a thousand H-bombs could be un-
leashed on them with the snap of fingers, they internalized them. I
often wondered how much they were affected by being born into and
having to function normally in that insane situation. And to answer
another why: it was satisfying for me to know where my financial
horizons were, since writing was to be adrift on a sea where every
wave brought shifting views and often no horizon at all.

The great majority of my students throughout my career were
white. (I wondered, therefore, was it they who were lowering the
standards that politicians and a not insignificant number of academics constantly complained of?) I had no problems with being "accepted" by students. Of course, there were times when I noticed that
flickering expression on some faces: "How came he here?" I was
never sure what they expected from me, and I didn't really care. I
was what they got, and I always did better with them than with some
of my colleagues. Black, and a number of other minority, students
discovered too late that, while I could big brother or father them, that
was when I asked a bit more from them than from others. (This was
the sneaky overhand punch, which they resented.) I was not required
to mentor students the way some junior members of departments
were. I held office hours during which I expected them to air problems or seek advice. Students, as a rule, rarely took advantage of office hours, even when they were mandatory. Instead, they preferred
discussions in the hallways between classes or other impromptu appointments.

Composition students were the toughest to teach, for you were trying to fill in a hole that should have been dealt with in grade school. This situation was true of students from both the inner and the outer schools, and the students *knew* it. Composition courses led to a series of psychological adventures, large and small. It was my sense that students felt cheated and angry. Without this foundation of basic intelligent communication, how does one move easily on to literature? to anywhere on the college level? Armies of adjuncts undertake to combine composition and literature as a solution. I have no idea how successful they've been, because no one tells you when a solution has not worked.

There may be too much literature or too much of the same literature, and not enough of it has meaning at the center or even the edges. Or maybe we are drawing the wrong conclusions from literature or cannot relate it to the world we inhabit. Maybe literature has become a fashion, a product (as it is called in the publishing industry these days), a thing of little intrinsic value, less a discipline than a game of Scrabble, where tossing about authors' names and book titles substitutes for learned discourse. Maybe we've drifted away from what matters to what is merely fashionable or unworthy of serious consideration or debate.

My eldest son was among the first students in the nation to take African American literature in the mid-1960s. A black friend also took it but did not do as well. I asked why. He said, "This was our thing, you know. Bust no butt here." So. A literature of no value! It was always distressing for me to run into the black students who thought like that, but I've even advised a few candidates for advanced degrees whose attitudes and work were quite similar. They were displaying the same contempt for the discipline that so many white academics did and do. This is not to say that I did not have some seriously bright, hard-working black students when I taught this course, for I did, students who, if I'd said "Nat Turner time" or "David Walker time," would have hit the bricks without hesitation. (And the same goes for a few white students who took the course with me as well.) But that's not all African American literature is about. It is about black people, but it may be as much about white people, who frame it absolutely and are graphically reflected in it. So-called American literature and Western literature are ninety-nine percent about white people, period, a trip through the hall of mirrors with a detached retina. Yet scholars of the West ignore the multiethnic and multiculturalist roots of Europe itself, which has undergone numerous invasions of Asian peoples and of the various Arab and Moorish peoples, not to mention early on, the Basques, or back near the beginnings, the old African himself. You would think that the academy would be delighted that African American literature, with a two hundred-year history, is so rich, has so much to teach and learn from on so many levels, so many branches, so endless a mine of mystery, linguistics, psychology, history, philosophy, adventure, music to draw on; but no, please not, the academy seems to say. Well, too late. The genie is out of the flask now; it cannot be stopped back up. *It is out!*

Students think journalism is television. Few journalism students want to write for newspapers; they're not even terribly interested in their school papers. Print journalism is a fossil, they think. Television journalism is glamorous; therefore, most journalism students want to be television anchor people. And maybe they should, because too many of them don't take writing seriously, maybe because they can't write very well, which gets us back to composition (which I hope, for the benefit of future journalists, these days is teaching the difference between *less* and *fewer*). Anchors don't necessarily have to write their own copy; reporters, edited to time (rarely language, sometimes sense), often do. Journalism in the 1970s was one way to prop up an English department whose student numbers were plummeting. At La-Guardia, it was a given that we'd not have equipment beyond a few typewriters. At Rutgers the administration thought to do without the technology that was starting to inundate the academy, but after pleading and grant writing by a colleague who knew about such things, we finally got our first computers (just as the third generation of them was coming out). Journalism is a real world, real time discipline. Varied, dangerously influential, ceaseless in its outpourings, opinions, and ability to shape for good or ill all kinds of events, and even itself, it is the kind of umbrella under which all other disciplines can gather. It could be truly interdisciplinary—if its handlers had any nerve and were less concerned with journalism as a moneymaker than with good journalism's being totally involved with the people's right to know the truth. Since the late 1960s all students have gotten used to seeing black newspeople on television reading and reporting the news. So white students were probably most comfortable with a black teacher who taught journalism courses. In any case, it was to me they usually came when they had problems, some very serious.

Creative writing was something almost all students thought they could do but soon discovered they could not. It was my job to tell them to forget it. Or to encourage them in written critiques and conferences. But one always had to be delicate; writing has become an almost sacred act for many students (what with the latest technology that seems hell-bent on keeping us all *electronically* in touch). A writer-teacher should approach these writings as though heading into a church. There may be laughing and joking, but the conferencing teacher and the student both know that what is occurring is something like breaking the code of the Rosetta stone. In my graduate writing courses there were usually a couple of students who were determined to remake the world. Increasingly though, I came to sense the other extreme, that it was far too late to make anything better, and even if it were not, the students had come to believe they were helpless anyway—and they were angry about that. More graduate writing students were coming from other parts of the world, so there was, close on, "the literatures of other places" set down in English. In many instances these were places where our "national interests" had had devastating effects on the population, in countries such as Iran, Nigeria, Egypt, Iraq, Guatemala, and Panama.

I am aware that I've used *angry* twice in regard to students. I think, though I pray I am wrong, that the classroom will be the next place where a person, a student, drowning in free-floating anger at finding himself or herself ill-educated to handle life, may walk in with an Uzi or M-16 and wipe out the place. It's happened in post offices, on a commuter train, and a couple of fast-food establishments. And it would not be the first time it happened on a college campus.

It was my white writing students who gave me yet another look at white America. There is something about writers and writing that always verges on the confidential that needs revealing—the Rosetta stone complex again. About every two or three years a few student stories or novels-in-progress would deal with family racism. In one sense the students wanted a measurement from me, a black person, of how far they'd grown away from it; in another they were asking forgiveness for being part of such a family. One of my graduate students years and years ago gave me what she called a "boogie doll"; that's what her parents called it. A three-inch black plastic doll in a hula skirt affixed to a pocket chain, it hung on the mirror of her parents' car, and they laughed at the way it danced and skipped around with every movement of the vehicle. I accepted the doll as an indicator of her separation from her parents' sensibilities. I have had but one or two white students who were oblivious to their own racism. It was as though they'd just arrived from another world. I let other white students deal with the situation—which many were happy to do—and put my most important comments in writing. They usually dropped the course after that.

I've often wondered why a college or university will hire a minority teacher, send her or him before a class to educate white kids, and otherwise treat him or her with contempt. Is the academy saying that the teacher is good enough for the kids but not for adults? How crazy is it to trust that teacher with the future yet debase her or him in the present? As it is, writers as professors of English are always suspect or held in contempt by the literature people. On the one hand, I found absolute polarization at one school where the literature people didn't even speak to writers. Writers, on the other hand, will usually talk to anyone. I am not sure if this is good or bad. It first surprised, then disheartened, me because were there no writers, there'd be no literature to teach. (You'd think there'd be a modicum of gratitude here.) To be a black writer and professor of English was to experience an academic semi-Coventry for which I was most grateful. I honestly never expected to be loved, because people who are handed rank and tenure when they enter never are. And if you are managing to publish with relative frequency, that doesn't garner you any bouquets either. And if you are black as well—oh, forget it. But I did survive the academy, and it was because I taught a variety of courses and so never became bored and because it was important that I not only teach as well as I possibly could (that would always be my sweetest revenge) but learn from my students in the bargain (a fact that leads me to believe that growing old at this time may be a blessing).

At Rutgers University, Newark, which is not, as many people believe, a school mostly attended by black students, the black people in administration were few, in the business end of things, and without power. At least this was the case when I was directed to them for some form of financial assistance for any hands-on journalism projects. There were no black deans or associate deans that I knew of, and my grapevine was very good. The one black department chair was, of course, in African American and African studies, although there had been, briefly, a black chair in drama. She had been brought in during one of those summer surprises when some senior faculty members meet to hire a person the administration wants, though the department where the person will work may not. During my time, two women, one from my department, served terms as associate deans. (The administration now seems to be grooming its new African American and African studies department chair as a candidate for associate dean.) The Rutgers-Newark faculty, by the way, is paid better than its counterpart in New Brunswick in order to attract people for presumed combat duty in the city of Newark.

One of the complaints among teachers these days is that students have too much power. If this is true, well, maybe it is about time. Over the years I've seen several groups of students protesting incompetent, unprofessional, or vengeful teachers — without moving a molehill. I've seen teachers promoted who hadn't written even a pamphlet since their dissertations and teachers who were disasters in the classroom, plain and simple; I've seen that for all the democracy symbolized by including student evaluations in the promotion process, the only times they were ever used were *against* teachers administrations wished to fire. As examples of students wielding power, at a couple of posts, my low grading of students who deserved it (but thought otherwise) brought me into conflict with administrations that had great respect for the parents who were paying the tuition and that did not approve of visiting professors who did not share this respect. At both schools I had the distinct feeling that the grades later would be changed. And at one of my several posts, a secretary caught a faculty member rifling files in the office of the chair that contained material on upcoming promotions. That person, who was a candidate (as it turned out a successful one), had a set of keys that opened every other office. This was clearly a criminal act, reliably witnessed. But from the chair up to the president, no one did anything. I have no doubt at all that had the person been black, the outcome would have been quite different. On balance it seems to me that if indeed students now have too much power, they need more. They're paying for it. Furthermore, like their parents' current seeming rejection of representative democracy through the ballot box, toward the end of my teaching career fewer and fewer students were taking the time to fill out the teacher evaluation forms. It had become common belief that they did little to reward good teachers and nothing to hasten the removal of bad ones.

At Rutgers-Newark we had an MA program in creative writing that was wedded to the MA in English. In all the years I ran this program, in conjunction with about four colleagues, I rarely had African American students. I'd had some in undergraduate creative writing courses, but they were indeed few. Two or three of these were very good and one was exceptional, and I let him audit the course for a year because he couldn't pay the tuition. Then I couldn't do that any longer. Letting good students of any ethnicity audit was something I usually did—in addition to reading and commenting on their work. A writer unwilling to do that for young writers probably has no business teaching. The United States since about the end of World War II has been unique in the teaching of creative writing. (It is or used to be considered silly in Europe.) Actually, I told the students who'd been accepted into the program that I could help them only if they helped themselves, if they produced, produced, produced. Cliché though it may be, I continue to feel that life is the teacher, and for most of the world's great writers that has always been the case. I also suggested to students they'd probably be better off doing anything but sitting in a classroom. But almost universally they insisted on the companionship, encouragement, and criticism of other students. Forget the tradition of rugged individualism that so many earlier writers seemed to embody. One student, however, did take a job on a yacht cruising up and down the American coast but jumped ship when the captain turned out to be a clone of Captain Bligh.

The graduate program in literature had not much better luck with African American or any other ethnic students. Advanced degrees were perhaps too much of a luxury. Clearly, affirmative action only opened doors on the first floor. For the minority student (and many others) part-time study and full-time work usually follow securing the BA, which delays entrance into the pool of academic faculty members or administrators.

The 1994 *Minorities in Higher Education* annual report also indicated that among African Americans, Hispanics, and Asian Americans, women on average held higher academic ranking than men did. Among some ethnic faculty members, approximately 40% were non–United States citizens (31). African Americans continued "to represent less than 5 percent of all full-time faculty in higher education" (28). The numbers of ethnic administrators—8.7% for African Americans, 2.5% for Hispanics (30), 1.6% for Asian Americans (31), and "fewer than one of every 200 college administrators was an American Indian" (32)—suggest that the future will not soon include any substantial increase in the numbers of ethnic academic administrators. This should not come as a surprise; it is just the way the system is and has always been. The system has been somewhat more willing to tinker with the teacher count than with the count of the administrators. I am not suggesting here that such administrators may merely be showpieces. I've had little experience in administration, usually declining to be a candidate for department chair in writing and at the earliest opportunity. Committee assignments cannot be avoided and perhaps should not be. I don't recall that my input, vocal or in proposal form, into any decision-making process save creative writing was given serious consideration, and for most of the African American colleagues I've known in the humanities this situation is not unusual. However, if one is an African American scientist whose work enables an institution to ask for and receive large grants for research and equipment from the federal government, naturally administrations tend to be far more attentive.

Finally, I want to note especially those teachers who have been farsighted enough to understand that the more literatures we open up to and understand, the more we come to know ourselves within the world and not in a self-serving, nationalistic context. It is not that these teachers have dismissed any of the canon; they have in fact extended it. Long, long ago I had a teacher (who later became a friend) at Syracuse University (in fact I had several good ones) named David Owen, called by some "C-minus Owen." Professor Owen was the first college English teacher I knew who, around 1959–60, systematically taught the writings of black authors *within* an American literature context. Over the years I've met many younger versions of Owen who, no doubt at some risk to their careers, have accepted the same intellectual challenge. They are white and brown Americans; they are Polish and Romanian, French and German, Italian and Spanish; they are also Japanese and Chinese and Indian. Several other teachers are on the faculties of African American studies programs or departments. Over twenty-six years the list has grown quite long, and over time these are the people who will continue to make it impossible to put the genie back in the flask.

And there are the students, I should also note, who have shared with me some of their lives, if not their literary successes, beyond our time in the classroom and over many years. They've made me wonder if, given another life and another chance to teach, I would consider it. Maybe. But not for long.

I would not have been able to write this without the benefit of the GI Bill of Rights, which I've always called the first affirmative action program. Under the bill, World War II veterans could enter or return to college with the federal government paying for tuition and books and a living stipend, whether or not the vet had a family. (By the end of the war there were ten million men and women in uniform.) How long the government paid depended on how long the former GI had served. I had been in service long enough to study more than four years. And the bill was color-blind. Of course there was abuse; of course racism occurred in the administration of the program on several levels. *But* it spelled opportunity for millions, and it created a tax-paying middle class larger than had ever existed in this nation. From a prewar depression mentality, the nation went to a postwar optimism in which the civil rights movement was delivered from its historical womb and the United States assumed a major role among nations. This group of beneficiaries became the parents of the baby boomers who are now starting to request their statements of accumulation from Social Security. In short, little investment, little profit; no investment, no profit at all. The GI Bill was an investment not only in education but also in the future of the nation.

Works Cited

American Council on Education. *Minorities in Higher Education.* Thirteenth Annual Status Report, 1981–91. Ed. Deborah J. Carter and Reginald Wilson. Phoenix: Oryx, 1994.

Gingrich, Newt, and Ward Connerly. "Face the Failure of Racial Preferences; Bankrupt Social Policies Will Not Educate Our Children." *New York Times* 15 June 1997, sec. 4: 15+.

Krauthammer, Charles. "Reparation for Black Americans." *Time* 12 Dec. 1990: 18.

Marzani, Carl. *The Education of a Reluctant Radical.* Book 3. New York: Topical, 1996.

A Stranger in the Department

C. L. CHUA

Of late, immigrant bashing has apparently become (again) a pop-ular political sport in America. There is the 1997 Balanced Bud-get Act debate threatening to take away food stamps, Supplemental Security Income, and Medicaid from indigent legal immigrants ("Budget Bill"). There was the 1994 California Proposition 187 threatening to deny public education to children of illegal immi-grants (Rodríguez 18). So let me say up front and unabashedly that I am a green-card-carrying immigrant and one who vocally supported the MLA Delegate Assembly's resolution against Proposition 187 dur-ing the San Diego MLA convention ("Minutes" 475–76). I am also an Asian, a part of that ethnic genus whose members (so say some ex-perts) are likely to be regarded as model specimens[1] of some exotic life form that thrives best when kept beneath glass ceilings.[2] And for invocation, I appeal to Zeus, patron of well-meaning strangers.

I came into the profession of teaching English in American col-leges during the1960s, in the times before affirmative action. (Some politicians nowadays would like to return us to those times.) But even then I was taken aback when my avuncular chair told me during the first week of the term that I would never be asked to teach the Intro-duction to Poetry course required of all English majors. He gave out that I was not born to it. I tried not to gape. I had turned down five other job offers to accept his! And if nothing else, teaching *was* my birthright. My maternal grandfather had founded the first school for children of Chinese immigrants to Singapore (then a British Crown Colony) at the turn of the previous century. My mother had been an

English teacher in a Methodist missionary girls' school, and when the Japanese Imperial troops occupied Singapore during World War II and banned the teaching of English, she had risked our lives by running an underground one-room English school in our village. My older cousins, who were some of her former students, still tell of their weekly drills of stuffing English texts and exercise books into chicken-feed bags and whipping out Japanese grammars in case an Army patrol dropped in. My lineage, I thought, had surely fitted me to be a teacher, and of English; my forebears had paid dues. But, of course, my then chair knew nothing about my family past; besides, what he meant by being born to it was probably not what I am laying claim to. Nevertheless, at the time I felt a little bit like Esau watching his expectations and rights slip away, and what was worse, I perhaps also had a fleeting regret that my complexion was not a smoother one, like my better favored brethren's. But I managed to summon a smile for that chair and swallowed my bitterness (we Chinese call it "eating bitter"); I built no barricades (I could call on no allies to man them anyhow) and did the best with whatever I was assigned to teach. I was taking lessons about living with your head in the lion's mouth from the Invisible Man's grandfather, yes, "overcome 'em with yeses" (Ellison 16). Some years later, the department developed a last-minute need to find a substitute for the faculty member originally assigned to the poetry course but who had received a research grant; I volunteered and was gratefully approved, and a couple of years later, I was nominated for a teaching award.

It was not until the late 1970s that affirmative action programs began to get under way and well-qualified women and ethnic minorities began to be recruited by universities. Unfortunately, the years when such a benign policy was in place often coincided with seasons of hard times when academic budgets were in decline. Such leaner years tended to bring out any latent meanness in people, even among people of color. Some African Americans whose lineage extended to antebellum days felt that the *nouveaux arrivés* from the Caribbean or from Africa should not receive consideration equal to that accorded to them. Analogous sentiments surfaced among Latinos/Latinas. Similarly, Asian Americans whose forebears were railroaders or prospectors on the Golden Mountain were cool toward an FOB (i.e., "fresh off the boat") like me. My experience of being given the cold shoulder by two established Asian American literati when they realized that I was an FOB still rankles in my memory of the MLA convention of 1975 in San Francisco. The Tony Award–winning playwright David Henry Hwang has captured that attitude when his character Dale scoffs:

> F-O-B. Fresh Off the Boat. [. . .] Clumsy, ugly, greasy FOB. Loud, stupid, four-eyed FOB. Big feet. Horny. Like Lenny in *Of Mice and Men*. [. . .] Boy FOBs are the worst, the [. . .] pits. They are the sworn enemies of all ABC — oh, that's "American Born Chinese"—of all ABC girls. Before an ABC girl will be seen on Friday night with a boy FOB in Westwood, she would rather burn off her face. (6)

Dale's views (and they are *not* Hwang's) are similar to those held by many native-born Asian Americans during the 1960s and 1970s. For instance, when Frank Chin and his collaborators compiled the then definitive anthology of Asian American writing, they proclaimed clearly their exclusion of immigrant Asian writers: "Our anthology is *exclusively* Asian-American. That means [. . .] American born and raised" (ix; emphasis mine—because I feel it ironic that a Chinese American would wish to tout exclusion). Understandably, though, they felt this way out of a sense of insecurity and "self-contempt" that their complex experience of American society had bred in them (Chin et al. x). On the one hand, native-born Asian Americans could not integrate with white America because American laws had treated Asians as unassimilable and undesirable by imposing repressive racist statutes on them. For instance, the Chinese Exclusion Acts from 1882 to 1943 banned entrance into the United States for working-class Chinese men and women and stripped American citizens of citizenship if they married Chinese (Kingston 154–59), while the World War II Executive Order 9066 shunted Japanese Americans into "concentration camps," to use President Roosevelt's phrase (Weglyn 217). To make matters worse, Chinese parents and grandparents of the immigrant generation would often deride their American-born offspring as "jook sing" (Chu 137), a derogatory epithet evoking an image of a hollow bamboo section (Dong and Hom 19–20) incapable of containing anything Chinese—culture, conscience, or couth. On the other hand, *Asian* art, thought, and literature were admired by white society, often with an "orientalizing" (à la Said) or exoticizing kind of "racist love" (Chin et al. x). *Asian American* cultural production, then, received little or no recognition; and it was only after the student protests of the 1960s at San Francisco State and Berkeley that Asian American studies programs began to emerge on the American academic scene and Asian American literature began to be studied seriously (Chan 181). Native-born Asian American scholars and writers in the 1970s, then, were clinging to a hard-won, barely acquired niche for Asian America in academe; their emphasis, therefore, was on the nativistic (Cheung 1) and "nationalist" (Wong 2) qualities of their subject. No wonder they were wary of me, an Asian from Asia, taking an interest in their project. Happily, this academic invidiousness has not persisted. By the 1980s, as the discipline of Asian American studies, literary and otherwise, gained ground and confidence, Asian American scholarship became less nativistic and began to tolerate a more international and "diasporic" outlook (Wong 9, Lim 289). Thus Elaine Kim observed in 1992: "As the world has changed, so have our conceptions of Asian American identity. The lines between Asian and Asian American, so important in identity formation in earlier times, are increasingly being blurred" (xiii).

But in 1975, the matter was a vexed one for me, and I felt discouraged from pursuing my interest in Asian American writing. I had no desire to make it on the backs of the forebears of those longtime Asian Americans, but this society's racism had exacted its dues on my hide as well as theirs. Indeed, this society made no fine discriminations between Asian Asians and Asian Americans as far as ethnicity was concerned. As the violent deaths of Vincent Chin in Detroit and Jim Loo in North Carolina illustrated (Chan 177–79), Americans at large could not usually tell the difference between Japanese, Chinese, or Vietnamese, much less distinguish between an FOB and an ABC. (To refresh the reader's memory, Vincent Chin was a twenty-seven-year-old Chinese American draftsman who was killed on the eve of his wedding after his bachelor party in June 1982 in Detroit. Two white men [stepfather and son] beat him to death because they had been laid off from their automotive jobs. They attributed their unemployment to Japanese automakers, mistook the Chinese Vincent Chin for a Japanese, and assaulted him. They merely received three years' probation and a fine of $3,000. Jim Loo, a twenty-four-year-old Chinese American, was pistol-whipped to death in Raleigh, North Carolina, in July 1989 because two white brothers mistook him for a Vietnamese, and they had lost a brother in Vietnam. In this case, at least, one of the killers did receive a thirty-seven-year jail sentence, though he was eligible for parole after four years.)

In 1982, after having moved through several universities in Asia and in America, I found myself elected to the chair of an English department in the United States, made up of twenty white folk and myself. I wondered whether I was not the first Chinese immigrant to chair a department of English in the United States; after all, the Chinese Exclusion Act was not repealed until 1943, when a quota of 105 Chinese were allowed to trickle into the United States annually (Takaki 111, 378). And certainly, when I attended the ADE seminar that the MLA organized for English chairs that summer in Seattle, I saw no other Asians attending. Nor were there any Asians at the annual state-level meetings of the chairs of English departments held during the Council of Teachers of English conferences. Apparently, with the exception of oddities like me, Asians in American academe were typed as nerds best for crunching numbers, frying microchips, or stalking quarks; the ability to appreciate the finer modulations of the English language, to hear the subtler cadences of American free verse, was apparently neither encoded into our DNA nor ordained in our stars. This, unfortunately, is a typification that even many Asians in America believe of themselves and of their children.

Having taken lessons from the Invisible Man's grandfather, I found that I had accrued a great deal of collegial knowledge and, consequently, of influence in my department. I knew how the personalities in it were likely to act in different situations; I had learned the dynamics of its committees by serving on every one of them; I had worked the ditto machine and freshman English registration — a nightmare of pencil and paper in the precomputer age. After I became chair, I found that this collegial knowledge and experience was invaluable in getting resolutions passed by the faculty and things done in the department. And I kept up my knowledge of the department by attending every meeting of every departmental committee. As can be imagined, these activities took up a great deal of time.

Effective department chairs need to be able not only to influence their faculty members but also to win over the administrators. Here again, I found collegiality a most useful tool. Immediately after I became chair, I volunteered for and was successful in gaining a seat on the university-wide Academic Policy Council that made decisions on faculty, curriculum, and the academic direction of the institution.

From my vantage point on the council, I could look out for the interests of my department, and I could be the first to bring important news (good or bad) to the department and present it in the way I felt best. I also volunteered successfully to serve on two key search committees: the search committee for the new dean of arts and humanities and that for the new academic vice president. During the candidates' campus interviews, I made sure to spend extra time with them, which they appreciated. After the successful candidates were installed, I found that their office doors were always open to me and that they valued my opinion, an opinion that had contributed to their being hired. Again, this cultivation of collegiality required a serious investment of time—the search committees sometimes met at 7 a.m., and departmental committees sometimes met until 7 p.m. But with the collegial influence gained, I could facilitate or hinder decisions on faculty promotions, course approvals, class size of writing courses. Sometimes it was almost as useful as having reason on my side. I also sensed that my presence as a person of color sitting on a committee acted to stop words from being spoken that might have been voiced if only the good old boys were there; occasionally, I could sense some people start a comment and catch themselves with a glance at me and a clearing of their throats. If my presence could not stop them from thinking certain thoughts, at least it deterred the open expression and use of those thoughts to form a camaraderie fed by bigotry.

In addition to collegial influence, the chair of a department is, of course, vested with a certain amount of administrative authority—to have some say, for instance, about the teaching schedules of faculty members, the classrooms they are assigned to, the number of courses assigned to part-time faculty members, and so forth. The exercise of this sort of administrative authority can create abrasive situations. In addition, a chair who is also a person of color should bear in mind that faculty members in a traditionally white department of English are not used to having administrative authority wielded by a nonwhite. (Perhaps that is one more reason for universities' creating ethnic studies departments where nonwhite chairs are likely to be in charge of mostly nonwhite faculty members.) One particular decision-making situation I was involved in did become extremely abrasive. It was a decision involving two part-time instructors, a man and a woman, both Caucasians. The man had been teaching a two-thirds load for a year, the woman a one-third load for a term. The department had a one-third load for me to assign to one of them. I assigned it to the woman because, among other factors, she had better qualifications — her MA was in English, his in philosophy. But the man felt that he deserved the extra third, which would have brought him up to full-time status, and he went off in a dudgeon to file a complaint with the union. There he was intemperate in his speech and made remarks about handguns and baseball bats. When these remarks got back to me, I immediately bought disability insurance, tripled my life insurance, rode my bicycle less (and then always on sidewalks), used different exits and entrances of my office building, and alternated between stairs and elevators in it. I also told my daughters to beware of white men bearing baseball bats. That was a stressful spring term for me. Providentially, I was able to distance myself from the situation because I left on sabbatical the following year. Before I left, I was notified that the angry white man's contract was not renewed at all and that he was hospitalized to undergo detoxification treatment of a long-standing alcoholism. As for the woman instructor, I noted with pleasure that she published a book in 1997 after having completed a doctorate at one of the two most venerable universities of Britain.

As a department chair and a senior faculty member, I was also able to exert some influence on personnel decisions and on curriculum. In both areas, I was, of course, very interested in promoting diversity. Surprisingly enough, I often found that, in my efforts to advocate diversity, the administrators were sometimes (not always) easy to work with and the faculty members were frequently grudging and sometimes downright obstructionist.

In matters of curriculum, faculty members can sometimes be as jealous of turf as any street gang. For instance, a starry-eyed newly hired instructor in English proposes a course on American ethnic literature. Hopes are even entertained that the new course might be cross-listed in the ethnic studies department. As the course proposal wends its way from department curriculum committee to school curriculum committee and beyond, the ethnic studies department takes a dislike to this new kid on the block. Instead of rolling out the welcome wagon for the new faculty member working toward a common cause, they roll out the tumbrel. They want the course proposal cut off and dead on arrival at the academic senate's curriculum committee. They do not perceive such a course as enhancing the diversity of the university's curricular offerings or as creating an opportunity for more students to be exposed to the richness of American ethnic literature. No, the moving spirits in the ethnic studies department see such an English department course as a trespass on their territory, a raid on their FTE pool—although they themselves do not offer such a multiethnic and syncretic course, listing instead discrete courses in, say, African American literature or Asian American expression. Eventually, it is only after ex machina jawboning by a conciliatory dean that the proposed course is approved and offered.

But curricular innovation can also be a rewarding experience. I recall with pleasure a project that a group of faculty members and administrators embarked on together to foster the formation of new multicultural courses and to infuse multicultural substance into existing courses. We were successful in obtaining a development grant from the state and a private foundation. Faculty members interested in participating in this project were invited to apply for summer stipends (about half the pay for teaching a summer course), and the successful faculty members (about twelve) then undertook over the summer to prepare new, multicultural courses or revise old ones to include multicultural materials. The last three weeks of summer were then spent in seminars (which I coordinated) in which participants presented the fruits of their labors for group suggestions and comments. This project went on for two summers and had a significant and salubrious effect on the multicultural diversity of the university's course offerings.

In personnel matters, administrators are often cast in the role of the villains of the piece. Indeed, they seem to be excessively stingy and retentive in approving full-time hirings. Of late on my campus, it seems to require the equivalent of four faculty retirements and one funeral in order to obtain one tenure-track replacement. But sometimes university administrations have to respond to extramural or student pressures, and inklings of diversity hiring creep into their five-year plans, whereupon windows of opportunity to hire women or ethnic faculty members are grudgingly cracked open. Having been involved in several such searches, I have been schooled to be disappointed and frustrated by my faculty colleagues even more than by administrators. Once, a small department of two full-time professors, both women, was allocated a tenure-track hire. Acting as the affirmative action designee to their committee, I was incredulous to hear them make the argument that we should only interview male candidates because their next hire should be a man—it was only fair to their students, they argued, that the young people should be spared from being harangued by yet another woman professor! On another search, a rather prominent immigrant ethnic writer and scholar surfaced as the English hiring committee's candidate of choice. However, the creative writing wing of the English department flew up in alarm over our nomination of the candidate: they objected vigorously to the candidate's fictional subjects, verse cadences, and insufficiently American accent during an evening's reading. To me, my very distinguished, talented colleagues of good will were missing the point of a *diversity* hire. Indeed, they seemed to want to hire clones of themselves, preferably their former students and disciples. They were especially difficult because sincere, and sincere because they felt themselves to be the keepers of the higher standards that were being threatened or eroded by the intrusion of a culturally different other. Despite my best efforts, the department voted to make an offer to the candidate to teach only literature classes to the exclusion of any creative writing classes. *Plus ça change . . . !* I was eating bitter yet again. After twenty years of social change and a decade of affirmative action, here was another eminently well-qualified immigrant ethnic candidate being barred from teaching certain courses!

In his wise and durable epic of a sojourner-protagonist, Homer sometimes seems to hold up the hospitality of strangers to each other as a measure of civility if not of civilization itself. I am sometimes led to wonder which of his many demesnes might best approximate the manner in which American academia hosts the duskier ethnic sojourners that wash up on its shores. Surely not like that of the island of Polyphêmos the Kyklops, who had his guests for dinner. Nor yet that of Skhería, where the Phaiákians were to suffer an earthquake for their zealous hospitality. But perhaps more like that of Aiaia, where Kirkê could treat you like swine or allow you to share her flawless bed (if you had a moly) and help you depart when you wished (though telling you first to go to hell).

Notes

1. I allude to the myth that Asian Americans are a "model minority" whose women make desirable wives, whose men are good workers, and whose children score above average. By this account, Asian Americans are all contented, law-abiding, and always able to pull themselves up by their own bootstraps

(Takaki 474–84). This myth began to be played up by the media in the 1960s to draw invidious comparisons between Asian Americans and African Americans ("Success Story"). It has taken strong and dangerous hold in the American imagination, so much so that a 1997 American Council of Education Report ranked its number one recommendation to be "demythologizing Asian Pacific Americans as a 'Model Minority' " (Yip 17).

2. Among Asian Americans the phrase is commonly used to describe the "pattern of Asian absence from the higher levels of administration; [. . .] 'a glass ceiling' [is] a barrier through which top [. . .] positions can only be seen, but not reached, by Asian Americans. [For instance,] at Berkeley's University of California campus where 25 percent of the students were Asian in 1987, only one out of 102 top-level administrators was an Asian" (Takaki 476).

Works Cited

"Budget Bill Restores Some Benefits for Immigrants, but Problems Remain." *Pacific Citizen* 5–18 Sept. 1997: 16.

Chan, Sucheng. *Asian Americans: An Interpretive History*. Boston: Twayne, 1991.

Cheung, King-Kok, ed. *An Interethnic Companion to Asian American Literature*. New York: Cambridge UP, 1977.

Chin, Frank, et al., eds. *Aiiieeeee!* New York: Doubleday, 1975.

Chu, Louis. *Eat a Bowl of Tea*. 1961. Seattle: U of Washington P, 1979.

Dong, Lorraine, and Marlon K. Hom. "Chinatown Chinese: The San Francisco Dialect." *Amerasia Journal* 7.1 (1980): 1–29.

Ellison, Ralph. *Invisible Man*. New York: Vintage, 1947.

Homer. *The Odyssey*. Trans. Robert Fitzgerald. New York: Doubleday, 1963.

Hwang, David Henry. *FOB and Other Plays*. New York: Plume-Penguin, 1990.

Kim, Elaine. Foreword. *Reading the Literatures of America*. Ed. Shirley Lim and Amy Ling. Philadelphia: Temple UP, 1992. xi–xvii.

Kingston, Maxine Hong. *China Men*. New York: Knopf, 1980.

Lim, Shirley Geok-lin. "Immigration and Diaspora." Cheung 289–311.

"Minutes of the MLA Delegate Assembly." *PMLA* 110 (1995): 466–82.

Rodríguez, Gregory. "The Browning of California: Proposition 187 Backfires." *New Republic* 2 Sept. 1996: 18–19.

Said, Edward. *Orientalism*. New York: Vintage, 1979.

"Success Story of One Minority Group in the U.S." *U.S. News and World Report* 26 Dec. 1966: 73–76.

Takaki, Ronald. *Strangers from a Different Shore: A History of Asian Americans*. Boston: Little, 1989.

Weglyn, Michi. *Years of Infamy: The Untold Story of America's Concentration Camps*. New York: Morrow, 1976.

Wong, Sau-ling C. "Denationalization Reconsidered: Asian American Cultural Criticism at a Theoretical Crossroads." *Amerasia Journal* 21.1–2 (1995): 1–27.

Yip, Alethea. "All Things Being Equal: The Realities and Myths of Asian Americans in Higher Education." *Asian Week* 5–11 Sept. 1997: 11–18.

Feathering Custer

W. S. PENN

George Armstrong Custer became a fantasy, an outright lie of bravery and victimization. It's a fantasy that must make us all — me, perhaps, more than anyone—wonder which fantasies we are allowing to be reinvented and which ones we are only playing roles in, like Sitting Bull in William "Buffalo Bill" Cody's Wild West shows. This role-playing is especially curious, since most of us lack both the wisdom and the sheer character of a man like Sitting Bull and most of us are probably a lot more like Custer—who wanted only to be publicly known and recognized and in the wanting became arrogant, foolish, and high-handed.

Custer, like Sitting Bull, came from somewhere: Custer from the poor family that belonged to the Democratic party in a Republican-controlled period; Sitting Bull from the long heritage of his people and their experiential contact with white European fantasies. One, Custer, actively created and re-created the foundation of his response to the world (which is what I mean by "identity" or "who you are") in order to construct and reconstruct a foundationless public image, which in turn was misconstrued to be his identity. The other, Sitting Bull, more passively allowed it to happen out of despair. In the one, it caused not only arrogance but also incredible risk taking, even to the extent that Custer hired Crow scouts and then ignored their repeated expressions of great worry over the sheer number of hoofprints they had seen near the Little Big Horn site. In the other, possibly, it allowed him to play a role for money, painfully setting aside the real pride and power of his medicine, and to act the warrior for a public willing to pay for their pornographic fantasies of belonging to an adventurous rugged individualism of a West they had never touched. For Sitting Bull it is probable that his power and identity were so secure, so firm that playacting did not affect or change them at all. It is hard to know.

Now that the Indian wars take place on different grounds, mostly in the academies where the spirit is separated from life and called committees, entire careers rest on invention of fantasies as people jockey for snippets of emasculate power that in our beery age is "fame" and that so corrupts humility and understanding, whether of success or failure. What if, we have to ask, the power jockeys, in some sense, don't begin with a core identity, a background? What if they don't come from anywhere or from an anywhere that can be clearly felt as a presence and not an absence, as in having a grandfather or father or as in not being adopted or not adopting a tribal family? Or what if, culturally, they begin their conscious public lives overlooked like Indians and yet the humidity of contemporary politics expressly says the opposite, that they should be noticed and even honored, not for merit but for background, and while they claim the blood they lack in that background? What if they just plain ole want to be other than they are, like a New Age feeler who collects the stuff, the appurtenances and appearances, of being an Other? What, in other words, happens on either side of the little Little Big Horn if those who would claim power are not remembered in their identity but constructed or reconstructed in it, especially in the late twentieth century when few Americans come from extended families, from geographies in which have lived generations of those who make them?

The reconstruction may, in some ways, be a piecing together out of whole cloth. You can become like the reductive image of George Custer jockeying for power and position, become an authority in name only, and hold "position" out of fear, not respect or admiration. Or you can become a Head Indian on campus who, in defending yourself against all the Custers, ends up skirmishing over turf with other Indians rather than dispensing the gifts of honor and respect.

Let's imagine. First, let's imagine the modern reconstructed Indian in situ, in a bend in the road, his offices and the offices of his allies hidden among the trees that line the river or canyon that divides the campus. It is a small river or canyon, and the offices, though small, are many and make up an "institute" that is given small amounts of money to dispense and that the institute's bureaucrats protect as though it were the lifeblood of their great-grandchildren. Our Head Indian, in other words, does not begin by earning the power and wisdom of Sitting Bull; he is granted it by a bureaucracy and comes already fully enrolled in the Wild West Show of the New Age university. He has shrunk in both purpose and stature. Indeed, he began small and has reconstructed himself as someone who has the power to hand out gifts, among which are his approval. In all likelihood, he has reconstructed himself as a "Native American," and the *Good Housekeeping* seal of his approval depends greatly on whether or not you are willing to accept that reconstruction without question.

Let's nickname this modern reconstruction Gyp Carnal.

When another Indian shows up in Gyp's department, Gyp greets him. As the Head Indian, he can afford to seem friendly.

"So how are you liking Michigan?" he asks at the department meeting.

It probably seems, somehow, inappropriate there in the midst of the newcomer's first department meeting to tell the details of how his wife stepped down from the airplane and burst into tears that were like the tears of a great grief—capable of appearing at any moment as though the sadness were stored in the sponge of her eyes. Nor does it seem wise to tell how their first visit to the twenty-four-hour superstore of food, lawn mowers, film developing, and dress shoes had frightened her with the look of its basic customer, as though warehouse food produces a strain of mutant shopper, pale-faced with searching Jell-O eyes beneath a fluorescent indoor moon.

So the newcomer makes a joke about how nice everyone is. Coming from New York ("New York isn't going to tell us what to do or not to do," the supervisor of campus security yelled when he tried to explain how his transit plates on a new car should be good for sixty days even in the swamp of Michigan, and besides all he wanted was a temporary parking permit to unload books in his office), not yet having lost his energetic sense of humor to the overcast flat of central Michigan, he may go on too long—which, in this part of the Midwest, means to go on at all. Hell, in New York you can stand at the market's checkout counter while the Dominican checker purposely ignores you, making it a point to finish her conversation about mascara and the plumage of orange lip gloss before deigning to lift your jug of milk and pass it over a scanner that beeps from curd on its screen. The surprise of having the checkout person ask after the health of your firstborn and give you tips on removing stains from bathroom tile while happily passing your purchases over a spotless scanner that generates money-saving coupons for your next "visit" is both pleasant and a little surreal to a New Yorker (which to the campus security supervisor, his brass belt buckle polished by the lap of his belly, his white hood hidden in his Ku Klux Kloset in Howell, Michigan, means not a place but a race and that race is "Jews").

"Everything is so nice, here," he concludes. "Sometimes I worry that I'll get niced to death." Ho ho. The day they move into their house the nice neighbor across the street nicely invites them over for a nice dinner to be eaten outdoors because it's such a nice night.

He arrives home with a truckload from storage and his wife meets him with, "Something awful's happened."

"What? Tell me."

"I'm sorry. I didn't know what to do."

"What? What happened?"

"The woman across the street insisted we come to dinner. I couldn't get out of it. I'm sorry."

"It's okay," he laughs. "That's probably how it is here."

"She's real pushy."

"Naw. She's just being friendly. That's all." (He is wrong there, but that's another story to be imagined at another time.)

He is cut short by a colleague who is concerned to make him feel welcome and right at home. "If it bothers you so much, why don't you just go back where you came from?" she inquires with all the gentle grace and humorlessness she can muster.

Our new Indian sighs. Relief. He isn't sure. But he thinks he hears in her dulcet voice the reminiscent timbre of the New York traffic cop pestered by an aging tourist for directions who says, "Lady, I ain't a fucking road map."

"Thanks for making me feel at home," he says, smiling.

This is pretty much the last conversation he ever has with Gyp Carnal, until he comes up for tenure. Gyp returns across the river (or canyon) to his entertainments at the institute. He never calls and, well, with getting settled, having children, writing books, and teaching, as well as with being a completely different, shy sort of person from a completely different sort of tribe, our new Indian never calls Gyp, either, until his department chair tells him that Gyp has written the provost in favor of denying him tenure. Then, being from a very different tribe in which telling the truth counts for something, he goes straight to his office and calls Gyp.

Being from a completely different background, Gyp assures him that he likes him fine, that he has not written the provost or composed the letter. "But," Gyp adds, "there are a lot of complaints I've heard about your lack of scholarship."

"Lack of scholarship" keeps coming up in this conversation like salmonella chicken, except that it seems almost like a joke. After all, it is well-known that Gyp himself has never published anything but a little monograph-sized book that he co-coauthored with two men who afterward accused him of doing none of the work and taking all of the credit. Since then, in pursuit of promotion, Gyp has argued that grant applications—applications, mind you—be considered as "publication" in the triadic research, teaching, and service of a large university.

To our not-so-new Indian, Gyp seems to be someone whose public sense of himself, his power, and his place is high-handedly disproportionate, like Custer. And yet he is not interested in getting into a battle with Gyp over territory. All that would do is damage the students and hurt the cause of Native American studies. ("See," the head of campus security would say, "they can't even get along with each other.") So he does what he was taught to do: he keeps a firm grip on his own identity and balance and lets it go.

Even when Gyp starts telephoning presses and, using the indirect power of rumor and innuendo, tries to stop the publication of his books, all the not-so-new Indian wants is for Gyp to stop his phone calls. Intrigues of this or any other kind don't interest him much. All he wants is for Gyp to go his way in peace and leave him to his way.

This is a fairly complete picture of the way Gyp Carnal works, and we have to interrupt the flow of the river to imagine and remember Gyp's very real enemy on the other side of the little Little Big Horn river (or canyon). He is a white bureaucrat whose career started on a successful note—he achieved a modest reputation and showed every promise of becoming a generally important scholar—but either the world has changed or he has, and his career seems to languish, his reputation having somehow fallen out of the sparrow's eye of academic repute. The notes of his success he can feel evaporating around him like humidity from a hot tub, and so he turns to bureaucracy and administration to get salary raises, chosen by the dean not because he is a good administrator who manages not to be high-handed with the barge pilots and postal mistresses but because there is no one else even adequate to the task who is as willing as Custer to make rules and bring order. To reconstruct himself fully as a petty bureaucrat, he has to forget who he once thought he was. He is pettifogging, pusillanimous, yet pugnacious, and for those qualities we'll call him Three Pee.

Rules are rules. And even minority faculty members cannot behave the way Gyp has. Like the head of campus security, Three Pee resents people who seem like seagulls, protected species who get paid more than he thinks they're worth because there are so few of them with PhDs. He gathers his forces and sends out scouts.

Meanwhile (now that he has his character and dimensions, the two dimensions that all of you will recognize as his real number, though not, perhaps, very realistic), back at the institute Gyp is telephoning, telephoning, telephoning—which for an Indian is probably a difficult technological task, but for Gyp, well he has "redial," and besides as a reconstruction he came fully versed in the use of modern tools—using what he thinks are his power and position to interfere with the not-so-new Indian's tenure review.

Where does Gyp get his sense of power and right?

Everyone knows he's wheedled an enrollment card out of a small and very newly federally recognized tribe where the elders are rumored to be angry that he has it, especially given the uses he put it to, and the people are said (by a member of the tribe) to regret ever granting him the privilege of calling himself one of them. But frankly, where (or how) I grew up, you either were or you weren't. A card was not going to make you any more Indian than dressing the part for the Wild West shows. Perhaps, as a reconstruction uncertain himself of who he is, Gyp tends to think of an enrollment card as a meal ticket and coup stick that he can use against those who, in his notional thinking, are not "Indian" or "Indian enough." With such limitations, perhaps he fails to imagine the possibility that other people are and are not afraid of who they are—or even that they have proof of who they are that they refuse to show just everyone because they morally object to having to show anyone.

Perhaps, too, Gyp thinks he gets some of his power and privilege from his own mentor who is, like General Pleasonton, a master of intrigue and innuendo who has played word warrior in the Wild West shows of the New Age for many years. After Wily Word Warrior calls the not-so-new anymore Indian—let's call him Big Little Man—to ask for his novel for his press, he has the press's editor "release" the manuscript when Gyp calls to wonder if Big Little Man is Indian at all. Gyp denies doing this. The press's editor denies it happened. The Mocassin Telegraph says he did and it did, but Big Little Man can't prove it and even if he could, why would he waste his time and energy? He is who he is though he, too, like everyone else, sometimes gets confused and has to spend time alone remembering just who that who is. He does what he does. And if his grandfather would not let the Feds tell him who he was, why would he let Gyp tell him who he was in the context of the university? He had been truthful, direct, and plain to Wily Word Warrior when he took his book that he is an urban mixblood; Wily, who likes publicly to claim he isn't an ID card essentialist, said clearly that it was no problem.

When Big Little Man went overseas and the press "released" his accepted manuscript, Gyp must have felt as powerful as Chivington at Sand Creek. He must have been, in his way of thinking, really happy, as happy as he could feel, preventing another Indian from passing him by in rank. For that was the subtext. In his constructed fantasy of self, he wanted to be the most important Indian on campus, and yet he did little to be important other than wear feathers, use acronyms like NAGPRA (Native American Graves Protection and Repatriation Act) liberally to show his currency, and whine to the provost. We can only imagine his disappointment hearing that another press accepted the book, a disappointment that doubled when, after hardcover publication and good reviews, Wily's press decided maybe it had been wrong and bought the paperback rights.

This, unfortunately, is not the end of Gyp Carnal's reconstructed love of the appearances of authority. He begins to take unnecessary risks — unnecessary because Big Little Man is not hostile and would never hurt him, if Gyp would just leave him alone. After the first failure, when Big Little Man comes up for promotion again, Gyp tempts fate and make another bold attack with another telephone call that begins with innuendo and devolves to slander. His first mistake is in ignoring his scouts: this editor is not in the grip of Wily Word Warrior, and the editor records the contents of the call and reproduces it in writing. His second mistake is to lie about it when asked by his department chair. Though guileful, Gyp, who is no Coyote, who thought he was protected by the medicine of behind-the-scene innuendo and false rumor that had always worked before, who deluded himself into thinking he was protected by the umbrella of a General Pleasonton's favor, has made the call from his office at the university—saved himself a dime, there—where all the times, dates, places of origin, and long-distance numbers called are recorded on a central computer. When Gyp realizes that he has bagged himself (which takes about a month), he changes his tack and admits to making the call while insisting that he, Gyp, The Gyp Carnal, does not have to abide by the rules of decency and professional collegiality that the university requires of its faculty. It is a high-handedness worthy of Custer himself.

Talk about role reversal and confusion. The world sometimes seems to be in connected pairings that are rarely binary oppositions and more the completions of an image like a shadow to Peter Pan. Three Pee sees his chance and takes it, getting Gyp removed to another department in another college on the distant frontier of the university's reservation, ostensibly on Big Little Man's behalf. Yet Three Pee begins to harbor a secret anger at Big Little Man because even then Big refuses to make Gyp's mistakes public, settling for a letter of retraction and apology and the promise that Gyp would never question his purpose or his identity again.

After all, who cares? Why does he need to make Gyp suffer any more than he suffers by being Gypped? In Nez Perce histories, if the teller of the historical story is corroborated by others who were there, it is enough. The historian doesn't gain any power from this corroboration, and the next time he tells it, it has to be corroborated all over again. Revenge is not his to have. Vengeance takes its toll on the vengeful, and opponents who are cowards and liars do not merit the status of "enemy"—whom a Nez Perce can respect thoroughly. All one should care, in the end, is that the truth be told in such a way that it is available to those who would look for it. Vindictiveness is for the Custers, the heads of campus security, the bureaucrats of the small heart. Three Pee believes in the kind of revenge that the federal government took on the "renegade" Indians by slaughtering the innocent and helpless Indians at Washita. For Gyp is little more than that.

Though not peaceful, fooled by his own sense of derived power and reconstructed insistency, Gyp has no power other than the tidbits the university feeds him when they need him to dress up and act the wild Indian. Gyp is, essentially, as helpless as an old woman in the frozen dawn.

Gyp Carnal barely exists. This is all imagined. But it is not all fantasy. It happens. Still, if it happened to me I know I would be content to do nothing more to Gyp (or the head of campus security) than ask that we meet no more again this or any other year.

The problem with imagined stories is they don't end easily. Three Pee's victory over Gyp at the little Little Big Horn adds to his confusion, gives him a feeling of power that was feeling only, and he begins to deal high-handedly in his turn with the barge pilots and post office clerks. He even begins to think that he can do in Big Little Man the way he did in Gyp Carnal. The differences are several: Gyp was camped at the little Little Big Horn, thinking he had power; Big Little Man may be naive or stupid, but not so stupid to think that he is visible for anything but his work. Other than that, he has no power. He is simply who he is. When Three Pee begins to do Custerly things, he lets him. He lets him deny legitimate reimbursements for trips taken in service to the department and at the request of Three Pee himself. He lets him try to insult him, calling him a "great man" in a voice dripping with the sarcasm of petty bureaucrats who assume you are like them in their fantasies. He lets it go, turns and walks away knowing that initial success followed by apparent failure (even if it is not really failure at all) creates a dangerous enemy for whom all that remains is administrative vindictiveness. And if there is proof of failure, it is in that very attempt at vindictiveness. For vindictiveness is not for the truly successful. Vindictiveness is the cauldron in which those who want you to fail find themselves, flailing about without any help from you. You don't get to put them there or dance about the boiling fire, unless you want to become like General Sherman, whose uncompromising policy was to treat surrendering Indians ruthlessly. To him is attributed the origination of the phrase, "The only good Indian is a dead Indian," and he was recorded in 1867 as saying, "The more [Indians] we can kill this year, the less will have to be killed the next war" (Josephy 615).

Thus, even after Three Pee begins to put memos in Big Little

Man's personnel file, for which Three Pee is reprimanded by the dean who oversees the memos' removal, Big Little Man should not feel ill will toward him. Even though he finds in these actions a much lesser Custer gone over the edge of the river (or canyon), he has to do the same as he did with Gyp. Let it go and wish that they will not meet again this year, or at least while he begins the process of letting it go.

Gyp and Three Pee are just extremes, made up or invented as a way to raise questions. As inventions, they must make us wonder if we really want to be "stars" in the bureaucracy of a university or anywhere else. Imagining these questions I am not sure how much I want to be publicly admired. I would be pleased if my work were. And I wouldn't mind reputation as long as it was earned, but if that ever happens it will be the work that maintains reputation, not me, who could just as well be dead and on another journey. If I ever have power, I hope (and I am as fallible as most people, if not more so) I use it to promote and not demote, to help younger or newer people find their way and not make them join mine.

George Armstrong Custer and Sitting Bull are iconographic myths, not unlike the powerful, double-barreled mythologies of Frederick Jackson Turner's and Buffalo Bill Cody's versions of the "Frontier." In their contemporary forms, they are once removed from the "real thing" that Coca-Cola lays claim to, but they are nonetheless similar in the reconstructions of their personalities.

As someone who likes to think himself unreconstructed—I just am, like a boulder in a stream—I do know that there are things about me that make people angry, that annoy them. In some cases, it's as simple as size, and I have five decades of experience of small males picking fights with me, wanting to prove themselves. Big men get all sorts of little men sticking their noses into their personal space in bars, in class, at jobs, in meetings, and essentially saying, Oh, yeah? Yeah? You want to fight about it? (I asked a big colleague if he'd experienced that. He thought a minute and said, "You know, I have. All my life. I'd never really realized it, though.")

I realized it because I changed schools so often, and I still remember Pete Wright and Dan O'Something, the thugs of my sixth grade school to which I was new, picking a fight and making me wrestle them to the ground and sit on their chests with my fist raised as though I would strike, making them say "uncle." (Pete? Dan? You probably don't read, but if you do, you could have won those tests by refusing to cry uncle because I don't think I am capable of hitting someone so helpless.)

And then there was the added lesson of Vicki O'Dell. Playing on the beach (Ventura, California) Vicki and I tossed sand at each other, and a grain got in Vicki's eye. My loving mother spent the next several hours as we drove Vicki to the emergency room and waited for the sand to be removed telling me that she could end up blind in that eye, that if Vicki never saw again out of that eye, it would be my fault entirely. I don't know if I was given to boyish violence before that incident. I do know that as that eight-year-old boy waited for the bandage to come off Vicki's eye to learn that her sight was not damaged, whatever desire I had to physically hurt someone vanished or buried itself so deep that you would have to threaten my children and wife before I'd strike out. So maybe mom did me a favor.

Nonetheless, I can be stubborn and aggressive for things I believe to be fair, just, or good. I have a Nez Perce way of speaking what I believe is the truth, and I have a Nez Perce willingness to have that truth corroborated or disagreed with. Maybe in a world of reconstructed people forming committees to give them a sense of life and importance, it is an attempt at directness coming from so unlikely a source (a poor boy from a democratic, relocated family)—is this what annoys?

Ultimately, I come down to my sense of identity, my sense of self that comes both from my background and (perhaps) from growing up with the knowledge that at birth I was never supposed to have lived. The two are hard to separate. But whatever the reasons, this boulderish ability to stay in contact with my own moral sense of things seems to drive some folks just plain paddleless.

So, like the name of any particular university, it isn't the Gyps or Three Pees who are important here, any more than the real reconstructed historical fake of Custer. Their places in this life and the afterworld are assuredly not the same as ours; they have to be who they are (or aren't), and we need to try to wish them no further ill. The important point is that they seem to lack a sense of being, of being who they are without the crutches of public acclaim or reputation or plasticized bureaucratic approval, reconstructing themselves with such thoroughness and lack of humor or self-awareness that they begin to confuse reality with appearance, authority with the outward shows of authoritarianism, and they begin to think they have the power to decide on peoples' fates or destinies. What they—and others like them —don't seem to understand is that people of intrigue like General Pleasonton and Wily Word Warrior protect you or remain loyal to you only insofar as it advances them and not you. Meanwhile, you have to go on being you—a depressing thought, I should think for some — without a moral compass.

A person of intrigue lacks what Wayne Booth and Henry James called the "moral sense." According to Booth, "[s]ome works [of literature] are marred by an impression that the author has weighed his characters on dishonest scales" not because "he explicitly passes judgment" but because "the judgment he passes" does not seem "defensible in the light of dramatized facts" (Booth 79). Earlier, quoting James, he suggests that the

> "moral sense of a work of art" depends completely "on the amount of felt life concerned in producing it." Though [James] qualifies this statement by including the "kind" and the "quality" of "felt life," he is still unmistakably clear that the morality of the work—that which gives the "enveloping air or the artist's humanity" — comes from the "quality and capacity" of the artist's "prime sensibility." (Booth 45)

I have written elsewhere that, as a dreamer, storytelling is all I believe in, that stories provide context and even analysis of human experience and that stories make or create the world and let us learn how we are to live in it and survive. Literature, to me, is storytelling. And much Native American storytelling involves the problem of identity. Stories, even implicitly, in the shadow of the implied or expressed author, construct who we are and, more important, how that who is. It is not a matter of "fiction" versus "nonfiction." It is all fiction, and much of it may be called true fiction, true storytelling, when the fictionizer demonstrates that "moral sense" and creates, along with the world of the story, our trust in his or her ability to tell that world accurately on a human or "felt" level.

When the constructors or creators of a story have their thumbs in the pan of the balance scales because they are involved in the reconstruction and maintenance of public reputation—like Custer— they lose all proportion in the perceptions and judgments of their continuously recontextualized (storied) lives.[1] If they are involved in intrigue and innuendo rather than straightforward attempts to "tell" the world, they soon achieve a kind of delusional madness that makes them take stupid risks because they believe themselves to be invulnerable or unassailable. They lose all proportion in their lives and their judgments.

We, then, can work backward to discover the intriguers—the way all readers of stories work backward to discover the implied author—whose lives or whose perceptual frameworks lack that simile to moral sense, lack what I might call foundational being.

The fake.

No matter how many feathers they wear, they will always be playing Indian, and until they reach the furthest extreme—which Gertrude Bonnin, in her claims of relationship to Sitting Bull, never quite reached—they will always suspect themselves of playing Indian, a fantasy they will try to hide by attacking other Indians—other Indians!—for being "not Indian enough."[2] No matter how many memos Custer sends, it is not merely history but also example that he teaches us. We can pity him, but we must not overlook the truth of what he is. He is, in the late twentieth century, the end product of committees using up precious energy to separate the spirit from life and then recycling the forms of life. The lives of these reconstructed or reconstituted people become all data and dullness.

It is madness.

And remembering the Little Big Horn, for me the results aren't really in need of imagining at all.

Notes

1. The phrase "thumb in the pan" is one I remember from graduate school thirty years ago and is, if I'm not mistaken, D. H. Lawrence's way of describing what a writer cannot do with his or her characters.
2. I was reminded of Gertrude Bonnin's claims of relation to Sitting Bull by my dissertation student and friend David Medei.

Works Cited

Booth, Wayne C. *The Rhetoric of Fiction*. Chicago: U of Chicago P, 1975.

Josephy, Alvin M., Jr. *The Nez Perce Indians and the Opening of the Northwest*. Lincoln: U of Nebraska P, 1979.

Penn, W. S. *All My Sins Are Relatives*. Lincoln: U of Nebraska P, 1995.

On Being Married to
the Institution

ROBYN WIEGMAN

This essay takes its title from a specific event in 1996 when the
dean of faculties at the institution that tenured me used the occasion of a celebratory reception for all newly promoted faculty
members to toast "our marriage to the institution."[1] I was struck
then, as I still am, by the inappropriateness of the language not only
because I believe that we need to approach the labor we do in the
academy as quite simply that—labor—but also because the collapse
of the public into the private on the one hand and the overdetermined heterosexual narrative of marriage on the other raise the
specter of the "family" as both metaphor and organizing principle of
academic life.[2] It was not that I had been unfamiliar with this
specter. The English department that tenured me regularly used its
departmental e-mail list to announce the births, marriages, and
deaths of faculty members and their families, and the intellectual
foundation of feminist knowledge that had given me the desire to
stay in the academy so many years before had long framed its understanding of the classroom and women's social relations through familial tropes, with sisterhood being the most famous and by now the
most critiqued. Few scholars who identify themselves under the sign
of the queer[3]—or who are thus identified—can have a relation to
their workplace that does not take into consideration the overarching and indeed oppressive atmosphere of heterosexual marriage,
family, and reproduction that structures the interpersonal codes, affective economies, and social practices of the academy.[4]

This is not to say that all "queers" understand their relation to the academy in the same way or that the critique I launch in this paper against the marital, familial forms of the institution represents a collective statement. In fact, there are many lesbian and gay people who believe that their assumption of the family form signals a profound political transformation, as E. J. Graff has asserted in the 1997 sex panic debates in the *Nation*. Writing in response to Michael Warner's defense of nonmonogamous sex as part of the political project of queer activism in the age of AIDS, Graff reasons:

> Of course stopping AIDS is urgent. But let's not fall for the idea that, in a consumer culture, sex is politically progressive. From where I sit, far more politically significant for all gay people is the lesbian baby boom, moving like a tornado through our nation's social institutions. Two-mom (and, less often, two-dad) families are fighting urgent and daily grass-roots battles [. . .] altering this country's minds about parenthood. (32)

For Graff, the difference between monogamy and promiscuity will ultimately outweigh the homosexual-heterosexual divide, as "allowing the home-and-hearth homos their gold rings will expose the fact that those who want to be the sexual avant-garde are most properly grouped with other sexual dissidents of whatever gender preference" (32). Much contemporary lesbian and gay political struggle is wagered precisely here, where civil rights means guaranteed access to the privileges and benefits of normative family forms, and the line being drawn in the sand, so to speak, functions to abject anything sexually queer from the public face of homosexuality.

How homosexuality can have a public face in a deeply heterosexual culture is of course no simple thing, and I don't mean to underestimate the difficulty of producing the queer family form that Graff renders above as a political goal. Normativities are valuable precisely because the practices that constitute them function as modes of exclusion and negation, which is to say that the struggle to achieve them is never a small or insignificant one.[5] For my former English department to announce on its e-mail list a non–birth mother's adoption of her son certainly breaks the heterosexual claim to reproduction that had been previously and repeatedly inscribed by the list's discourse and in ways that no doubt challenged the ideology of family collectively (if unconsciously) shared among many of our colleagues. But even as the heterosexual patent of the list is forced to give way, its general function as a bulletin board for the family as the department's primary social form has hardly been undone, nor has that form's structural service as the institution's general mode of social reproduction begun to wane.

To think about the reverberations of being married to the institution means, then, differentiating the horizons of individual and local struggles for inclusion and recognition from the ways in which the contemporary academy organizes itself as a social community through heterosexualized, bourgeois practices of marriage and family. By trying to talk concretely here about these practices, I hope to aid both faculty members and administrators in their pursuit of the political project I elsewhere call queering the academy, which entails opening the academy's social and collegial forms to the prospect of a queer sexuality that does not reproduce intimacy's disciplined horizons of monogamy, marriage, or the family form. Thus seeking the concrete detail of heterosexuality's institutional familial privilege, this essay understands its political contribution to reside not in prescriptions for a utopian future but in the assemblage of practical information that makes visible the mundane contexts, activities, and discursive hegemonies of heterofamilial ideals.[6]

The Dean's Desk and Other Recruiting Matters

In *The Psychic Life of Power*, Judith Butler writes in passing that "[o]ne should not underestimate how exhausting it is to be expected to be an 'out' homosexual all the time, whether the expectation comes from gay and lesbian allies or their foes" (94). In the context of her conversation about Foucault and disciplinary power, this comment seeks to foreground the psychic work that disclosure entails in a culture that assumes not only an individual's heterosexuality but that individual's desire for and imbrication in heterosexuality's normative telos of marriage, reproduction, and family as well. At the same time, Butler's point is aimed at the assumption within gay and lesbian discourses that political commitment necessitates our repeated self-disclosure and further that such disclosure can guarantee our political representation and viability. Butler's comment thus cites a recurrent dilemma in which the queer subject is constrained within heterosexuality's inability to exhaust itself and a political demand that forces the queer subject to exhaustively produce a queer self.

While Butler's language for this dilemma puts stress on the *expectation* that one must be "out," the force of the exhaustion that she notes can arise more from the unevenness of normativity's demands than from a pervasive cultural insistence that queers incessantly perform their sexually eccentric selves. The "foes" of homosexuals, for instance, may expect an out performance under certain conditions, but more often than not they expect heterosexual conformity, and with a vengeance. This expectation comes in a variety of forms, many of which are located in the mundane practices of everyday life: in the narratives and images of popular culture, in the educational and religious pedagogies of institutions, in the spatial layout of homes and communities, and in the discourses of friendship, gossip, and love. While much contemporary queer studies scholarship takes aim at the ideological production of heterosexuality and its material basis in institutions of law, government, and education, little has been written that specifically analyzes the academy in its everyday constellation of heterosexual reproductive forms and social practices.[7]

Let's begin, then, at the beginning of one's marriage to the institution, with the dilemmas posed by recruitment rituals that tacitly assume a normative heterosexual subject. Consider, as you read, the options facing the queer subject who seeks employment in such real-life scenarios as the following:

1. At the MLA convention, the chair of a department you are interviewing with knows your dissertation director and arranges a friendly drink for the three of you. After the chair and your director catch up on social issues, including how each of their children is fairing, the social-cum-business meeting turns to the issue of your potential relationship with the chair's department. When the dissertation director mentions your same-sex female partner, who happens to have a gender-neutral name, the chair asks, "Oh, what does he do?" Besides restraining yourself from kicking your director, who has now put you in the position of self-disclosure or self-effacement, what do you do?

2. At the campus interview, when the dean is late for your meeting, his secretary and administrative assistant greet you and begin to chat in a cordial way. After inquiring about the children you may or may not have, they ask if you are married and what work your husband does. The dean does not arrive in time to rescue you from this conversation. What can—or do—you say?

3. When the dean arrives, you are led into an office that is decorated with three or four family photos, each propped in appropriate direction for the gaze of the visitor who sits in a nicely padded chair. You know the appropriate sociality dictated by the photos—the sentimental inquiry—but you decide to ask about the university's sports teams. Just your luck: this dean went to small private schools and thinks that sports are detrimental to the educational mission of the institution. When he scans your undergraduate transcript for possible details of your prior failures, focusing on that single term in 1973 when your family pulled you out of school because of your sexual activities (rush that child to the shrink!), you have the job-landing choice: tell him about the familial trauma of coming out or suspiciously blink.

4. After your job talk, the department has planned a reception and dinner at a faculty member's home in your honor. Several of the faculty members in the department bring their children, and dinner consists of conversation that revolves around the various kinds of local activities the department's "kids" have been doing. When the children talk to you, you maintain a cordial niceness, but it is only with a certain rudeness that you can avoid listening to the oldest child's brief piano recital in the living room.

5. On the second day of the campus visit, you meet with the campus housing officer, who shows you around various neighborhoods, describing the school systems, their influence on property taxes, and the benefits of raising children in the area. When it is time to discuss the university-funded mortgage that would be a part of your recruitment package, should you land the job, you discover that only an opposite-sex spouse can inherit the property purchased through this mortgage program should something, as they say, "happen" to you. Further, you learn that the university calculates your mortgage amount on the basis of your marital status and the number of your legal dependents.

The wise and seasoned academic queer likes to believe that she will no longer get angry or even flustered in any of these situations. She has spent a great deal of time, after all, studying her first-time-job-hunting self who was startled anew at the way that heterosexuality, family, and a marital social form insinuated themselves into the so-called public and professional life of the university. But she doesn't fool herself: securing an academic position *is* about the intellectual and affective, if not libidinal, attachments that faculty members in a department—and deans—feel toward one as a potential member of their group, and that group is so powerfully invested in the reproduction, indeed reproducibility, of itself that the queer academic is no minor threat to protocols of sociality, whether we are speaking of the "cordial" and seemingly benign discursive encounter or the institutionalized forms of support that ensconce the reproductive heterosexual family as the academic norm. What's important here is not to dismiss the categorical dilemma that the queer academic subject faces, where resisting the normative codes and social forms is to render herself fully (as opposed to partially) outside what we might call the academy's social mode of production; to acquiesce, through silence or misleading speech, is to defer but not to escape the problematic of expectation and disclosure. In the scenarios that accompany the pursuit of benefited employment, the queer subject confronts the difficulty—some might say the socially constructed impossibility—of forging a simultaneously public and private "self."

Becoming Collegial

The occasion of this essay, for a volume published by the MLA, makes possible the airing of certain kinds of critical "complaints," and it is no doubt the hope of the editors of this volume that such complaints will be treated less as individual tales of woe than as symptomatic sites for understanding the academy's institutionalized modes of producing and perpetuating the historical privileges accompanying socially dominant identities and identifications. In the state of California, where I now teach, of course, even the hard-won "privilege" of addressing historical privilege has been undermined by the anti–affirmative action backlash, as issues of social deprivation based on race, ethnicity, and gender are being legally dismissed as legitimate sites of inquiry or address. In such a climate, where the issues of heterosexuality and its performative reproductions have failed to garner the kind of historical and political urgency that we might say race, ethnicity, and gender have (if tenuously) held, this essay's devolution into the common or mundane, indeed into some of the most transparent acts, encounters, and modes of social relationality, risks at the very least its own critical dismissal. I say this because academics, especially liberal ones, often place a great deal of their liberal political capital, if you will, at the level of personal intention, which means that firmly held democratic beliefs in equality are staged more often as inclusivist gestures—including gays and lesbians in university programs for spousal benefits, for instance—than in the reconsideration of the ways in which their individual lives tacitly reproduce the culture of heterosexuality and family that serves as this essay's critical target.

To be married to the institution is part and parcel, then, of the formation of social bonds with one's colleagues and peers, and it is only through their concerted attention to the institutional plotting of their own seemingly benign normativities that the academy will not simply make room for but also itself be interpellated by the queer. This is not to rely on an individualist response to the matters I pose in this essay but to insist that prototypically inclusive intentions that do not risk the critical reassessment of the personal formation of marital reproductive heterosexuality are little more than pretentious liberal gestures. In this context, faculty members need to consider the extent to which the heterosexual family form serves as a primary means for the articulation of their own social bonds, shaping many of the activities and services provided by the institution and offering temporal and spatial opportunities for community outside work. Many colleges and universities, for instance, run child care programs, even elementary schools for the children of their workers; house organizations devoted to family fun (picnics, plays, holiday festivities, vacations); build faculty and student residence communities designed for children; and provide newsletters for newcomers detailing the area in terms of the specific needs of families. While some of these services evince a hard-won victory for feminist organizing around issues of women's reproductive labor, it is nonetheless crucial to confront the way that the social bonds developed through child rearing and child care also produce conservative institutional cultures dependent on reproduction as a social form.

It is not unusual, for instance, for women's studies programs to have at their core a group of scholars whose ties to one another arose through shared child care, and it has been a regular practice in every program I have ever worked in for the discourse of "one's family" to function as an unquestioned caveat for arranging and postponing program meetings and events. The point here, let me be clear, is not that we should dismiss the everyday lives of women who are caught in the double bind of career and family, for that would surely be a misunderstanding of the way that heterosexuality as a mode of compulsory reproduction, in Adrienne Rich's now familiar formulation, has a deep systemic tie to patriarchal social formations (see "Compulsory Heterosexuality"). Rather, I am seeking to foreground the way that even the feminist articulation of reproduction has been less nuanced in its rendering of the complexities of heterosexuality's normative modalities in the daily life of the institution, where reproduction as part of academic culture structures political bonds between queer feminists and their heterosexual, reproductive colleagues. For the queer subject, whose lack of status as a mother or spouse marks her eccentricity to the codes of institutional sociability, there is no recognizable "outside" to her work or workplace identity; she is in this regard without a public narrative of her own private life, since it is paradoxically the family form that enables professional women today to claim a private life that can have legitimacy in the public sphere of academic labor. This is, I think, an odd historical emergence, where the absence of the marital family form leaves the queer subject without the kind of legitimating labor that allows one to make public the affective intimacies she may form in the so-called domestic, private sphere.[8]

The legitimating relationship between public and private (and the full force of normative sexuality to condition the transit between the two) must be understood as a profound factor shaping both the perception and the possibility of academic collegiality. I say this because at most institutions, collegiality is measured less by the collective generosity and struggle that accompany knowledge debates than by the forms of social life that colleagues collectively inhabit. Because of the asymmetry between the heterosexual's ability to tacitly claim both the public and the private and the queer's inability to render herself complexly knowable as queer in either domain, the social or collegial life of the department must be understood as always already permeated by heterosexuality's normalizing injunctions. What this means is that the alienation that many queer faculty members experience, as they attend—or refuse to attend—the bar mitzvahs, graduations, weddings, and baby showers of their colleagues and their children is of an order far more significant than a simple individual antifamilial disposition. That alienation is about the inhospitality of the institutional lives of departments to render "difference" at the

level of the social, and it affects not only the queer academic's relation to her colleagues but often the very path of her career in—and
too often out—of the academy. The exhaustion that Butler cites
might be thought of, then, as the repetitive affective economy within
which queer subjects inhabit the everyday sociality of the academy,
where exhaustion registers simultaneously the necessary performance of an out queer identity and heterosexuality's inexhaustive
power to reproduce itself as the horizon of intelligibility for social
forms and practices.

Exhaustion

In the February 1998 issue of the *Women's Review of Books*, Dale
Bauer joins other feminist scholars from across the United States to
address the current dilemmas and opportunities facing women's studies programs and faculty. In "The Politics of Housework," Bauer
launches her own critique against the heterosexual marital form,
reading it less, as I have done here, as the horizon of departmental
and campus sociality than as the overall underlying structure of academic work. Citing studies that demonstrate how men in dual career
households continue to do quantitatively less labor than their female
counterparts in the home (and usually only the labor that they
choose to do), Bauer links the sexual division of labor of home and
family to the exploitation of women's labor in the academy. "Women's
studies teachers do the second shift of academia," she writes (19).
This second shift comes in two primary forms: that of joint appointments, which feature a double burden of teaching and service that is
rarely compensated (and more often than not a liability in tenure and
advancement); and that of interdisciplinary affiliations, which subordinate the labor that scholars perform in women's studies programs
to the intellectual and institutional priorities of the traditional academic department. "[W]omen's studies work is perceived along domestic lines: taking care of the 'family' or one's sisters, addressing the
extra-systemic needs—often emotional—of women and men" (19).
Not only do administrators enforce this division of labor, but as Bauer
rightly points out, women's studies scholars routinely accept their domestic institutional chores as the labor of feminism in the academy.[9]

Bauer's analysis makes possible an understanding of the way that
even the alternative site in the academy—women's studies in this

instance—does not escape the tenacious power of the heterosexual familial form as a kind of material framework for organizing academic labor. What this means for queers in particular Bauer doesn't say, but it is no great leap to contemplate how such subordinating conditions of labor extend the scope and deepen the hold of the heterosexual familial form that I have been tracking in this essay. For the queer who seeks the alternative site as a way of countering the suffocating heterosexual and familial culture of the institution, the confrontation with that site's own embeddedness in such social and material forms contributes to identity's exhaustive features. Most acutely, it demonstrates the extent to which the labor that is performed in the academy is unevenly developed both within and across the bodies of the scholars who inhabit the institution, as even the alternative site extracts the psychic and material toll that the difference of the queer elsewhere pays for her own alterity.

Does this mean, then, that there is no alternative to being married to the institution? Or that queer critical resistance to it cannot amount to much? It is hardly the project of this volume to underestimate the power of defining in precise ways the academy's failure to transform the institutional culture of privilege and exclusion that has characterized professional life in the United States. Indeed, it seems to me that the labor we do in the academy is so profoundly untheorized and the complexities of the relationship between traditional departments and identity-based sites so markedly undermanaged that the project of articulating these issues does matter. But its "matter" is no simple thing, especially as the issue of the academy's heterosexual family form goes to the heart of departmental practices, collegial relations, and the everyday protocols of institutional life. My provisional attempt to make legible the implicit and pervasive structure of the heterosexual family form aims to interrupt its seemingly inexhaustible reproductivity. But more than this, it aims to make possible an academic culture that bears within it the legibility of the queer.

Notes

1. I have written about this incident in "Queering the Academy."
2. The struggle to unionize graduate student labor in the United States offers an important opportunity to foreground the linkage I am citing between the misrecognition of institutional labor as labor and discourses of the family and reproduction. The paternalistic notion that institutional intimacies will be compromised—that faculty-student relationships will be perverted and intel-

lectually undermined—by the recognition of graduate student labor pivots on a submerged familial framework that not only requires infantilization as a precondition of intimacy but also posits mentorship and generational succession as a vehicle for institutional reproduction. Greater attention to the relationship between familial reproductive logics and the labor issues of the institution might make important political connections between unionization and what I am calling in this essay the legibility of the queer academic subject. Certainly such connections are crucial for expanding the political critique of labor in the academy that unionization currently and often too narrowly signals.

3. While I use *queer* to refer to gay and lesbian people and to nonmonogamous, nonreproductive bisexuals or heterosexuals, the term has been in tension, at times overt conflict, with the use of *gay* and *lesbian* to define the political horizon of sexuality studies in the academy. For some critics, including myself, *queer* references sexual practices, social forms, and knowledge formations that do not arrive at identity as an ontological or epistemological destination (see esp. Sedgwick; Butler, *Bodies That Matter*). For others, however, *queer* threatens to erase the specificity of same-sex desires and identity formations—especially the legacy of lesbian-feminist critical theory and political culture. Bonnie Zimmerman, for instance, writes, "It is curious indeed to find Queer Nation—even a totalizing Queer Planet—emerging to replace a discredited Lesbian Nation" (4). For a crucial counterpoint to the critical divide that separates *lesbian* from *queer*, see Lauren Berlant's "lesbian/queer challenge to the sexual imaginaries of feminist and gay politics" ("'68" 301).

4. While the savvy reader will note that I move in this introductory paragraph from marriage to reproduction to family in ways that might improperly suggest their critical indistinction, I am assuming that it is heterosexuality's normative telos that generates this powerful consolidation of social practices and forms and further that the occasion of this volume makes imperative a tracking of such consolidation within the social practices of the academy.

5. One might think here of the way that the normative forms of reproduction and the family are used as mechanisms for the racialization and abjection of specified populations, so much so that welfare laws in the United States have long functioned to produce the very stereotypes of illegitimate reproduction and pathological family forms that the economic formation of slavery had itself generated. As should be clear, my critique of the family and reproduction as normativities limits itself to the context marked out by this collection, that of the academy, and to the ways in which the academy's production of a professional class of workers both borrows from and intersects with family and reproduction as bourgeois ideals.

6. I am interested, then, in the political project of making "apparent" the unrecognized dominant forms of academic sociality and intimacy. For faculty members and administrators who want a more pointed answer to the question, "What should we do?" I would say that, at this point in the nearly universal illegibility of the queer in academic institutions, a full-scale interrogation, assessment, and critical understanding of the scope of the imperative of heterofamilial forms would be not simply politically responsible but also a welcome form of political engagement.

7. For an interesting exception, see Crew.

8. Certainly the language of public and private betrays its own ability to maintain separate entities here—and elsewhere. A number of important scholarly conversations have emerged in the last few years to challenge the way that public and private as conceptual categories have framed our understanding of nineteenth-century social life. See especially Lora Romero's *Home Fronts* and the special issue of *American Literature* called *No More Separate Spheres*, edited by Cathy Davidson. In addition, Lauren Berlant's *The Queen of America Goes to Washington City* details the contemporary privatization of the public in United States culture in ways that demonstrate how a New Right political agenda underlies the production of a family-centered "intimate public sphere" (1).

9. The resistance among some women's studies faculty members to pressuring administration for full-time tenure-track lines is often presented as the necessary move to protect the supportive and collaborative "ethos" of a program. In doing so, feminist faculty members are guaranteeing the continued "volunteerist" culture of many women's studies programs by extracting women's labor for the institution without renumeration. This "housewifing" of the feminist scholar perpetuates the academy's own diminishment of the seriousness of feminist knowledge and works to convince feminist scholars that the work we do is so marginal that doing it overtime is the only way it can be done at all.

Works Cited

Bauer, Dale M. "The Politics of Housework." *Women's Review of Books* Feb. 1998: 19–20.

Berlant, Lauren. *The Queen of America Goes to Washington City: Essays on Sex and Citizenship*. Durham: Duke UP, 1997.

——— "'68, or, The Revolution of Little Queers." *Feminism Beside Itself*. Ed. Diane Elam and Robyn Wiegman. New York: Routledge, 1995. 297–311.

Butler, Judith. *Bodies That Matter*. New York: Routledge, 1993.

———. *The Psychic Life of Power: Theories in Subjection*. Stanford: Stanford UP, 1997.

Crew, Louie. "Before Emancipation: Gay Persons as Viewed by Chairpersons in English." *The Gay Academic*. Ed. Crew. Palm Springs: ETC, 1978. 3–48.

Davidson, Cathy, ed. *No More Separate Spheres*. Spec. issue of *American Literature* 70.3 (1998).

Graff, E. J., et al. " 'Thinking Queers' vs. 'NeoCons.' " *Nation* 29 Sept. 1997: 2+.

Rich, Adrienne. "Compulsory Heterosexuality and Lesbian Existence." *Signs* 5 (1980): 631–60.

Romero, Lora. *Home Fronts: Nineteenth-Century Domesticity and Its Critics in the Antebellum United States*. Durham: Duke UP, 1997.

Sedgwick, Eve Kosofsky. *Tendencies*. Durham: Duke UP, 1993.

Warner, Michael. "Media Gays: A New Stone Wall." *Nation* 14 July 1997: 3–4.

Wiegman, Robyn. "Queering the Academy." *Genders* 26 (1997): 3–22.

Zimmerman, Bonnie. "Introduction." *NWSA Journal* 7.1 (1995): 1–7.

Raising Standards
While Lowering Anxieties

Rethinking the Promotion and Tenure Process

ANNETTE KOLODNY

> Alice: "Would you tell me, please, which way to go from here?"
> Cheshire Cat: "That depends a good deal on where you want to
>   get to."
> — Lewis Carroll, *Alice's Adventures in Wonderland*

"Maybe I should just pack it in right now," the young woman suggested hesitatingly. "When I started graduate school, I left a pretty good job in publishing—and I'm sure I could still get that job back, if I tried." She was standing, third in line, in a hotel corridor outside the entryway to a large suite in which job interviews were being conducted. Indeed, all along the corridor of this midtown Manhattan conference hotel, men and women stood (or sometimes sat on the floor) next to doors or entry foyers, waiting their turn. No one was smiling. The word was out that the 1992 MLA *Job Information List* had fewer entries than any year's list since 1976. What troubled this young woman, as she explained to me, was not just the paucity of jobs but the prospect that, even if she found a position, she still might not enjoy a full career. In her eyes, women in academe seemed to be faring no better in 1992 than when her mother had attempted to climb the tenure ladder twenty years earlier. "If all the statistics are right," she insisted, "then very few of us have any chance of making it to full professor. So why bother even trying?"

Just starting out her professional career, this newly minted PhD had every reason to be concerned. A 1991 article by Debra Blum in the *Chronicle of Higher Education* revealed that although the total number of women in tenure-eligible ranks in all fields and disciplines had steadily increased since the early 1970s, their proportion of the total faculty nationwide nonetheless remained relatively steady (since the total itself increased). As a result, the greatest gains were registered at the rank of assistant professor, where the proportion of women went from 24% in 1972 to just over 30% in 1989. As Blum pointed out, however, only 13.6% of full professors in 1989 were women (A20). Figures compiled in 1992, just as this young woman first entered the job market, were even less encouraging. In an article in the 24 January 1993 *New York Times* that appeared three weeks after the MLA meeting, Anthony DePalma reported that "women make up only 11.6% of full professors nationwide" (A11). "And even that figure is misleading," he continued. "The more prestigious the institution, the fewer women there are" (A11). The example offered was the Ivy League where, as the reporter noted dryly, "women make up 7% to 13% of full professors, excluding those in the medical schools" (A1). To his credit, DePalma emphasized the discrepancy between these figures and both the numbers of women college students and the numbers of women earning doctorates. "While women make up more than half of all college students, they make up just 27.6% of faculty members." The article then concluded with the observation that "the pipeline argument" could not explain these figures, "since women receive 36% of the 38,000 doctorates conferred each year" (A11).

Even before DePalma's article appeared, statistical studies from the MLA's Committee on the Status of Women in the Profession had confirmed that women were making "dramatic gains at the PhD level" between 1970 and 1986, a period in which "they almost doubled their share of the doctorates granted in English and increased their representation among foreign language degree recipients by just over half" (Huber 59). But as Bettina J. Huber cautioned in a summary essay, those same studies also indicated that while "women made significant gains at all ranks between 1977 and 1987," their gains "were less dramatic at the full-professor rank" (Huber 59–60). In reviewing this data, Huber cited a number of factors, including the "rapid shift in undergraduate interests" to vocational studies in the mid-1970s, the shrinking college age population, and the consequent "severe contraction of the academic job market, which hit the humanities particularly hard because of the simultaneous decline in majors." As Huber observed, "It would appear, therefore, that just as women were starting to join the faculty in significant numbers, the doors of the academy were swinging shut" (58).

Notwithstanding the stagnant job market that began in the 1970s and has continued through the 1990s, the dramatic increases in the percentages of women earning doctorates should have resulted by now in some statistically significant realignments at the senior ranks. But the explanation offered by Huber in 1990 holds true at the end of the decade and not just in the humanities disciplines: "women have been hired in relatively large numbers at the assistant-professor level since 1980, but once in tenure-track positions, they have advanced more slowly than men to tenured ranks and full professorships" (66). As the century draws to a close, therefore, women are still predominantly clustered in the generally untenured ranks of assistant professor and lecturer. Unless hiring and promotion patterns change dramatically, data from the United States Department of Education predict a growing bulge of under- or unemployed women PhDs. According to that department's projections, the percentage of doctoral "degrees awarded to women is expected to grow from 37.9 percent in 1996 to 49.5 percent by 2006." And even though this gain is "not quite large enough to reach parity with men," it nonetheless signals the markedly increased number of women available for academic employment ("The Future"). While optimists can always tease modest signs of progress from these and other recent statistics, overall the picture remains bleak. Whatever their field or discipline, women continue to hit the proverbial glass ceiling at two crucial points: in the initial promotion and tenure review and then, again, in advancement to full professor.

Given this picture, the young woman who stopped me in the hotel corridor in 1992 was right to have second thoughts about her chosen career path. She and every female graduate student with whom I have had similar conversations in subsequent years faced not only a depressing job market but, in addition, twenty years of stalled progress in admitting women into full partnership within academia.

To be sure, under pressure from affirmative action laws and organized women's groups—and often with genuine good will—colleges and universities around the country have attempted to increase the numbers of women and minority faculty members hired and promoted. The problem with these efforts is that they have been largely aimed at simply adding women and others from underrepresented groups to institutional structures designed by and for a white male professoriate. Thus, even when a disproportionate number of women and minority faculty members fail to succeed in the promotion and tenure process, few schools have felt compelled to examine the process itself. Instead, the common response is to abandon aggressive affirmative action recruitment altogether or to hire another cohort of junior women and minority faculty members in hopes that these *new* people will better adjust to or "fit into" the system as it currently exists.

Only rarely is such institutional inertia an expression of viciousness or intentional insensitivity. There is another, more obvious explanation: those now in power in academe are those for whom the promotion and tenure system worked. Indeed, it is the very system that conferred their present status. The urgent need for change, therefore, is felt only by those for whom the current system is not working or at least not working as well. But these individuals are usually without a voice in policy making. And when these individuals do raise their voices, more often than not they are dismissed as "uncollegial," while their legitimate charges of systemic bias are greeted by accusations that they are merely trying to lower academic standards. As a result, women and minorities continue to be disproportionately underrepresented in the senior ranks across all fields and disciplines, and existing promotion and tenure documents remain unexamined at most institutions.

To the best of my knowledge, there exists no comprehensive national survey of the obstacles to advancement encountered by women faculty members. Nonetheless, anecdotal wisdom abounds, and most academics have a ready list of problems facing women in the promotion and tenure process. What follows is hardly exhaustive, but it does summarize my own observations and those that colleagues have shared with me over the years.

UNFAMILIAR RESEARCH AREAS. Many women and minority scholars have been drawn to the academy by their interest in subject areas that are innovative and still developing, including, for example, women's studies, ethnic studies, African American studies, or disability studies. While these fields can prove personally rewarding to junior scholars and their students, and while these scholars' work adds substantially to the creation of new knowledge, both their research materials and their experimental methodologies can be unfamiliar to senior departmental colleagues who abide comfortably entrenched in more orthodox approaches. In too many cases, *un*familiarity breeds contempt (or, even worse, suspicion and devaluation). When the promotion and tenure review begins, senior professors may be unable to recognize a junior colleague's contribution to an emerging field, instead dismissing her or his work as eccentric or merely faddish.

HIDDEN WORKLOAD. Whatever their rank, women and minority faculty members repeatedly find themselves burdened with responsibilities that have never been demanded of their white male peers. The consequences for junior faculty members can be career-threatening. An assistant professor in her fifth year who ought to be concentrating on preparing her promotion and tenure file for review may feel compelled to devote long hours to mentoring a first-year colleague—especially if there are no women available in the tenured ranks. Minority and women junior faculty members alike find themselves mentoring women and minority graduate students as well as undergraduates—even when these students are not in their classes or are not their own dissertation advisees. Although these kinds of activities drain substantial stores of time and energy, I have rarely encountered women or minority faculty members who felt they could turn away from such responsibilities. As an African American colleague at another institution explained to me years ago, "If we're going to open up the pipeline and get these young folks through it, then I've got to make sure they have a friend and a helping hand along the way. In my department, I'm the only black person—so who else would they turn to?"

National surveys demonstrate that women and minority faculty members tend to spend more time on student advising and in office hours than their white male colleagues do.[1] My own observations over the years have led me to conclude that the majority of male faculty members are comfortable scheduling ten-, fifteen-, and twenty-minute slots for students during office hours but that women, by contrast, rarely give a student *less* than twenty minutes. Indeed, during my own years as a faculty member, before I became a dean, I regularly spent more than six hours each week in office hours. Like many of my women colleagues, if I deemed it potentially helpful, I afforded students time to talk about personal matters that were impinging on their academic performance. Most male colleagues shied away from such conversations.

Because women and minority faculty members are often numerically underrepresented in their home department and across the campus generally, they tend to be overburdened with committee assignments. In the laudatory attempt to seek diversity, most universities try to include at least one woman and one minority member on almost every committee. While this practice may amount to no more than tokenism, it does not diminish the fact that the few women and minority faculty members available are consistently overutilized in committee assignments. And when the appointment to a committee is couched in terms like, "If you don't serve, there won't be any voice for women's issues," it is very difficult for even the most junior assistant professor to decline. In fact, the stronger the faculty member feels regarding issues of gender, ethnic, or racial equity, the more susceptible he or she is to burdensome invitations. At the same time, that faculty member must be on guard against the trap of being asked to speak "on behalf of" a particular race or gender, constantly reminding committee colleagues that she or he speaks—as they do—as an individual. In trying to maintain individuality while simultaneously bringing unique or alternative group perspectives to any committee, the lone woman or token minority often exhibits heroic capacities for overcoming marginal status and inserts a vital new voice into the discussion. But these individuals always walk a psychological tightrope, and the emotional cost is enormous.

Perhaps less well understood is the fact that women and minority faculty members spend more time than their white male peers in preparing for committee meetings. The only woman in the room may be asked to take the minutes. (And unless she refuses or suggests a rotation system, she will be asked to take on this task repeatedly.) More important, because the woman or minority faculty member has often been invited to serve on the committee specifically to represent women's or minority perspectives, this individual feels compelled to do the extra work that will make those perspectives comprehensible. As a result, unlike their white male peers, these committee members spend hours researching statistics, gathering reports, or surveying colleagues in order to bring a firm database to an upcoming meeting. The majority on the committee may rest content to put forward their personal observations and opinions; women or minority members do so at their peril. They know that to be persuasive they will have to present irrefutable evidence. And because they know that a lone voice is too often lost within the larger group, they also know that to be heard they will have to spend additional hours in one-on-one conversation, personally lobbying key committee members on "their" issues.

Inescapably this makes the role both more stressful and more time-consuming.[2]

Less subtle indicators of the hidden workload are the differential course assignments given to junior faculty members. Again, although no surveys exist, many junior women tell me that they are assigned fewer graduate seminars than their male peers are and that they are repeatedly asked to teach large undergraduate courses or endless sections of basic French or English composition. By comparison, male peers enjoy course assignments closer to their areas of research interest, and department chairs are often more responsive to the men's need for lighter teaching loads as they complete a book or an article. When I have pointed out this phenomenon to department chairs, men and women alike, they acknowledge that such disparities exist, even in their own departments. Their most common explanation is that male junior faculty members approach them directly and request lighter teaching loads when they are heavily involved in completing a research project before the tenure review. By contrast, junior women faculty members rarely make such requests explicit. Moreover, women appear to be more cooperative and flexible in accepting course assignments, while men declare themselves limited to their specialty. And department chairs—both men and women—readily admit that they do not monitor carefully enough for such disparities or consciously seek to offer women the same opportunities as men. In most cases, it may be an innocent oversight—but for the woman who is its victim the oversight can be devastating.[3] Not only does she enjoy less research time than her male peers do but also, when she is reviewed for tenure, she may be judged a less valuable colleague because she has not demonstrated proficiency in teaching graduate seminars or advanced undergraduate courses in her particular field of expertise.

Unquestionably the most obvious aspect of the hidden workload is that, even in two-wage-earner heterosexual families, women continue to shoulder the major responsibilities for home keeping and child rearing. The young male assistant professor, full of enlightened views and feminist sympathies, "helps" his wife at home with the cooking and child care. But the young woman who is an untenured assistant professor typically spends up to twice as many hours as her husband in organizing these same chores, and more likely than not, it is *her* book (not his) that gets left unwritten on the dining room table (see Banner et al., esp. 4–6).

LACK OF ACCESS TO INFORMAL MALE NETWORKS. Senior male faculty members express no hesitation at inviting a new junior male colleague to join them for a beer at the end of the day or to try out for the noon basketball league at the gym. And many powerful male bonds have been forged at the Friday night poker game. Women are rarely invited to partake of such activities. Married women are generally invited only to social gatherings to which spouses (or other guests) are also invited. And single women are sometimes altogether shunned (or, even worse, "hit on" sexually). As a result, the informal networks of friendship and collegial exchange that silently influence the promotion and tenure review remain largely unavailable to women. As long as informal networks provide opportunities for senior males to advise their younger colleagues on publication venues, to recommend fellowship opportunities, to facilitate introductions to other major researchers, and to assess the collegiality and the intellectual worth of their juniors, the prevalence of these male-only gatherings continues to be a serious problem for women.

DIFFERENTIAL STANDARDS. A frequent complaint from women who have experienced difficulty in the promotion and tenure review is that the standards they were held to were higher than or different from those for male peers going through the review at the same time. A woman's ten articles in prominent refereed feminist journals may be deemed less consequential than a male colleague's three articles in more familiar (even if nonrefereed) journals. In the humanities disciplines, men are usually tenured on the basis of an original, single-authored book published by a reputable university press. The woman whose book has also been published by a university press is often asked, in addition, to demonstrate that she is now embarked on a further scholarly project. The variety of differential standards becomes even more problematic where the evaluation of "quality" is wholly subjective. How, for example, do we compare the archival recovery of a forgotten woman author and the most recent exegesis of a William Faulkner short story? The familiar may be judged of superior worth simply because it *is* familiar.

The most common complaint from women who have had difficulty in the promotion and tenure process, however, is that they were being held to standards to which the senior members of their promotion and tenure committee were never held. In other words, the men on the committee were requiring levels of scholarly productivity from junior women that they had never demanded of themselves. When trying to vent their outraged sense of injustice, women in such situations repeatedly offer the analogy of Alice in Wonderland, wandering through a landscape in which the rules are always arbitrary.

Let me offer just one example. At a small midwestern university, Professor X, a promising young Americanist, was denied promotion and tenure despite consistently high praise from students and even though she had won a dissertation prize at the Ivy League institution from which she had received her PhD and had published an original book with a major university press, as well as five articles in well-respected refereed journals. Not a single member of her all-male promotion and tenure committee had published a book, and the chair of the committee had only one article to his credit, a brief review essay in a small journal. The committee had expressed itself as unimpressed with the quality of her book, in part because it introduced what they perceived as nonliterary concerns into a discussion of canonical American texts. As Professor X later said to me, "They just don't understand feminist or American studies interdisciplinary approaches."[4]

When I was invited to the same institution as a commencement speaker, the chair of this young woman's promotion and tenure committee happened to be seated to my left at the awards dinner. At some point in the conversation, I expressed my surprise that Professor X had not received promotion and tenure. "Oh," replied the tenure committee chair, "I haven't published any books myself, you know, but I have my standards." He then proceeded to explain that Professor X's book had not received universally laudatory reviews. I responded, in vain, that no scholarly book ever does. But only scholars who have themselves produced a book for peer judgment would know that.

INAPPROPRIATE STATEMENTS BY EXTERNAL REFEREES. Without malice or intent, even the most supportive referees sometimes write letters that hurt the woman candidate for promotion and tenure. A statement like "She is one of the top women in Shakespeare studies today," rather than "She is one of the top scholars in Shakespeare studies today," is a typical example. By measuring the woman scholar *only* against other women in her field, the external referee subtly suggests that her work cannot support larger comparisons. Too often, referees may discuss a woman candidate's nonacademic assets, such as her charming personality, her ability to throw a great party, or the excellence of her fudge brownies. These may be well-intentioned expressions of personal warmth, but they undermine the profile of the candidate as a serious professional. And review committees are quick to interpret such sentences as covert signals that the candidate's professional talents are weaker than her personal ones.

Other letters by external referees can be intentionally damaging. Many referees try to hide their biases, while others openly identify themselves as hostile to or ignorant of feminist approaches, cross-disciplinary analyses, or women's studies. Yet, in both cases, such referees proceed to evaluate a candidate's publication record as though their comments were wholly objective. If, in their haste to read dozens of candidates' files, members of a promotion and tenure review committee overlook a referee's admission of prejudice—or if the committee members are not aware of that bias—they will give the referee's negative comments a weight they should not have.

Because change in academe is gradual and incremental, any overhaul of the promotion and tenure process that seeks to address the obstacles I've listed here must itself also be gradual and incremental. Understanding this, during the years that I was dean, the College of Humanities at the University of Arizona, Tucson, decided to reexamine promotion and tenure in two separate steps, beginning first with a clear set of *criteria* and then moving on to the invention of new promotion and tenure *procedures*. The first step, in fact, strategically prepared the way for the second. The faculty, department heads, and I all felt reasonably confident that we could build consensus around appropriate criteria for evaluating teaching, research and scholarship, and service because we had ready referents in national norms and discipline expectations at peer institutions. Had we begun with a wholesale invention of new procedures, the effort would have been sabotaged by some individuals' suspicion that we were simply attempting to find ways to promote women and minorities without regard to quality. By beginning with a criteria document, therefore, we constrained anxieties that standards would be lowered in what was already an aggressive campaign to recruit and retain women and minority faculty members.

After an eighteen-month collaboration between faculty members and department heads, a document was hammered out that both clarified and upgraded criteria for promotion and tenure within the College of Humanities. Among other things, the criteria document explicitly acknowledged the new kinds of scholarly productivity that we were striving to accommodate. For example, our new "Promotion and Tenure Criteria" recognized traditional forms of publication, including books, articles, and monographs; in addition, it accepted the fact that, in certain humanities disciplines, "an innovative textbook, software programs, video presentations, translations, or the like" might well be "of such high quality as to constitute a significant contribution to the field in the opinion of nationally recognized experts" (9). We thus made room in our promotion and tenure criteria document for people whose research resulted in the curatorship of museum shows or in innovative software for foreign language instruction.

The criteria document also emphasized the need to have a candidate's record assessed by those with expertise in the field. Although the document largely shied away from procedural issues, the faculty saw the need to guarantee—even in this document—the fairness of the review process. As a result, the criteria document stipulated that "in every case, the candidate must be guaranteed fair representation by scholars sharing his or her area of academic specialization" on departmental promotion and tenure committees (3). Because of the signal importance of this guarantee, departments with limited areas of specialization began to appoint to their promotion and tenure review committees those from other appropriate departments or programs who were knowledgeable about a candidate's field or methodological approach. This informal practice was later codified as part of the procedures document.

Finally, the criteria document raised one more quasi-procedural issue: the need to protect women and minority faculty members from a debilitating hidden workload. In one of the boldest statements in that document, all department heads and the dean were put on notice that "care must be taken [. . .] on the part of both candidates and administration, not to overcommit assistant professors by demanding a level of service that interferes with their development of a coherent research program and of teaching skills." The document explicitly cautioned that, "while women and minorities are under-represented on the faculty, it will be particularly important to resist the temptation to overutilize their contributions to service" (7).

Soon after the new "Promotion and Tenure Criteria" were adopted by faculty ballot in the spring semester of 1990, each department within the College of Humanities began to revise its own department-level promotion and tenure materials accordingly. Equally important, junior as well as senior faculty members quickly recognized that guidelines were now required to help us implement the review of our enhanced and upgraded criteria. In other words, having agreed—as a community —to clarify and raise our standards as well as to embrace new forms of scholarly productivity, we needed a set of procedures that would truly level the playing field. As dean, I was concerned that after refining and raising the threshold of expectation we also lower the anxiety level by assuring all promotion and tenure candidates that the review process, as much as possible, was scrupulously fair *and* designed to ensure their success so long as they met our clearly articulated written criteria.

In May 1992, after marathon committee meetings and nine drafts, the College of Humanities voted to adopt its first promotion and tenure procedures document. This second document was the result of a collaboration between all department heads and program directors, the faculty as a whole, and the newly formed Faculty Planning and Policies Advisory Committee. Appointed by me specifically to provide me with advice and counsel on a whole range of policy issues, the committee was gender-balanced, with minority participation, and included faculty members from all three tenure-eligible ranks (assistant, associate, and full professor) in equal numbers. Every program and department was represented, along with a full spectrum of faculty views and political dispositions. (In subsequent years, at the committee's recommendation, half its members were elected by the faculty.) A large and potentially unwieldy group, the committee broke into subcommittees, divided up its many tasks, and began work on its first charge: drafting procedures for fair and open promotion and tenure reviews. Over a two-year period, the committee circulated successive drafts for faculty-wide comment, and committee members presided over open forums to allow for further faculty input. The committee also met regularly with the department heads and program directors.

The committee's charge was not an easy one because few units on our own campus or nationwide had documents that could serve as models. Still, the goal of the group was clear: they wanted to build on the spirit of the criteria document and address the obstacles that had traditionally thwarted the successful advancement of women and minorities. They also wanted to protect the career advancement of those in nontraditional or marginalized areas of study—like the lone linguist in an English department or the single Portuguese specialist in a Spanish department. To accomplish this goal, they did a great deal of reading, gathering relevant materials from other universities and from professional organizations. Probably more important, they did much sharing. Once the group members felt sufficiently comfortable with one another and a certain level of mutual trust and respect had been established, individuals on the committee began to talk about their own career histories. Several women revealed details of experiences that had been both personally and professionally wrenching and talked frankly about the difficulties they had encountered because of their gender. One woman's candor emboldened another to speak out in turn. And by the end of their first year together, three men on the committee told me privately that they had come to understand the plight of women and minorities in the profession. As one senior male observed to me, "I think this is what you feminists call consciousness-raising."

Perhaps because the committee had developed this quality of candid exchange and had watched one another go through a sea change in attitudes, many members were unprepared for the outright hostility directed against them by some on the faculty when an initial draft was circulated. One open forum degenerated into a three-hour "encounter session," the subcommittee chair reported, with ten very vocal faculty members assaulting the committee with "sputtering" invective and personal attack. "It was an ugly outburst of self-protection," one committee member later told me. "They just don't want anything to change, they're scared," added another. The major objections, according to the committee members, centered on recommendations to involve promotion and tenure candidates in the choice of external referees and to set minimum qualifications for those faculty members within the college who would serve on promotion and tenure review committees. As some faculty members apparently viewed the matter, junior faculty members could not be trusted to supply names of appropriate off-campus experts in their field, while service on review committees was seen as an automatic right conferred by tenured status rather than as a professional responsibility earned by merit.

Recognizing that there would be resistance to any redesign in promotion and tenure procedures, the Faculty Planning and Policies Advisory Committee repeatedly redrafted their recommendations with a view toward mollifying anxieties and incorporating responsible suggestions. But they gave up the illusion that their hard work would be universally applauded. Their perseverance in circulating all drafts for additional input (thus ensuring widespread faculty ownership), their willingness to meet with each department, and their continued openness to debate and discussion finally proved persuasive to a large majority of faculty members ready for meaningful change. In the end, reason and good will prevailed.

With each redrafting, I consulted with the university attorneys' office to ensure that we remained in compliance with university and Board of Regents policies. In only one instance was there a problem. Together the Faculty Planning and Policies Advisory Committee and the department heads and program directors had recommended enhanced procedures for stopping the tenure clock that included paid "family responsibility" leaves. The draft of that recommendation spelled out provisions for stopping the tenure clock on the basis of "family care responsibilities [. . .] or other appropriate reasons" and made it possible for a faculty member to remain on full salary during any leave period (up to two semesters) connected with "family care responsibilities." Those who proposed these paragraphs were convinced that until and unless women faculty members were permitted paid family care leaves while stopping their tenure clock—and men faculty members were given an incentive to do the same—the playing field would never be level. Despite the persuasiveness of these arguments, university attorneys restricted us to the terms for stopping the tenure clock that had appeared in a recent memorandum from the provost. And they told us that because the state of Arizona had no policy for granting paid family care leaves, we could not—as state employees—institute them on our own.

As a result, the first version of the "Promotion and Tenure Procedures" carried a copy of the provost's memorandum at the end, along with a statement that urged the development of campus-wide paid family care leave policies in the future. Amended by faculty vote in later years, the "Promotion and Tenure Procedures" document dropped the provost's memorandum (because improved provisions for stopping the tenure clock had now become university-level policy); and our recommendation for paid family care leaves became a topic of discussion across campus, as other deans began to take notice of our arguments. In the meantime, the College of Humanities pursued other methods for achieving equity in family care issues.

The amended version of the "College of Humanities Promotion and Tenure Procedures" is printed as an appendix to this chapter, so that readers may go through the document in detail. Let me point out some of its salient features. First, the procedures offer a plausible level of fairness by enjoining the dean to appoint to the college-level promotion and tenure review committee "only faculty members who have met the current criteria by which the candidates under consideration are being judged." Most—but not all—faculty members have welcomed this condition because it secures the most professionally active and engaged faculty members in the crucial task of evaluating their junior colleagues. Second, candidates no longer suffer the anxieties of protracted uncertainty because "at each stage in the review process every candidate is to be promptly informed of the recommendations (including any minority reports) made regarding her or his tenure and/or promotion." The principle of openness enunciated in that sentence is further guaranteed by the stipulation that candidates receive verbatim copies of all committee recommendations as well as the department head's recommendation to the dean and the dean's recommendation to the provost. At both stages, moreover, the candidate can compose a written response to be included in the promotion and tenure file; among other things, this gives the candidate an opportunity to correct any factual errors that may have crept into a head's, a dean's, or a review committee's letter. According to one senior faculty member, this lifting of what he called "the veil of silence" not only introduced real accountability into the process for the first time but, in addition, contributed substantially to improved morale among his junior colleagues. All along, this had been one of our major goals.

Other significant features of the document include the following:

Candidates for promotion and tenure are integrally involved in helping to identify appropriate internal and external reviewers. The purpose here is to ensure that a reviewer known to be irretrievably hostile to a candidate's field of study or hostile to the candidate personally is not invited to sit on a departmental committee or submit an external letter of reference.

Moreover, in addition to being consulted in the choice of external reviewers, candidates are assured that their external referees are appropriate persons to review their work.

Any unprofessional or inappropriate information about a candidate that appears in an external referee's letter must be clearly noted as such in the department head's letter. The referee's letter can then be weighed accordingly.

Informal or "overload" participation in an interdisciplinary program, such as women's studies, African American studies, or American Indian studies, is evaluated as part of the promotion and tenure file. The candidate thus receives full credit for all his or her contributions.

Like the earlier criteria document, the cover page of the "College of Humanities Promotion and Tenure Procedures" mandates that, "immediately upon assuming their duties, all newly hired tenured or tenure-eligible faculty members" will receive copies of these and other pertinent promotion and tenure materials. From their first day, thereby, faculty members know what is expected of them and how they will be evaluated.

Admittedly, the promotion and tenure procedures document of the College of Humanities at the University of Arizona represents no panacea. Written policies are only as fair and unbiased as those who implement them. Even so, because the document was developed within a larger matrix of strategies designed to enhance the performance of women and minorities—including the cluster hiring of women and minorities, a buddy system, blind-submission research grant competitions for faculty members, awards for innovative curriculum development, and a gender-balanced Faculty Planning and Policies Advisory Committee—it played a significant role in contributing to an environment in which all faculty members could know that they were invited to succeed. Together with these other strategies, the new procedures effectively changed the culture of decision making during the years that I was dean and, as well, helped us to build a sense of community. What we wanted, after all, was to encourage the best from every faculty member and to transform what had once been a gate-closing function into a gate-opening function for everyone who was qualified.

Appendix

UNIVERSITY OF ARIZONA, TUCSON, COLLEGE OF
HUMANITIES PROMOTION AND TENURE PROCEDURES

The specific qualifications required for tenure and/or promotion are discussed in full in the departmental promotion and tenure documents and in the College of Humanities (COH) Promotion and Tenure "Criteria" document. What follows here pertains only to the "procedures" to be followed in conducting tenure and/or promotion reviews.

Immediately upon assuming their duties, all newly hired tenured or tenure-eligible faculty members, regardless of rank, will receive from their respective department heads copies of three sets of promotion and tenure materials:

1. the Promotion and Tenure Guidelines adopted by their respective departments
2. the COH Promotion and Tenure "Criteria" document, together with the COH Promotion and Tenure "Procedures" document, and the COH Promotion and Tenure "Timetable"
3. all relevant university promotion and tenure documents

Department heads will also provide copies of these promotion and tenure documents, where appropriate, to all candidates for hire into tenured or tenurable positions.

COLLEGE OF HUMANITIES
PROMOTION AND TENURE PROCEDURES

I. *Appointment of Committees*

The procedures to be followed in the College of Humanities (COH) for the constitution of promotion and tenure committees must conform to those regulations which, by regental authority, are binding upon the university as a whole. We therefore note the following governing paragraphs from the *University Handbook for Appointed Personnel (UHAP)*, first edition, 1988 (3.11.01):

Standing Committees

Provided there are sufficient faculty members in a department to warrant such a committee, each college and department shall have a standing committee on faculty status to advise the dean and department head before recommendations are forwarded to higher administrative levels concerning all faculty personnel matters. Each committee shall be composed of at least three tenured members of the faculty.

In promotion to tenure matters, the committees shall be so constituted that recommendations shall be made only by faculty
members holding rank superior to the rank of the candidate
being considered, except in the case of full professors where the
committee members shall each be a full professor. Normally
standing committees shall meet without the administrator whom
they advise.

A. The College of Humanities Promotion and Tenure Committee (aka
"the Dean's Committee")
   1. Each year the dean will appoint a COH promotion and tenure
       committee and will name its chairperson. The committee will
       be charged to act in the best interest of the College of Humanities
       as a whole.
   2. The dean will make appointments to the COH Promotion and
       Tenure Committee in such a way as to ensure compliance
       with the equitable gender and minority representation require-
       ments of federal and state antidiscrimination laws and with
       ABOR [Arizona Board of Regents] and university policies and
       rules against discrimination. No one who is otherwise qualified
       shall be barred from service on promotion and tenure com-
       mittees on the basis of religion, race, color, national origin, phys-
       ical disability, or sexual orientation.
   3. The committee will consist of no fewer than six members.
       Four of those members will be from four different departments
       of the College of Humanities; two will be from departments or
       programs in other faculties or colleges. Appointments will be
       for one or two years.
   4. The dean will appoint to this committee only faculty members
       who have met the current criteria by which the candidates under
       consideration are being judged. Members of the committee
       from units other than COH shall be those who have met the cur-
       rent criteria for promotion to full or associate professor in
       their respective fields. In accordance with the provost's guide-
       lines, associate professors may serve when there is no candi-
       date for promotion to the rank of full professor.
   5. The committee will be presented with a detailed statement of
       the university's affirmative action policies and guidelines,
       which will be explained by a representative of the affirmative
       action office. Also, it will be explained to the whole committee
       at their first meeting that, should there arise in the course of
       deliberation any questions regarding race, gender, or other
       sorts of bias, then, at the request of one or more members, the
       committee will consult with a representative of the univer-
       sity's affirmative action office for advice and guidance in such
       matters.
   6. In any given year, it is likely that the committee will include
       members from departments that are presenting candidates. It

is therefore stipulated that a committee member may not participate in discussions concerning candidates from his or her own department, that he or she must leave the room during such discussions, and that he or she must abstain from voting on those cases.

7. The membership of this committee will be considered public information, and the dean will announce the names of its members at the beginning of each academic year.

8. Faculty under review for possible promotion and tenure are to have no direct or indirect contact with the committee or its members regarding their own cases.

9. At each stage in the review process every candidate is to be promptly informed of the recommendations (including any minority reports) made regarding her or his tenure and/or promotion, in order that her or his response may go forward to the next level with the recommendation. Therefore, before the dean's recommendation concerning a candidate is sent to the provost, the candidate will be furnished with a complete and verbatim copy of that same recommendation. The candidate will also be provided at this time with a copy of the COH committee's report to the dean, which shall include a record of the committee's numerical vote. However, the votes of particular members of the committee, as well as their individual judgments and comments, shall be kept confidential. Moreover, any quotations from external reviewers included in the dean's recommendation or the committee's report shall be referred to as having been made by "Reviewer A," "Reviewer B," "Reviewer C," etc. Each candidate will indicate that she or he has received and read these documents by signing a copy of each and returning it to the dean's office, along with any comment or reply she or he may wish to make. At this point the file will be forwarded to the next level.

B. Departmental Promotion and Tenure Committees

Membership on standing or ad hoc departmental promotion and tenure committees is by appointment. In each department, it is the department head who appoints the members of that department's promotion and tenure committee, after thorough consultation with the department faculty. However, a department head's discretion in this matter is subject to the following constraints.

1. In accordance with *UHAP* regulations, a standing departmental promotion and tenure committee "shall be composed of at least three tenured faculty members."

2. Department heads will make their appointments to the promotion and tenure committees in such a way as to ensure compliance with university affirmative action and nondiscrimination guidelines and policy. To this end, whenever

feasible and appropriate, department heads may appoint to their committees tenured faculty from other departments and programs who are qualified to evaluate the candidates' work. No one who is otherwise qualified shall be barred from service on promotion and tenure committees on the basis of religion, race, color, national origin, physical disability, or sexual orientation.

3. Whenever possible, the departmental promotion and tenure committee will include at least one member with expertise in the candidate's particular field. The committee should also include as many members as possible conversant with the candidate's general area of specialization.

4. The committee will be presented with a detailed statement of the university's affirmative action policies and guidelines, which will be explained by a representative of the affirmative action office. Also, it will be explained to the whole committee at their first meeting that, should there arise in the course of deliberation any questions regarding race, gender, or other sorts of bias, then, at the request of one or more members, the committee will consult with a representative of the university's affirmative action office for advice and guidance in such matters.

5. Each candidate, in consultation with the head, will compile a list of five University of Arizona faculty members with the rank and expertise necessary to evaluate the candidate. The list may include former or present members of the departmental standing promotion and tenure committee. The department head will select from this list two persons who, if they are not already members of the standing promotion committee, will join it as ad hoc members to participate in discussion of, and to vote upon, that particular candidate's case. Appointment of such additional, ad hoc members is also subject to the qualifications listed immediately above (B1, B2, and B3).

6. Whenever the department's workload so demands, a department head may appoint more than one promotion and tenure committee.

7. Members of the promotion and tenure committee are not permitted to discuss the candidate's evaluation with her/him, unless the committee as a whole should formally request such a discussion. Any such request on the part of a committee must be communicated to the candidate through the department head. Likewise, any questions the candidate may have regarding the committee's procedures must also be directed to the department head.

8. At each stage in the review process every candidate is to be informed, promptly, of the recommendations (including any minority reports) made regarding her or his tenure and/or promotion, in order that her or his response may go forward to the

next level with the recommendation. Therefore, before the department head's recommendation concerning a candidate is sent to the dean, the candidate too will be furnished with a complete and verbatim copy of that same recommendation. The candidate will also be provided at this time with a copy of the departmental committee's report to the department head, which shall include a record of the committee's numerical vote. However, the votes of particular members of the committee, as well as their individual judgments and comments, shall be kept confidential. Moreover, any remarks from external reviewers quoted in the department head's recommendation or in the departmental committee's report shall be referred to as having been made by "Reviewer A," "Reviewer B," "Reviewer C," etc. Each candidate will indicate that she or he has received and read these documents by signing a copy of each and returning it to the department head, along with any comment or reply she or he may wish to make. At this point the file will be forwarded to the next level.

II. *Preparing the Promotion and Tenure File*
(Note: The following procedures are to be understood as subordinate to and governed by the procedures outlined in the document issued every spring by the provost's office [hereinafter referred to as the current Provost's Guidelines], which deals with continuing status and the promotion process and preparation of dossiers. This document, which must be studied carefully by all involved in the promotion and tenure process, is subject to change. Changes that it may undergo in the future may necessitate changes in COH procedures and thus may require alteration of the directions given below.)
A. Identification and Notification of Candidates
By March 1 of each year department heads will write to all members of their departments who are eligible for tenure and/or promotion, inviting candidates for mandatory or optional review to submit their candidacies to the department head and the chairperson of the departmental promotion and tenure committee. (For dates of all subsequent steps, see the most recent COH Promotion and Tenure Timetable.)
B. Proper Format for the Preparation of Dossiers
1. Dossiers must be prepared using the outline form (headings and subheadings) from the most recent version of *"Provost's Guidelines for Preparing Promotion and Tenure Cases"* issued each spring by the provost.
2. All published or forthcoming works listed in a dossier must be cited according to the complete citation form, i.e., all citations must include title, publisher, place and date of publication, and page numbers.

3. In the event that a candidate for promotion and tenure presents published or soon to be published materials which cannot be given adequate critical evaluation because they are written in a language insufficiently known to members of the departmental or the COH committee, the chairperson of either committee may request that the candidate prepare an English translation of selected portions of the materials (or a précis of them) that would permit the committee to make an informed evaluation. In certain cases it may be deemed necessary to invite a consultant, fluent in the language in question, to participate in the committee's discussions (but not to vote).

C. Referees and Letters of Evaluation

1. Each candidate may submit up to ten names of potential reviewers from outside the University of Arizona, but in so doing must take care to nominate only those persons whose objectivity will not be put in question (for example, by previous close association with the candidate as a research collaborator, coeditor, or dissertation adviser).

2. To the list of possible reviewers nominated by the candidate the department head will add the names of other persons of his or her own choosing who are knowledgeable in the candidate's field.

3. The full list of potential reviewers—i.e., the list of all those whom the candidate has suggested together with all others whom the head is considering—will be discussed with the candidate, who will be given the opportunity to present compelling and legitimate reasons for removing any person(s) from the list. A list of all potential reviewers to whom the candidate has objected will be kept as a part of the official promotion and tenure file.

4. The final decision as to which persons will serve as reviewers will be made by the department head, in consultation with the departmental promotion and tenure committee—this in accordance with the current Provost's Guidelines, which specify that "candidates may suggest names, but the department head or review committee should select the individuals to be contacted." It is understood, however, that in any case in which a candidate has presented compelling reason for removing a particular person from the list of potential reviewers, the department head will respect the candidate's wishes and not solicit a reference from that person.

5. Some (but no more than half) of those finally selected to serve as reviewers will be from the candidate's list of nominees.

6. The names of all reviewers finally chosen, including those suggested by the candidate, will be kept confidential. At no point in the process will the candidate contact, either directly or indirectly, external reviewers or potential reviewers regarding the tenure and/or promotion review. If contacted by a reviewer, the candidate shall refrain from responding to questions about

the promotion and tenure case and, instead, shall direct the reviewer to the department head or the chairperson of the departmental promotion and tenure committee for any required information or directions.

7. By the date established in the current COH Timetable, the department head will write a standard letter to all outside reviewers requesting an evaluation of the candidate. (A sample letter is usually provided in the current Provost's Guidelines.) Referees will be assured that their letters of reference will be held in strictest confidentiality, within the limits of applicable law, ABOR policy, and university regulations. The letters to all reviewers must be substantively identical.

8. At least three of the letters of reference included in any promotion and tenure file must be recent.

9. In order to ensure the confidentiality of the reviewers, once their letters have been received, the department head shall label them "A," "B," "C," etc., and prepare a separate list of the reviewers identifying them as "A," "B," "C," etc. All subsequent references to external reviewers in written documents shall refer to them as "Reviewer A," "Reviewer B," "Reviewer C," etc. Reviewers' letters, with their original signatures, shall remain part of the candidates' files.

10. In the department head's letter to the dean, the department head shall call attention to letters that are not in accordance with federal and state antidiscrimination laws, or with ABOR and university policies and rules against discrimination.

11. For further information on outside reviewers, consult the current version of the Provost's Guidelines.

D. Collection of Supporting Documents

1. It is the responsibility of the candidate to provide a copy, offprint, or preprint of each work published or accepted for publication. Each manuscript accepted for publication but not yet actually published must be accompanied by a letter from the publisher, journal editor, or other responsible person indicating its acceptance.

2. A candidate's teaching record must be documented, not merely asserted. It is the responsibility of the department head and the candidate to provide an evaluation of teaching and advising, as directed in the current Provost's Guidelines.

3. Proof of professional honors or recognition and proof of professional service, both within and without the university, is the responsibility of the candidate. He or she should submit all pertinent documentation when citing such honors, awards, or service— e.g., letters of appointment to committees; letters of recognition from local, regional, national organizations; etc.

4. In any case in which a professional honor or award is cited, the candidate should also provide some information or documentation about the award or honor.

5. The candidate should discuss with the department head submission of any other documents that may be deemed pertinent to promotion or tenure action.

6. Significant new materials may be added to the candidate packet during the review process in accordance with the procedures described in the current Provost's Guidelines.

7. The department head shall ensure that the candidate's file remain intact and the identical file as was reviewed at the department level be forwarded intact to the dean's level.

III. *Procedures for Evaluation of Research, Teaching, and Service*

A. Evaluation of Research

1. As noted above, the candidate must provide copies of all her or his published and soon to be published works. The candidate should also provide copies of any published reviews of those works which he or she wishes the committees to consider.

2. It is possible that an external reviewer's initial letter will prompt further questions on the part of the department head or the departmental committee. In such cases the department head may request a second letter of reference from the reviewer, asking him or her to provide clarification of points in the initial letter or requesting additional information. All such follow-up requests, and all responses to them, must be in writing. Referees will again be assured that all such correspondence will be held in the strictest confidentiality within the limits of applicable law.

3. The departmental committee will summarize the content of all available reviews of the candidate's publications.

4. The departmental committee will evaluate anthologies, books, and journals in which the candidate's works have appeared or will appear, and will summarize their relative standing in the candidate's field.

5. The departmental committee will summarize and evaluate invited and volunteered conference papers, talks, poetry readings, performances, etc., that the candidate has given, while also assessing the relative importance of the meetings (conferences, colloquia, etc.) at which the contributions were made.

6. The departmental committee will summarize the relative importance to the department and institution of the candidate's scholarly and creative production. If the candidate is said to have national or international standing, this claim must be substantiated.

7. In addition to judging the quality of the candidate's individual contributions, the departmental committee will also assess the coherence, quality, development, and potential value of the candidate's overall research program and will assess the relevance to that general program of all individual research products.

8. Scholarly editing, where it can be shown to require sustained research and original or critical activity, may be offered as another example of scholarly activity. In most instances, however, journal editing or similar activity will be understood as "professional service."

B. Evaluation of Teaching

A full statement of what information to provide on teaching, and what not to provide, is contained in the current Provost's Guidelines. The following procedural points are for use by the candidate, the department head, and the promotion and tenure committees, in implementing those guidelines.

1. The committees will evaluate local, regional, and national awards or recognition the candidate may have won for teaching and determine their importance.
2. The departmental committee will appoint qualified individuals to provide peer review of the candidate's teaching. This may include actual classroom visits arranged in consultation with the candidate.
3. The head will provide summary statements of the results of teaching evaluations conducted since the candidate's last formal promotion evaluation, or for at least the three years preceding the year of the current review. The departmental committee will evaluate and comment on the candidate's teaching effectiveness.
4. The departmental committee will include any other pertinent information concerning the quality of the candidate's teaching.

C. Evaluation of Service

The committees will evaluate and summarize all evidence provided by the candidate concerning service to the department, university, region, and/or profession and will carefully weigh all claims made about the significance of such service.

IV. *Supplementary Procedures to Be Followed in Considering the Tenure and/or Promotion of Faculty Engaged in Interdisciplinary Programs*

Participation in the activities of interdisciplinary programs may comprise an ongoing and integral part of a faculty member's professional activities. To the extent that this is so, these efforts should be recognized, alongside other relevant activities, in the evaluation procedures for promotion and tenure.

If the candidate's formal workload includes a significant portion within graduate and/or undergraduate interdisciplinary programs, then it shall be evaluated according to the procedures outlined below, consistent with current graduate college procedures. Moreover, if the candidate, in consultation with the department head, considers his or her informal or "overload" participation in teaching, research, or service within the framework of an interdisciplinary program to constitute a significant portion of his or her workload, the head of the home department shall seek a written evaluation of the candidate's performance from the director of the interdisciplinary program, according to the procedures outlined below. These procedures are to be followed in addition to—not in place of—all the other procedures prescribed above.

1. The candidate will be asked to include, as part of her or his promotion and tenure dossier, a detailed statement of all teaching, research, and service activities that she or he has undertaken as a participant in the relevant interdisciplinary program.

2. The head of the candidate's home department shall request from the director or chairperson of the relevant interdisciplinary program an evaluation of the degree and quality of the candidate's contributions to the interdisciplinary program.

3. This evaluation will be written by the director or chairperson of the interdisciplinary program in consultation with an ad hoc committee comprising three tenured faculty of appropriate rank. The evaluation document will be sent to the head of the candidate's home department for inclusion in the candidate's promotion and tenure dossier.

4. Ordinarily, membership on such an ad hoc committee will be drawn from the interdisciplinary program's executive council and will include the director or chairperson of the interdisciplinary program. However, in the case of a candidate being considered for promotion to full professor in an interdisciplinary program the director or chairperson of which is not a full professor, that director or chairperson will join the ad hoc committee as a nonvoting member (that is to say, he or she will participate in the discussion of the candidate's case but will not vote), and an additional full professor shall be added to the committee.

5. In cases in which the ad hoc committee mechanism appears unnecessary or redundant (e.g., when the candidate's involvement in the interdisciplinary program's activities is minimal, or when there is a large overlap between the membership of the home department's promotion and tenure committee and the interdisciplinary program's ad hoc committee), one or more tenured members of the interdisciplinary program's executive council may be invited by the head of the home department to serve as pro tempore and ad hoc voting members of the home department's promotion and tenure committee.

6. In the case of a member of a graduate interdisciplinary program, additional input may be solicited from the university's director of graduate interdepartmental programs whenever this is

deemed appropriate by the candidate, by the head of the home department, or by the director or chairperson of the interdisciplinary program.

7. Once documentation of a candidate's interdisciplinary program activities has been incorporated into the candidate's dossier it will be considered — at all stages of review and by all reviewers — as integral to the evaluation of the candidate.

V. *Appeals*

Should a candidate feel that procedures have not been followed at the departmental committee level, a written appeal may be directed to the department head. Should a candidate feel that procedures have not been followed at the department head or COH Promotion and Tenure Committee levels, a written appeal may be directed to the dean.

VI. *Deferred Teaching Assignments and Delays of the "Tenure Clock"*

We call attention to the Provost's Guidelines of June 29, 1989, regarding "stopping the tenure clock." COH is seeking ways further to enhance candidates' ability to delay the "tenure clock." A proposal to this effect was drafted in 1992 by the Planning and Policy Advisory Committee (see the italicized matter, below), but it was not accepted by Central Administration because general university policy in this area has not yet been formulated. The following are therefore recommended:

1. That candidates consult regularly with their department heads regarding the current status of proposals and procedures to delay the "tenure clock."
2. That the COH Planning and Policy Advisory Committee, together with the COH department heads and program directors, the university affirmative action office, and the Committee on the Status of Women consider the possibility of including, in a future version of the COH Promotion and Tenure "Procedures" document, a procedure like the following:

In addition to, or in lieu of, the provost's provisions for stopping the "tenure clock" (outlined in the June 29, 1989, "Provost's Memorandum on the Promotion and Tenure Process"), the College of Humanities offers the following further options:

A faculty member who has urgent "family care responsibilities," or who can offer other appropriate reasons, may request of her or his department head, and of the dean, a semester of deferred teaching assignment at full salary.

> At the time such a request is made the faculty member may also request, again of both the department head and the dean, a commensurate delay of the "tenure clock."
>
> All such arrangements will be made upon the written and legally binding understanding (signed by the faculty member, his or her department head, and the dean) that the faculty member has a contractual obligation to reimburse the department in one of the following ways:
>
> 1. By teaching, without pay, one summer session course in each of two consecutive summers; or
> 2. By teaching, without extra compensation, a one-course "overload" in each of any two semesters within the four semesters following the semester of the deferment; or
> 3. By some other negotiated combination of additional teaching and/or advising duties to be fulfilled within a specified time after the semester of the deferment.
>
> Such deferred teaching assignments are not automatically granted, but every effort will be made to accommodate those with clear and pressing "family care responsibilities" or other appropriate reasons.

Note: Throughout this document, the terms *publication, publisher,* and *published* shall be understood to refer both to work available in printed form (books, articles, etc.) and to work available in electronic media (computer programs, software, etc.).

Notes

1. A 1990 survey by the Carnegie Foundation, published in *Change* magazine, also reveals that women "are the most conscientious members of the campus community" when it comes to "contributing to the process of governance on campus" (39).

2. To avoid this kind of damaging tokenism, the College of Humanities at the University of Arizona, Tucson, sought to make *all* committees gender-balanced and inclusive of significant minority representation. Until we had employed sufficient numbers of new faculty members to make this a reasonable goal, however, we were in danger of severely overburdening the women and minority faculty members already in place. As a result, as dean, I authorized department heads to reduce the teaching loads of women and minority faculty members carrying unusual service burdens. In this regard, a feminist dean can make a difference, and no one suffered unduly from our efforts at balance and diversity. Happily, at the end of two years of active and successful recruitment, no department or program within the humanities any longer needed repeatedly to call on the services of the same few women and/or minority faculty members.

3. This pattern can often be predicted by disparities in treatment of men and women in the initial recruitment process, as when male candidates are asked to deliver a research paper while women candidates are asked to "guest teach" an introductory-level class. Antidiscrimination laws prohibit this kind of gender-inflected treatment, of course, but some departments persist in it unthinkingly.

4. My own experience at the University of New Hampshire twenty years ago was remarkably similar. See Kolodny, "I Dreamt Again That I Was Drowning."

Works Cited

Banner, Lois, Eileen Boris, Mary Kelley, Annette Kolodny, Cecelia Tichi, and Lillian Schlissel. *Personal Lives and Professional Careers: The Uneasy Balance*. Report on the Women's Committee of the American Studies Association. College Park: ASA, 1988.

Blum, Debra E. "Old Issues Unresolved: Environment Still Hostile to Women in Academe, New Evidence Indicates." *Chronicle of Higher Education* 9 Oct. 1991: A1+.

Carnegie Foundation for the Advancement of Teaching. "Women Faculty Excel as Campus Citizens." *Change* Sept.-Oct. 1990: 39–43.

DePalma, Anthony. "Rare in Ivy League: Women Who Work as Full Professors." *New York Times* 24 Jan. 1993: A1+.

"The Future: Women Get More Degrees than Men Except at Doctoral Level." *About Women on Campus* 6.2 (1997): 7.

Huber, Bettina J. "Women in the Modern Languages, 1970–1990." *Profession 90*. Ed. Phyllis Franklin. New York: MLA, 1990. 58–73.

Kolodny, Annette. "I Dreamt Again That I Was Drowning." *Women's Writing in Exile*. Ed. Mary Lynn Broe and Angela Ingram. Chapel Hill: U of North Carolina P, 1989. 170–78.

University of Arizona. College of Humanities. "Promotion and Tenure Criteria." Rev. May 1992.

Minority Hiring in the Age of Downsizing

CARRIE TIRADO BRAMEN

The 27 April 1994 issue of the *Chronicle of Higher Education* devoted a number of stories to the academic job market. One of the articles, entitled "Tales from the Front: Husband and Wife Experience the Extremes in Search for Jobs as Literature Professors," featured my husband, David Schmid, and me, and it compared our experiences on the job market at the Toronto MLA convention in 1993. The article begins: "He is white. She is half Chicana. He had one job interview. She had fourteen [interviews] and four offers" (Heller). It doesn't take a PhD in English to realize how we were made to signify, namely that my husband did not find a tenure-track job because he is white and that I found employment because my mother is Chicana. The article makes no mention that I work in two fields of study, late-nineteenth-century American and contemporary multicultural literature, which are considered valid by the academy, while my husband's work is not. He researches and teaches in a field that is still considered ill-suited for the rigors of academic pedagogy, namely contemporary popular culture.[1] Rather than interrogate the multiple factors that led to my success on the job market, the *Chronicle* instead got up close and personal, reporting how the racial politics of academia permeated the private sphere of the domestic: How does a marriage function when the wife, and a minority at that, is the main breadwinner?

Not surprisingly, I received hate mail from this article, one from an anonymous angry white man in New York City, who kindly listed in descending order the various racial and ethnic groups who were most likely to find jobs. For good measure, he also added the category of gender. So in what he perceived to be a grotesque inversion of the great chain of being, black women were at the top and white men at the bottom. Scott Heller, the author of the *Chronicle* article, would have been proud of this anonymous reader, since he read the piece as it was intended to be read: as an implicit indictment against affirmative action, since minorities, and even half-breeds, are taking all the jobs. We cannot underestimate the appeal of this reading to make sense of a depressing job market. For someone who has been on the job market three or four times and who teaches part-time as an adjunct at a local community college, this article feeds a festering sense of anger, frustration, and despair. The desired reading of this article, that minority wives are taking jobs away from their white husbands, has tremendous explanatory power: it reduces the complicated dynamic of corporate restructuring (of which the academy is a part) to a simple question of race. Race explains corporate downsizing.

In the same issue of the *Chronicle,* Heller interviews two white males with doctorates, Matthew Stafford, a PhD in mathematics who tried for four years to find work in the academy before returning to graduate school for another degree ("Discouraged Mathematician"), and David Guest, an adjunct in the English department at Austin Peay State University in Tennessee. Guest mentions that the department is offering two tenure-track positions, and he has applied for one of them. But Guest's dissertation adviser, Vereen Bell, of Vanderbilt University, is not optimistic about his student's chances of landing a tenure-track job: "I'm sure his sex and his Caucasian-ness don't help. I'm not bitter about that and he's not bitter about that. The market is making corrections for crimes it committed 20 years ago" (Heller, "English Instructor" A20). After reading this, I assumed that Austin Peay State University was making numerous minority hires, or even one or two, given the fact that Guest's "Caucasian-ness" was a strike against him. In 1996, I called the English department at Austin Peay State asking about recent hires. Since Heller's article was written, they have filled three tenure-track positions, all with "Caucasians" and none of them with Guest. I asked if there were any minority faculty members in the English department. There was one.

"Was?" I asked. "Yes." The graduate student's voice became grim: "He died last week."

In 1988, Heller offered a far more sympathetic view of affirmative action in his column "Personal and Professional," where he examined the difficulty that small colleges in predominantly white rural areas have in attracting minority faculty members ("Some Colleges"). He features Joanne Washington, a black single mother and her son, Clinton, who moved to a small college in rural Pennsylvania. The college provided a number of personal and professional incentives, including a work-study student to assist her in completing her dissertation. Heller underscores the fact that her dissertation is incomplete by referring to administrators of small colleges, who believe that work-study students are "very effective in luring candidates who haven't completed their degrees." Heller ends the article with a Spielberg-esque portrayal of this rural idyll, where Joanne Washington judges floats in the homecoming parade, while Clinton rides his bike in the children's event. Perhaps one way to account for the difference in tone between Heller's two articles is the fact that Washington, as a single mother, is not in direct competition with patriarchal authority, her role as concerned mother does not conflict with another role as "ambitious wife." What does unite the two articles is the emphasis on casting female scholars as mothers and wives, in relational terms that underscore women's connections to the domestic.

The danger of Heller's "Personal and Professional" approach to the serious problems confronting the academy is that it individualizes the political; it recrafts the 1960s and 1970s slogan, "the personal is political," into the 1980s version, "the political is personal." Chandra Talpade Mohanty effectively summarizes the dangers of this individualist approach:

> [A]ll politics is collapsed into the personal, and questions of individual behaviors, attitudes, and lifestyles stand in for political analysis of the society. Individual political struggles are seen as the only relevant and legitimate form of political struggle. (204)

By focusing on the personal, Heller successfully evades implicating the power of institutions and structural relations that connect the academy to outside spheres of authority. This individualist approach is safe for Heller; it allows him to address complicated issues like affirmative action and academic hiring without actually discussing them as policies and practices but solely in terms of individual sagas of triumph or tragedy.

Whether as representations in the academic press or as idle gossip in the corridor, the discourse of minority hiring falls too readily within this "personal and professional" tradition of individual anecdote. Academic hiring has been taken too personally. As an attempt to break out of this tradition, I want to shift the discussion of minority hiring away from individual experience and toward institutional policies, because race thinking is an impoverished way to account for a shrinking job market. The focus on race and the related rhetoric of white male attrition serve only as red herrings to detract from the issue of downsizing, which involves, among other policies, the replacement of permanent academics with temporary ones.

My objective is to situate discussions about affirmative action hiring in the context of the current assault on higher education in order to insist on the need for academic unions to address the intersection of race and class in challenging the two-pronged attack against the ivory tower and the people of color who work within it. The attack against affirmative action, or what one journalist refers to as "the epidemic of rage," is currently employed to obfuscate the economic changes now occurring in the academic workplace. Corporate restructuring within the university affects *all* academic employees regardless of race or gender. An exclusive focus on the "color line" prevents us from noticing and adequately responding to the other lines that are being drawn within the profession, lines that divide tenured and tenure-track faculty members from adjuncts and part-time employees, lines that divide faculty members with health care and pensions from those with no benefits, lines that divide those who have representation in faculty governance with those who have no voice in their departments and institutions. Despite the current vogue of W. E. B. Du Bois's work, few critics have actually referred to his writings from the height of the Great Depression, where he argues that "white labor in its ignorance and poverty has been misled by the propaganda of white capital, whose policy is to divide labor into classes, races and unions and pit one against the other" ("Communism" 406). For Du Bois, unions have historically represented both the problem of the "color line" and its panacea; its potential for the latter, a point I will return to later, is in its ability to link contemporary attacks against affirmative action with more general assaults on higher education and to defend members against both.

From the Personal to the Institutional

The historian Nell Irvin Painter has led the way for an institutional analysis of minority hiring. In an article on affirmative action and the academic marketplace in the American Historical Association's monthly newsletter *Perspectives,* Painter addresses the concern that minorities are taking all the jobs.[2] By referring to National Research Council statistics indicating that only 3.1% of doctoral recipients in 1991 were women of color, she concludes that "there simply are not enough women of color receiving doctorates in history to affect the chances of white men in any but the slightest degree. The main competition of white men in the history profession continues to be first, other white men, then white women" (10). Painter views the scapegoating of black women as a mode of evasion, a strategy that avoids confronting the larger economic picture: "[White men] focus less on economic hard times than on people of color, especially black women, who seem to represent a kind of competition that can never be beaten" (10).

Painter's article provoked vociferous criticism in the following issue of *Perspectives,* when Andrew Gyory of New Jersey, among others, wrote a letter to the editor, arguing that white graduate students' fears about finding a job are legitimate and not a sign of "paranoia." Although he spends most of his letter decrying Painter's reliance on anecdote and her lack of hard facts, his own points remain unsubstantiated. He concludes that "minority candidates will gain teaching positions at a much higher rate than their white counterparts [. . .]. [T]he reality—and not the fear—is that minorities are now hired before whites" (22). Not only does Gyory offer no evidence to support his claim that "minorities are now hired before whites," he also refuses to acknowledge the vast racial disparity among PhD recipients. In the same year that Gyory published his letter, over 89% of the doctorate degrees in history went to whites, and most PhDs who received tenure-track appointments in history were also white. But then again, Gyory does not need facts to substantiate this claim, since his views are already ideologically natural-ized as common sense.

Take, for instance, the view of one renowned professor, who sim-ilarly observes that in today's university "white males are the distinct minority":

> It is also true that comparative literature, in its first U.S. phase, was the pursuit of a very specific Eurocentric canon and that this canon had been designed largely by a group of white male multilingual refugees from totalitarian Europe [. . .]. Today, in a university where white males are the distinct minority, this situ-ation clearly *must* change and indeed has changed appreciably.
>
> (Perloff 183)

Marjorie Perloff, a professor of English and comparative literature at Stanford University, claims that "white males are the distinct minor-ity" in the context of a promulticultural position. She acknowledges that the field of comparative literature must have "more options" in different national literatures and cultures to accommodate the new student body. It is unclear whether Perloff is speaking generally about the university population in the United States or about the specific demographics of Stanford University, but on either front white men do not constitute a "distinct minority." According to Bettina Huber, the former director of research for the MLA, minorities received an average of 8% of the PhD degrees granted in literature each year be-tween 1980 and 1988.[3] At the undergraduate level, minorities re-ceived 11% of the bachelor's degrees granted in English in 1992 ("Minorities" 8). These national trends even hold true for Stanford University. According to the university's own statistics, whites consti-tute 50.1% of the undergraduate population and 50.7% of the gradu-ate. Rather than represent a "distinct minority," white male students comprise the largest proportion of the student body with 26.6% and 32.8% at the undergraduate and graduate levels, respectively.[4] White women constitute the second largest group, with 23.6% and 17.9%, re-spectively. Perloff's homage to multiculturalism betrays a hidden anx-iety about the perceived demographic changes of certain universities, specifically her own.

The rhetoric of white attrition within the academy is indicative of a larger national trend, where white perceptions of the demographics of the United States substantially differ from the reality. According to one study sponsored by Harvard University, the *Washington Post,* and the Kaiser Family Foundation, whites perceive that they constitute merely 49.9% of the United States population, where in fact, according to the 1992 census, they represent 74%.[5] Conversely, whites believe that blacks constitute 23.8% and Hispanics 14.7%, where they actually represent 11.8% and 9.5% (Morin A1). The designers of the study conclude that white anxieties about their perceived minority position in the nation directly influence policy decisions as well as attitudes toward affirmative action, welfare, and white flight from American cities.

Whether it's "minorities are taking all the jobs" or "white men are the new minorities," shibboleths such as these function as "factual" observations of an actual reality rather than the pseudointellectual sound bytes of a virtual reality. They illustrate forms of "inferential racism," which Stuart Hall defines as

> those apparently naturalized representations of events and situations relating to race, whether "factual" or "fictional," which have racist premises and propositions inscribed in them as a set of *unquestioned assumptions.* These enable racist statements to be formulated without ever bringing into awareness the racist predicates on which the statements are grounded.
>
> (qtd. in San Juan 40)

This is not to say that all critiques of academic hiring, and particularly minority hiring, are inherently racist, but when they are predicated on unquestioned assumptions or claims that are based on hearsay or personal anecdote, then they epitomize instances of "inferential racism." The most common example of this type of racism is in the rhetoric of white attrition, where white men, in particular, are cast as the "vanishing Americans" of the late twentieth century. This rhetoric also assumes that minority success depends on tokenism, while white success results from merit.

Such assumptions about the marginalization of whites almost defy belief, but they can be easily refuted by examining the number of PhDs awarded to minorities in history and English, numbers that have not substantially increased in twenty years. In the discipline of history, 0.3% of PhDs in 1975 went to Native Americans, while in

1992 the figure was 0.8%. In 1975, 1.3% of doctorates in history went to Asians, while in 1992 it was 2.4%. In 1975, 1.6% of PhDs in history went to African Americans; in 1992 it was 3.9%. In 1975 only 1% of PhDs in history were awarded to Latinos; in 1992 that figure still remained a mere 1.4%. And the same lack of change also holds true for whites. In 1975, 90% of doctorates in history were awarded to whites; in 1992 it was 89.2% (qtd. in Painter 7).

The figures remain similar for doctorates in English and American literatures. In the United States in 1992, 6 Native Americans received a PhD in English, as did 18 African Americans, 37 Asian Americans, 3 Puerto Ricans, and 7 Mexican Americans. Compare these numbers to the 1,080 whites who received doctorates in the same year (National Research Council 108). These statistics hardly support the widespread assumption that minorities are taking all the jobs, and it is a sad testament to the times that I even need to be making these statements. Far from taking over the academy, minority scholars are still in the minority. Among those graduate students, faculty members, and others who have expressed such outrage toward minority dominance in the academy, their silence about the real dominance of whites in the profession continues to be deafening.

But my purpose is not to refute the claim that minorities are taking all the jobs, since I find this debate ultimately specious and dangerously close to the end of last century when white workers blamed blacks, Chinese, and Mexicans for white unemployment. The issue is not who is taking all the jobs but where have all the jobs gone? This more difficult question moves us further into an institutional and structural critique that can get at some of the sources of white resentment toward minority success and ways to redirect this anger toward more constructive ends. The Modern Language Association annually publishes statistics that monitor the shrinkage of the humanities. According to Bettina Huber in *Profession 94,* the total number of positions advertised in the English *Job Information List* between 1988 and 1993 decreased by 38% ("Recent Trends" 101). Minority literature accounted for 1% of all positions advertised in 1982 but increased to 9.5% of all positions in October 1994. From a survey of departments that advertised positions in the 1987-88 issues of the English *Job Information List*, minorities were hired for 12% of the 896 positions that were filled (Huber, "Minorities").

I predict a gradual decrease in the number of minority jobs

advertised and a return to the figures of the 1980s. Once departments have their token minorities in multicultural literatures, they will likely return to hiring in traditional Anglicist and Americanist fields, which will include primarily, if not exclusively, whites. María de la Luz Reyes and John Halcón call this trend the "one-minority-per-pot syndrome" and the "typecasting syndrome." The first term refers to the reluctance of departments to hire more than one minority faculty member, while the latter represents the underlying belief that minorities should be hired to teach exclusively minority literatures, bilingual education, or "foreign" literatures. Although the 1994 statistics demonstrate a vast improvement in minority hiring, 88% of the jobs still went to whites, which hardly supports Andrew Gyory's claim that minorities are hired before whites. The two sets of statistics, the number of PhD recipients versus the number of hired PhDs, demonstrate that receiving a PhD is not equivalent to obtaining a tenure-track position; however, both sets of statistics indicate that whites receive the vast majority of doctoral degrees as well as tenure-track positions.

What these statistics do not disclose is the number of white women who are doctoral recipients and tenure-track hires. The debate over academic hiring has been primarily framed in terms of race, despite the fact that white women have been arguably the primary beneficiaries of affirmative action. In higher education, for example, between 1981 and 1991, the number of full-time faculty members grew by 54,247, with women accounting for 40,283 of the total. White women represented the bulk of the increase, garnering 32,579 positions (Phillip 15). The invisibility of white women in this debate is evident in the very way that these statistics are collected. Both the National Research Council and the Modern Language Association arrange their data according to racial affiliation and gender but not in terms of their intersection. White women are the silent winners of affirmative action and they, not people of color, are the main competitors for white men. According to Barbara Christian of the African American studies department at the University of California, Berkeley, "The affirmative action issue will create a debate among Black and white feminists that has gone underground, but needs to be continued" (qtd. in Phillip 17). The necessity of this debate not only within the academy but also nationally is evident in a California poll that found a majority of women of color opposed to the anti–affirmative action proposal—called the California Civil Rights Initiative—while a significant majority of white women, 66%, favored it (Phillip 13).

Higher Education under Fire

Despite improvements in the percentage of minorities hired, the academic marketplace overall is in an ongoing state of crisis.[6] Thousands of PhDs are without jobs or are underemployed at a time that was once predicted to be a golden age for higher education. The mid-1990s, it was once said, would mark the changing of the guard, when one generation would replace another. Quite the opposite has happened. Although one generation is retiring, the new generation is not allowed to enter, except at a slow trickle. Economic retrenchment has hit the academy hard, and in the name of "tax revolt" we are currently witnessing the dismantling of public institutions, social services, and state-funded education. Public education today is viewed as a government subsidy, a wasteful form of expenditure that needs to be dramatically curtailed. In his acceptance speech for the presidential nomination at the 1996 Republican convention, Bob Dole expressed nationally what many Republican legislators are already doing locally: he launched a frontal attack against teachers' unions, which included vilifying their opposition to school vouchers for the private sector.[7] This strategy of pitting the public against the private sector is one that New York's Governor George Pataki has already implemented in appointing Candace de Russy in 1995 to the State University of New York Board of Trustees. Her platform is quite clear: cut SUNY's professional schools—health science, the medical school, the law school, and dentistry.[8] Why should the state subsidize professional training when private institutions offer these same programs? My prediction is that this same logic will be applied to graduate and undergraduate education in the humanities, and SUNY, which has only been public since World War II, will become increasingly privatized once again.

Perhaps at one level Masao Miyoshi is correct in saying that the distinction between public and private universities is becoming increasingly vague, since professors at both are "now corporate employees who can be underemployed, outsourced, and displaced" (78). Although I take Miyoshi's point that faculty members and instructors in both the private and the public sectors are vulnerable to downsizing, I would argue that they are now being pitted against each other for limited state resources, and private schools are often coming out ahead. In his transition team on higher education, Pataki appointed only representatives of private colleges and universities. Not surprisingly, he took their advice, which included a stiff SUNY tuition hike to decrease the gap between private and public. Now they will be on more equal footing to attract the state's middle-class and upper-middle-class high school seniors, who are increasingly choosing SUNY as a cost-efficient alternative to expensive private tuitions. Can you imagine a more effective way to discourage students from coming to SUNY than to disassemble it, thus guaranteeing New York taxpayers a mediocre product? Not only did Pataki increase tuition by nearly $1,000 in two years, preventing more than 11,000 students from returning, but his budget proposal for fiscal year 1997 included a $164 million reduction in state aid to SUNY (on top of the $36.6 million cut in 1995), to be offset partly by a $400 tuition increase (qtd. in McCaffrey).

As Michael Bérubé and Cary Nelson have observed, higher education is indeed under fire, but let me add that public institutions will be the first ones to fall. The proposed New York State budget will cut SUNY's funding by 31.5%, while reducing other agencies an average of 6.5%. New York State, which ranks forty-seventh in the nation for state support of public higher education, is implementing cuts that are disproportionately aimed at the university. These cuts to SUNY are not unique. According to Paul Lauter, funds for higher education have been slashed since 1990 in thirty states, affecting two-thirds of all public colleges and universities. The University of Connecticut has absorbed cuts of $47.5 million in four years and has lost about six hundred jobs. Tuition went up 42% between 1991 and 1992. The University of California system incurred some of the most draconian cuts. According to an April 1993 draft report for the California Assembly Committee on Higher Education,

> In only the past two years, the state has withdrawn more than $550 million from its $6.5 billion in annual support for higher education. The workforce of the two public universities has shrunk by 6,800 faculty and staff—the only sector of state government employment to have declined—in the last ten years.
>
> (qtd. in Lauter 74)

Lauter concludes that the furor over political correctness functioned to "discredit higher education. Behind that screen, conservatives have implemented a well-orchestrated and financed campaign to cut budgets, downsize universities, and thus sharply restrict access to higher education" (73). Now after the political correctness wars have been fought and the smoke has dissipated, it has become increasingly clear that this argument functioned as a red herring, as a way to direct attention away from policies that have systematically made higher education increasingly inaccessible and have subsequently made the ideals of the GI Bill of 1944 obsolete (see also Soley).

From Tenure to Temp

Although higher education is certainly disproportionately cut, it is important to view these cuts within the larger context of corporate restructuring, downsizing, and Orwellian "right sizing." Take, for example, the rising tide of adjunct instructors, who teach part-time or full-time for usually a third of what tenured faculty members earn, with no pensions or health benefits. According to Ernst Benjamin, only 22% of faculty members held part-time positions in 1970, compared with 36% in 1989 (56). When a senior professor retires, the position more than likely reappears in the next year's job listing as one for a temporary instructor or a visiting assistant professor, if it appears at all. The Modern Language Association has responded to this trend by publishing its "Statement on the Use of Part-Time Faculty" in each October issue of the *Job Information List*, which concludes that the "primary motivation for many of these [part-time] appointments has been to reduce the cost of instruction" (qtd. in Belatèche 64). Adjunct faculty members represent a bargain: they often have the same credentials as tenure-track faculty members but cost less. This trend must be seen in the national context of the increasing reliance on temporary and part-time workers, who receive 20% to 40% less than their full-time counterparts. One out of every twenty workers in the United States is temporary. In fact, the largest employer in the country is no longer General Motors but a temporary employment agency called Manpower (Scheuerman).

At the same time that the public sector faces a scarcity of jobs and a lack of revenue, a recent front cover of *Fortune* magazine reads, "Why Profits Will Keep Booming" (qtd. in Chomsky). The 1980s and especially the 1990s have been very good years for the captains of industry; capital gains have increased 66%, corporate salaries have increased 66%, and 60% of the new wealth has gone to the top 1% of the population. Between 1980 and 1994, corporate profits climbed more than 200%. According to Sean Reilly, back in 1972 the CEOs of the nation's largest companies made 40 times the pay of the average worker. Today they earn better than 140 times more (qtd. in Scheuerman).

The crisis of higher education must then be situated in the economic context of rising profits and increased concentrations of wealth, which benefit, to borrow Noam Chomsky's phrase, "the minority of the opulent." Yes, the minorities are taking all the jobs, but it is the minority of the rich, not people of color, who are systematically robbing the public sector of much needed revenue. As William Scheuerman, president of the United University Professions (UUP), the SUNY chapter of the American Federation of Teachers, has noted, the tax burden of the country has shifted away from the well-to-do and onto the backs of the middle and working classes.

The academy is not immune from these changes. As Masao Miyoshi argues, the university is fully "integrated into transnational corporatism," since the academy in both style and substance functions as a corporation. Miyoshi sees the current restructuring as permanent, with senior faculty members vigorously encouraged to retire early, student-faculty ratios increased, teaching loads enlarged, and budgets for basic research reduced. He predicts that "we may, in fact, some day find ourselves being hauled outside of academia among those disempowered whom we haven't taken note of for the last half century"(79). Miyoshi's *Blade Runner*esque portrayal of University 2000 is a rather dismal forecast for the next generation of academics.

I want to conclude this article not with a dirge of inevitable doom but rather with an urgent plea for intervention. Although the process of downsizing is in some respects inevitable, the degree of retrenchment is still uncertain. Academic unions are important institutions of mobilization that have provided, and will continue to provide, a degree of resistance against these draconian cuts, and in many cases, they have successfully lobbied legislatures to reduce the extent of the damage. The three academic unions, the American Federation of

Teachers, the National Education Association, and the American Association of University Professors are all at the fore in combating the assault against public higher education.[9]

Despite ongoing struggles, there have been success stories, including one at the University of Connecticut, where the AAUP led a successful campaign against continued state funding cuts. From 1987 to 1992 the University of Connecticut's general fund budget had been cut by $33.5 million; tuition for in-state students had risen 82% (Pratt 46). In 1992, the University and the AAUP ran ads and mailings on the theme that the university budget had already been cut to the bone. One ad featured a skeleton dressed in University of Connecticut track clothes and wearing a mortarboard. In 1993 the Connecticut legislature added $8 million back to the university's budget and slated an additional $9.5 million to be returned the following year. The AAUP succeeded in making a convincing case that further damage to the University would hinder the general economic recovery and limit the state's future (Pratt 48). Similarly, in 1995 the UUP succeeded in getting $85 million in proposed cuts returned to the SUNY system.

Such examples, whether at the University of Connecticut or SUNY, could not have been achieved without a union. According to Linda Ray Pratt, however, less than one-fourth of faculty members in higher education are in unions, in contrast to K–12 teachers, who are thoroughly organized in every state (36). At a time when efforts to unionize graduate students are on the rise, with recent victories at SUNY and the University of Wisconsin, Milwaukee, faculty members also need to organize around issues of slash-and-burn budget cuts, job retrenchment, and part-time labor.[10]

For many employees of state universities, the union organizations are already there; the key is to join them, to work for them and thus revitalize them. This, however, is easier said than done. For junior faculty members, there are structural disincentives against working actively in the union. No tenure committee will be impressed with your work as a delegate for the statewide convention or the reports you circulate on discretionary funds. With hiring freezes at many colleges and universities, young faculty members are burdened more than ever with large class sizes, increased graduate advising, administrative work, and greater publication expectations. In addition to the challenges confronting junior faculty members, the issue of unions raises larger questions about the potential incompatibility between the individualism of intellectual labor and the collectivism of unions. Or to put it another way, how can a profession that awards and indeed depends on individual achievement expect to unite its faculty? Jo Schaffer, UUP's membership development officer, recently responded to this question in a matter-of-fact way: "When you come right down to it, it is the union that affords us the opportunity to teach, to think, to function as academics" (qtd. in "Strengthening Membership" 6).

We seem to have lost sight of the conditions of our labor, that our intellectual independence is in large part dependent on unions, which have helped build the ivory tower that we now inhabit in its rather dismantled state. The benefits of the union include better working conditions through collective bargaining, promotion of professional and academic development, equitable resolution of grievances, and collective clout through political action. Yet for two full generations, as Cary Nelson has remarked, faculty members have been deluded into thinking that they transcend politics and economics and have embraced a powerlessness that trades "safety from public scrutiny and rage for any chance of influence" (128). Cloistering ourselves from the current onslaught will prove more difficult, since early retirement packages for senior faculty members, staff reductions, and canceled departments and programs will demand that we make decisions about the future direction of our departments and programs, our institutions, and our profession. To paraphrase Miyoshi's argument, we are not immune to the corporate reorganization of academic institutions.

As an organized way to challenge such corporate reorganization of higher education, academic unions can only be revitalized if more tenured faculty members begin to view themselves as intellectual workers whose interests as employees converge with those of others who occupy different positions in the university's hierarchy. Academic unions need to address the growing diversity of their membership not only in racial and ethnic composition but also in the increased numbers of adjuncts and part-time employees. Typically, the union devotes most of its time and resources to issues that concern tenure-track and tenured faculty members as well as professional staff: the protection of tenure, pensions, health benefits, discretionary funds, and merit increases. This is not to say that such issues are insignificant; when tenure is under attack, it is a critical time to defend the principle of job security, which has been for so long an assumed perk of the profession. But at the same time, academic unions need to acknowledge that they also include adjuncts, who are more concerned about gaining access to basic health care than they are about the preservation of tenure, which may seem to them a privileged debate.

What is both promising and frustrating is that the three national teachers' unions (AFT, NEA, and AAUP) have official statements advocating protections and benefits for adjunct labor (see Douglas). All three documents recommend the integration of adjuncts at the level of department meetings, faculty governance, and benefits. They even support awarding tenure to part-time faculty members or converting part-time appointments to full-time tenure-track status. What is frustrating is how few of these recommendations are actually implemented in the day-to-day business of the institution. Even provisions that can be offered to part-time teachers by an individual department —such as an office, a vote in department and committee meetings, the opportunity to advise students, or just a mailbox—are ignored or even resisted. This gap between the tenured and the temporary worker creates an unfortunate obstacle to the protection of both types of employees' jobs. An important way for professional unions to strengthen their organization is for them to address more volubly and emphatically the concerns of part-time or non-tenure-track instructors, who constitute nearly 38% of the teachers of higher education (qtd. in Cassebaum).

I take the recent unionizing efforts of Yale's Graduate Employees and Student Organization (GESO) as an exemplary model in establishing alliances with all workers of the university community. As a strategy for their own institutional survival, GESO created a coalition with two existing unions of clerical and technical workers (Local 34) and service and maintenance workers (Local 35). That the graduate students found greater support among the service and clerical workers than among many of their own professors illustrates the extent to which tenured faculty members resist the image of themselves as employees.[11] This attitude actually worked to the benefit of the Yale graduate students, who claim unequivocally that the trilocal alliance has "permanently breached some of the visible barriers of class, race, and gender between the different groups of employees on campus" (Janette and Joseph 8). According to Michele Janette and Tamara Joseph, two students active in the unionizing efforts, the trilocal community with clerical and service workers "is not based solely on ideas, but on the physical reality of having marched and yelled together, of learning the names of people whom we have learned not to see, of developing strategies together, and of knowing we are willing to take risks for one another" (8).

In 1933, W. E. B. Du Bois similarly observed that the effectiveness of unions depends on their inclusivity: their ability to create alliances with workers of different occupations and different races. An all-encompassing union is necessary, because as Du Bois has insisted, like Masao Miyoshi, there is "no escape" from the "organized industry of the world today, the organized finance and commerce, the empire of concentrated capital" ("Where Do We Go" 152). The most powerful way to challenge organized industry, finance, and commerce is still to unionize, to offer an organized and powerful body on the other side of the collective bargaining table. To invoke Du Bois again, who is speaking on behalf of the *Crisis:*

> *The Crisis* believes in organized labor [. . .] and that all American labor today, white, black and yellow, benefits from this great movement. ("Organized Labor" 301)

By focusing our energies on organized labor, we can address the *cause* of the dearth of tenure-track jobs and the plenitude of temp teaching rather than merely respond to its *effects*, namely in the form of scapegoating minorities for taking all the jobs. Invoking the "color line" blinds us to the actual divisions that are plaguing our profession and our university communities. To apply Du Bois's words, which were originally intended for working-class labor at the early part of this century, to the situation of faculty members in higher education today demonstrates the extent to which the "empire of concentrated capital" has permeated the halls of the ivory tower.

Notes

I wish to thank David Schmid and the *Socialist Review* collective for their helpful and generous comments on an earlier draft of this essay. I am also grateful to Lora Romero for suggesting that I write on this topic. A slightly different version of this article originally appeared in *Socialist Review*.

1. I would argue that there is a notable gap between popular culture's vogue in some academic journals and presses and the actual hiring practices of university English departments.

2. I am grateful to the historian Leslie Harris at Emory University for bringing these debates to my attention.

3. I want to thank Bettine J. Huber for sending me a revised and updated version of her paper, "Minorities in the Modern Languages," which she presented at the MLA convention in 1991.

4. Many thanks to the Office of the Registrar at Stanford University for these statistics.

5. The study was based on an update of the 1990 census, which involved projecting the figures for 1992.

6. One other positive change to occur in the job market in recent years is that nearly two-thirds of writing positions are tenure-track, compared with 44% in 1982. Composition and rhetoric positions (including creative writing) constitute the largest proportion of job hires in the profession (see Huber, "Recent Trends" 102).

7. In a bizarre abuse of the acceptance speech for the presidential nomination, Dole said, "To the teachers' unions I say, when I am President, I will disregard your political power for the sake of the children, the schools and the nation. I plan to enrich your vocabulary with those words you fear—school choice, competition and opportunity."

8. De Russy outlines her position in a 1995 memorandum to her fellow SUNY trustees and the chancellor.

9. I include the American Association of University Professors (AAUP) with reservations. Although they did lead the charge against Governor Lowell Weicker's cuts from the budget of the University of Connecticut in 1992, they have not been a strong advocate for adjunct labor, as the American Federation of Teachers (AFT) has been (see Friedberg). Furthermore, the ACUP is not affiliated with the AFL-CIO and lacks collective bargaining power.

10. When I delivered an earlier version of this paper at the 1995 American Studies Association Conference in Pittsburg, an audience member from Virginia claimed that unions are not an option for faculty members in "right to work" states. This is not true, since public school teachers (K–12) are unionized, according to Pratt, in all fifty states. If public school teachers are already unionized in these states, they why shouldn't teachers in higher education also be?

11. A number of graduate student unions, which now represent over 21,000 students in eight states, have chosen to ally not with traditional teachers unions but with the United Auto Workers (California's Association of Graduate Student Employees) and the Communications Workers of America (State University of New York's Graduate Student Employee Union). Their coalition with these unions resulted from a concern that a combined faculty–graduate student employee union could potentially raise a conflict of interest, since professors supervise both the academic and the employment aspects of graduate students. But another reason why many graduate student unions have sought alliances with such organizations as the UAW and CWA is also strategic: they provide more money and more muscle than traditional teachers' unions (Barba 44).

Works Cited

Barba, William C. "The Graduate Student Employee Union in SUNY: A History." *Journal for Higher Education Management* 10.1 (1994): 39–48.

Belatèche, Lydia. "Temp Prof: Practicing the Profession off the Tenure Track." *Profession 94*. New York: MLA, 1994. 64–66.

Benjamin, Ernst. "A Faculty Response to the Fiscal Crisis: From Defense to Offense." Bérubé and Nelson 52–72.

Bérubé, Michael, and Cary Nelson, eds. *Higher Education under Fire: Politics, Economics, and the Crisis of the Humanities.* New York: Routledge, 1995.

Cassebaum, Anne. "Adjuncts with an Attitude? Attitudes Encountered in the Struggle for Fair Pay and Job Security for Adjunct Faculty." Conf. on College Composition and Communication Convention. Washington. 25 Mar. 1995.

Chomsky, Noam. Speech sponsored by the Martha's Vineyard Peace Council. C-SPAN. 23 Aug. 1995.

de Russy, Candace. "A Personal Vision of SUNY's Future." Memo to State Univ. of New York trustees and chancellor. 15 July 1995.

Dole, Robert. "Text of Dole's Acceptance Speech." *Baltimore Sun,* 16 Aug. 1996: 22A.

Douglas, Joel. "Collective Bargaining for Adjunct Faculty." *National Center for the Study of Collective Bargaining in Higher Education and the Professions Newsletter* 16.2 (1988): n. p.

Du Bois, W. E. B. "Communism and the Color Line." 1931. *The W. E. B. Du Bois Reader.* Ed. Eric Sundquist. New York: Oxford UP, 1996. 406–08.

———. "Organized Labor." *The Crisis* 4 (July 1912): 131; rpt. in *The Seventh Son.* Ed. Julius Lester. Vol. 2. New York: Random, 1971. 301–02.

———. "Where Do We Go from Here?" 1933. *W. E. B. Du Bois: A Reader.* Ed. Andrew Paschal. New York: Collier, 1971. 146–63.

Friedberg, Leslie. "The Sad Lot of Adjuncts." *On Campus* 15.4 (1995–96): 7.

Gyory, Andrew. "Nothing Irrational about Job Fears." *Perspectives* Dec. 1993: 20–22.

Heller, Scott. "A Discouraged Mathematician Ponders His Future, and It's Not in Academe." *Chronicle of Higher Education* 27 Apr. 1994: A19.

———. "English Instructor at Austin Peay Waits to Hear If He'll Be Around for a While." *Chronicle of Higher Education* 27 Apr. 1994: A19+.

———. "Some Colleges Find Aggressive Affirmative-Action Efforts Are Starting to Pay Off, Despite Scarcity of Candidates." *Chronicle of Higher Education* 10 Feb. 1988: A16+.

———. "Tales from the Front: Husband and Wife Experience the Extremes in Search for Jobs as Literature Professors." *Chronicle of Higher Education* 27 Apr. 1994: A18.

Huber, Bettina J. "Minorities in the Modern Languages: How Well Represented Are They?" American Literary Pluralism Forum. MLA Convention. San Francisco. 29 Dec. 1991. Updated and revised version.

———. "Recent Trends in the Modern Language Job Market." *Profession 94.* New York: MLA, 1994. 87–105.

Humanities Research Council. *The Humanities Doctorates in the United States: 1989 Profile.* Washington: Natl. Research Council, 1991.

Janette, Michele, and Tamara Joseph. "Making It Work: Scholarship, Employment, and Power in the Academy." *National Center for the Study of Collective Bargaining in Higher Education and the Professions Newsletter* 22.2 (1994): 4–8.

Lauter, Paul. " 'Political Correctness' and the Attack on American Colleges." Bérubé and Nelson 73–90.

McCaffrey, Shannon. "SUNY Panel Backs Interim Chancellor for Post." *Buffalo News* 15 Apr. 1997: A7.

Miyoshi, Masao. "Sites of Resistance in the Global Economy." *Boundary 2* 22.1 (1995): 61–84.

Mohanty, Chandra Talpade. "On Race and Voice: Challenges for Liberal Education in the 1990s." *Cultural Critique* (1989–90): 179–208.

Morin, Richard. "A Distorted Image of Minorities." *Washington Post* 8 Oct. 1995: A1+.

National Research Council. Office of Scientific and Engineering Personnel. *Summary Report 1992: Doctorate Recipients from United States Universities.* Washington: Nat. Acad., 1992.

Nelson, Cary. "Lessons from the Job Wars: Late Capitalism Arrives on Campus." *Social Text* 44 (1995): 119–34.

Painter, Nell Irvin. "The Academic Marketplace and Affirmative Action." *Perspectives* Dec. 1993: 7–11.

Perloff, Marjorie. " 'Literature' in the Expanded Field." *Comparative Literature in the Age of Multiculturalism.* Ed. Charles Bernheimer. Baltimore: Johns Hopkins UP, 1995. 175–86.

Phillip, Mary-Christine. "Antidote to an 'Epidemic of Rage.' " *Black Issues in Higher Education* 18 May 1995: 12–19.

Pratt, Linda Ray. "Going Public: Political Discourse and the Faculty Voice." Bérubé and Nelson 35–51.

Reyes, María de la Luz, and John Halcón. "Racism in Academia: The Old Wolf Revisited." *Harvard Educational Review* 58.3 (1988): 299–314.

San Juan, E., Jr. *Racial Formations / Critical Transformations: Articulations of Power in Ethnic and Racial Studies in the United States.* Atlantic Highlands: Humanities, 1992.

Scheuerman, William. "To the Point: Middle Class Overboard!" *Voice* [Publication of the United University Professions] 23.1 (1995): 4.

Soley, Lawrence. *Leasing the Ivory Tower: The Corporate Takeover of Academia.* Boston: South End, 1995.

"Strengthening Membership: Active Participation Needed More Than Ever." *Voice* [Publication of the United University Professions] 23.5 (1996): 6–7.

Tropicalizing
the Liberal Arts
College Classroom

SUSANA CHAVEZ SILVERMAN

> I have the hybrid vigor [. . .]. Mixed is better.
> —Kelvin Christopher James

> There is no theory that is not a fragment, carefully preserved, of some autobiography.
> —Paul Valéry

I want to begin this essay by assuming the "risk" of the autobiographical.[1] Although the links between autobiography, confession, and women (or women's writing) have traditionally been overdetermined, Nancy K. Miller, in her book *Getting Personal*, has shown us how elements of the autobiographical, such as the anecdote, while they often "characterize the essays of black women writers like Alice Walker and June Jordan [. . . have also] been a way for some men to experiment with self-representation while writing critical theory" (27). My essay intends to inscribe itself between and among both these poles; my discourse is at once self-representational and critical. For an essay on pedagogical praxis this risk is, for me and my particular pedagogy, ineluctable.

Racism compels the designated inferior race to ask [. . .]
"In reality, what am I?"

—Lewis R. Gordon

Instances of labeling and mislabeling have become something of an obsession in my life and work. I am sure that this obsession is anything but coincidental, given our particular historical conjuncture, in which, on the one hand, ever more precise shadings of difference are codified and celebrated on the multiculti altar (academic and popular) while, on the other hand, reactionary, backlash measures to this perceived "excess of diversity" are enacted by the dominant culture, academic and otherwise. Some recent examples from my home state of California are the University of California Regents' decision to abolish affirmative action in faculty hiring and student admissions; Proposition 209, the so-called California Civil Rights Initiative; and the passing of Proposition 187, which would deny schooling and social and medical services to non–United States citizens, *gracias* Governor Pete Wilson.

So what am I, anyway? *Pues, soy "pura bicultura,"* as the cultural critic Coco Fusco writes in her aptly titled book *English Is Broken Here: Notes on Cultural Fusion in the Americas* (x). Fusco's felicitous oxymoron, poignantly bearing the trace of both truth and impossibility, identifies me also. I was born on Sunset Boulevard, *en el mero corazón de* Hollywood, to a second-generation Mexican American mother and a first-generation Jewish American father, of Russian and Romanian background. My sisters and I were raised between and among several cultures but always with an accent on *"lo hispano."*[2] By this I mean that my first and several subsequent school terms were spent in Madrid; we spent summers, until I was seventeen, in Guadalajara, México, returning for the school year to our Los Angeles home. These geocultural locations, coupled with a fierce attachment to my mother's California-based New Mexican family (along with the estrangement my sisters and I felt from our father's New York Jewish family, who, like the mother in Sandra Cisneros's eponymous story, did not want their boy to "marry a Mexican"), resulted in my strong identification, as far back as I can remember, with "the Mexican in me" (Cisneros 4). This identity began to take shape in a less inchoate way and became increasingly politicized under the rubric "Chicana" during my undergraduate years, when I was privileged to study with María Herrera-Sobek and Alejandro Morales in one of the first national Chicano studies programs, at the University of California, Irvine, from which I graduated with a major in Spanish.

Mientras tanto, however, all was not quiet on the western front: with my alabaster skin, green eyes, and perfect Spanish I was inevitably perceived as other: usually too Mexican for the Jews, too *güera* for the Mexicans, and too *algo*, something unidentifiably, disconcertingly exotic, for the Anglos.[3] Fusco expresses the frustration of this in-betweenness eloquently:

> To this day I despise having people, especially those who claim some intelligence, ask me what I "really" feel that I am, or to begin to question the authenticity of my claims on the basis of some eugenics equation [. . .] that was always a losing proposition for me, since I didn't look oppressed enough for white liberals or black enough for cult nats. I just signaled confusion. (ix)

Fast-forward to the official beginning of my professional life in the United States. Shortly after accepting my first tenure-track job in this country in 1989 (after having worked in and out of academe, in South Africa and California, for about eight years), the then head of women's studies at Pomona College was quoted to me by a Chicana undergraduate as having been asking students and faculty members if I was a "real Mexican." Conversely, however, the current chair of women's studies, herself then an untenured Chicana historian, began to articulate a welcoming space for me at our institution by calling me —paradoxically but poetically—a "real mestiza." My problem is different from the one described by Indira Karamcheti in her essay "Caliban in the Classroom," in which she discusses Daphne Patai's concept of "surplus visibility." Karamcheti's essay examines "the problem of the personal as it establishes or works against authority in the classroom for the teacher marked by race or ethnicity" (139). Marked by a kind of "surplus exotica" yet "famine/phantom visibility" in each of the cultures my identity derives from (Chicano, Jewish, Anglo), my physical appearance is not recognizably visible enough to be subsumed completely under any one of them.[4]

In recent years, because of the publication of important works on hybrid subjectivities in various disciplines,[5] my career has allowed me to begin reconceptualizing intellectually what was, during my childhood, only a site and source of pain or "confusion," as Fusco calls it, and during my adolescence and early adulthood a site of re-

ductive identificatory practices. (If I call myself only a Chicana, for
example, what happens to the interplay of sexuality and Jewish-
ness?) Challenged and inspired by the writings of multiply positioned gendered, ethnic, or racial subjects, I have begun to embrace
and to theorize my own biracial, culturally hybrid self. I have begun
to embrace and to theorize and teach from—as a position of strength
—a deliberately performative site of liminality, ambiguity, and hybridity.

The title of this essay is a sort of conflation of one of the courses
I teach at Pomona College and the title of a collection of critical essays I edited with Frances R. Aparicio, called *Tropicalizations: Transcultural Representations of Latinidad.* The term *tropicalizations,* as
we conceptualized it several years ago, owes its most obvious debt to
Edward Said's seminal orientalism, and, following Said, Aparicio and I
deploy the term to theorize and explore hegemonic representations,
both of Latin America by the United States and of the "domestic third
world," to use Gayatri Spivak's term (263), most particularly Chi-
canos/Chicanas and Latinos/Latinas, by the dominant culture *within*
the United States. In addition, we attempt not simply to reproduce by
inversion the prevailing "us against them" binary, the self-other paradigm endemic to early cultural studies and still prevalent in some sectors today. Thus we pull the notion of "tropicalization" across to
another valence (hence our insistence on the pluralized form), by
using it also to describe the aesthetic productivity of United States
Chicanos/Chicanas and Latinos/Latinas such as Guillermo Gómez-
Peña, Victor Hernández Cruz, Sandra Cisneros, Marcia Ochoa, Alicia
Gaspar de Alba, John Leguizamo, and Coco Fusco. Their work critically recirculates, subverts, and contests available stereotypes and
images, "giving back [to] the world" (in Gaspar de Alba's phrase [50])
a radically "re-tropicalized" Latino/Latina body and *obra.*

What do I mean by "tropicalizing" in relation to the liberal arts
college classroom? If this question seems to suggest that I don't find
the liberal arts college a very tropical space, I would have to concur.
Even at Pomona College,[6] a nationally ranked western liberal arts college, I was until 1997 one of only two—and the only still untenured
—Chicana faculty members in a tenure-track position.[7] In the
strictly census-type sense then, one can observe that my very presence on campus, in its necessarily surplus representativity, overde-
terminedly tropicalizes the classroom.[8] In terms of another kind of

tropicalizing, described in relation to the *Tropicalizations* volume, above, my work has continued to evolve in ever more interdisciplinary, boundary-blurring directions. Thus in my research and in the pedagogical practice that inevitably emerges from and returns to it, I attempt to tropicalize the liberal arts classroom by engaging the various disciplines I work within (and without) and the institution itself in a contestatory manner.

I was academically trained as a Latin Americanist, specifically as a twentieth-century poetry specialist. Notwithstanding the disciplinary rigors of my very traditional graduate training, I have worked on issues of gender and sexuality for the past twelve years. And it is my work focused on gender, sexuality, and representation that has been the common thread enabling me to forge interdisciplinary, "extra-canonical" links between the Latin American women's poetry I have been studying since I was an undergraduate and the hybrid, poetic-theoretical writings by United States Chicanas and Latinas that occupy much of my research time today.[9] My pedagogical goal is to encourage these various disciplines—Chicano studies, gender and sexuality studies, Latin American literary criticism and theory—which have emerged from very different epistemological traditions, to talk to one another. It is also, in Debra Castillo's phrase, to compel these disciplines—through my multiply situated teaching body—to "talk back" to the institution whose administrative and departmental structures sometimes seem to practice a sort of disciplinary apartheid.[10]

Ironically, I have come up against institutional restraints even as precisely the sort of engaged, interdisciplinary pedagogy that I practice has been solicited officially at Pomona College.[11] I was hired by the college "as a" twentieth-century Latin Americanist, a specialist in poetry. However, as is widely known, the liberal arts college differs from the research university in that liberal arts college professors must wear more hats, so to speak. Whereas there may be as many as twenty or even more Hispanists alone in one department at a large research institution, there are far fewer of us in our departments. It is axiomatic that the sort of specialization we were accustomed to during our graduate training cannot exist in our current jobs. This does not mean, however, that the border crossing I am discussing here was welcomed with open arms by all my colleagues. As I began to develop new courses and revise the standard, disciplinarily sanctioned ones I was hired to teach (Latin American survey, for example, or twentieth-century poetry) in response to my growing research interest in gender and sexuality issues, hybrid subjectivities, and United States Chicano/Chicana and Latino/Latina literature, this development was at one level of institutional discourse applauded and on another critiqued.[12]

At the departmental level, I was subtly taken to task by a senior colleague who, after seeing my syllabi, suggested that my courses were not especially useful for preparing our Spanish majors to take the senior comprehensive exams (the reading list for which, at the time, had not been updated in nearly ten years). This recourse to "the" canon—even in postmodern times—has not been the only negative reaction to the perceived threat of my interdisciplinary endeavors. Although I do not officially hold a joint appointment with Chicano studies, my upper-division courses have been embraced by many Chicano studies faculty members and students (who constitute a large percentage—over half, consistently—of my constituency), and my courses are routinely cross-listed with Chicano and women's studies. There have been several moves to draw me back to the proper disciplinary fold, however. In 1994 as faculty members worked to establish a Latin American studies program, the then-chair of the steering committee, a Hispanist, requested that I quantify the percentage of "Chicano versus Latin American content" in several of my courses (so that they could be counted as either "core" or "related" courses).[13] In another instance of disciplinary boundary policing, several years ago the chair of the intercollegiate literature program (a faculty-driven comparative literature–type major with a self-proclaimed heavily theoretical orientation) sent me several memos inviting me to submit my upper-division courses such as Tropicalizations and Surrealism and After in Latin America for "inclusion" in the literature program. I responded that I had submitted my courses various times but—in an ironic move for a program purportedly devoted to crossing boundaries of all types—they had always been rejected on the grounds that they were taught in a "foreign" language or that their deep theoretical foundation was not readily apparent from my (translated) syllabi.[14]

> In disturbing the Eurocentric professorial way-of-being, have I
> resisted assimilation?
>
> —Ana M. Martínez Alemán

In the upper-division courses I regularly teach at Pomona College, I follow a paradigm laid out in Frances A. Maher and Mary Kay Thompson Tetreault's *The Feminist Classroom* in using some specifically feminist, extracanonical strategies. I teach Introduction to Literary Analysis in Spanish and Advanced Composition and Spanish Phonetics each year. Once every two or three years I teach the Latin American literature survey sequence. Every other year I alternate among several upper-division seminars: Surrealism and After in Latin America, Woman as Sign and Subject in Latin American and United States Latino/Latina Literature, Tropicalizations: Beyond Self and Other in Latin American and United States Latino/Latina Literature, and El deseo de la palabra: Twentieth-Century Latin American Poetry and Poetics. The literary analysis, phonetics, and survey courses I inherited from my senior colleagues and have adapted to suit my pedagogical style; the seminars I have never taught to precisely the same purpose (or using the same syllabus) twice. Responding to my own research interests, a desire to experiment and innovate, and student input, for example, I have team-taught the surrealism course with my colleague Karen S. Goldman, formerly of Pitzer College, whose research interests coincide with mine. We deliberately followed a collaborative model of curricular planning, something not widely practiced among faculty members at the Claremont colleges, at least not in our field. This way, we could share rather than compete for students and bring to bear our common interest in poetry as well as our different strengths, hers in the avant garde and Spanish surrealist cinema and art, mine in contemporary poetry and gender theory. Poetry is generally regarded—particularly by undergraduates—as the "difficult" literary genre; however, the two times we cotaught this course we had to turn away many students and ended up with enrollments of nearly thirty students.[15]

Even during my first year at Pomona College, I taught the survey courses I inherited *contracorriente*—"against the grain." Constrained by the weight of tradition (and, admittedly, by fear of reprisals at tenure time for my lack of conformity), I used Enrique Anderson Imbert's (now, thankfully, out-of-print) anthology of Latin American literature because it was the text that had been used for years by the senior Latin Americanist in my department.[16] However, I guided the students through a critical deconstruction of this anthology. We arrived together at a contextualized reading of the gaps and silences and of the historical specificity the anthology's organization revealed: the "poetisas" section alone, with its notes about the physical appearance and the scandalous love affairs of the women poets, was deemed subjective, dated, and *machista* by the students and me. This deconstructive reading of an out-of-date, inherited text is but one example of what I attempt to develop, articulate, and put into practice in all of my courses, what the acclaimed educational theorist Henry Giroux calls a "critical pedagogy":

> [T]his means providing students with the opportunity to develop the critical capacity to challenge and transform existing social and political forms, rather than simply to adapt to them. It also means providing students with the skills they will need to locate themselves in history [and] find their own voices.   (74)

What [to make] of all those other bodies in the room?
                                                —Susan Wolf

In *The Feminist Classroom*, the authors highlight four qualities or nuclei around which the professors they interviewed for their study construct feminist, "positional" pedagogies. I found my own pedagogical praxis deeply connected with these nuclei even before reading the way they were named in this insightful book. These nuclei are mastery, voice, authority, and positionality. In considering and critically articulating my own pedagogical praxis for this essay, I found it difficult to keep these nuclei in discrete categories. In fact, the authors seem to have encountered this same difficulty, as the book manifests a great degree of overlap. To me, perhaps the most important quality for the *aula tropical*, as I call it—for a feminist, extracanonical classroom—is *authority*, but I have grappled with all of them.

One of the most important pedagogical moves, in the post- or extracanonical and feminist classroom, is redefining the notion of *mastery*. "Critical pedagogy," claims Giroux, "needs to create new forms of knowledge through its emphasis on breaking down disciplinary boundaries and creating new spheres in which knowledge can be produced" (76). "New spheres" are precisely what I attempt to create in the tropicalized classroom—at the same time widening my institution's and department's definition of "the" field and of "legitimate" areas and modes of research within—by making women, sexuality, race, and ethnicity central subjects of inquiry in every course I teach, regardless of its "original" departmental or disciplinary affiliation. True multiculturalism "challenges the authority of traditional paradigms, showing them to be embedded in history rather than enshrined truths" (Maher and Tetreault 5). This is what I attempted to do with the Latin American literature survey course the first time I taught it, by contextualizing the Anderson Imbert anthology.

After my first couple of years—during which I was quite intimidated by the liberal arts college undergraduates—I have found myself lecturing less and less, hardly at all, feeling less urgency to demonstrate my mastery of the material and more the pedagogical exigency of allowing student voices and interests to shape the classroom.[17] In this, my teaching style overlaps squarely with that of the professors interviewed for *The Feminist Classroom*, many of whom praised the efficacy of having student journal entries or questions on the material, rather than faculty questions, guide the discussions. In the Latin American literature survey course I taught several years ago, I found this approach the only consistently effective one with the inexplicably passive group of students I had. Student summaries and questions structured nearly every class meeting; furthermore, I turned some of their own questions back on them for the final exam and was rewarded by essays of unusual depth and sophistication. One potential red flag to this student-centered approach to mastery of the material, however, is its relative unpredictability. Control—or the illusion of control sustained by authoritarian, traditional lecture-style pedagogy—is abdicated here: you risk getting voices from the wild zone.[18]

The second quality discussed by Maher and Tetreault is *voice*. For me, voice is a metaphor for my most powerful, abiding commitment in education: giving voice to those who are traditionally muted or silenced, both in the prestigious liberal arts college community and in the dominant culture. In my institution as in many, especially the private colleges, this means students of color, women, and queer students.[19] I deploy specific strategies to empower different groups of students, in terms of their relation to language. Paradoxically, Advanced Composition and Spanish Phonetics (which sounds like the most discipline-driven, canonical course—and indeed, to my horror and frustration, that is how it began) has become one of my most innovative, radically contestatory courses. It has subversively evolved into what is fundamentally a Spanish for Spanish-speakers course. Nevertheless, in an important way, it also continues to address the needs of the (few) "traditional" Spanish students who enroll and for whom, ironically, the course was originally designed years ago, when Pomona College's Spanish section, like most traditional Spanish departments even today, enrolled very few—and made little if any concerted effort to attract or serve the interests of—Chicano/Chicana and Latino/Latina students.

Now, over half (and usually closer to between 70% and 80%) of the students who enroll in Spanish 102 are Chicano/Chicana and Latino/Latina. Their greatest anxieties are overwhelmingly about their writing skills. I strategically empower these students by emphasizing their oral Spanish ability and their enjoyment of, and cultural competency with, the readings, especially the examples of Chicano/Chicana and Latino/Latina writing in the literature packet I put together for the course.[20]

The female students of all ethnicities are generally far more reluctant to speak than the male students are. Pedagogical research and my own observations over eighteen years of teaching confirm that the larger the class size, the less likely that female students will feel empowered to speak out and participate. Because of my commitment to feminist pedagogy, I insist on maintaining the small teacher-student ratio I find is most effective for empowering women's voices in the classroom.[21]

Many of Pomona's students are materially privileged and intellectually gifted and have attended excellent, often private, college prep secondary schools. For the Anglo students, I bolster their confidence in their writing skills. Their confidence in this ability can help to offset anxiety about their spoken Spanish and about the perceived necessity of their "competing with natives." In sum, Spanish 102 has been, overall, unusually effective for all the students it caters to, although I am most sensitive, probably, to the fact that for students of color "voice" is always about race, class, and gender (Maher and Tetreault 96).[22] I try to attend to this fact always, but particularly and passionately in the face of student-generated formal reports about faculty members who dismiss the "race thing" in their courses with cavalier remarks such as "I'm so sick of all this PC stuff" (this from a so-called feminist professor in a women's literature class!).

For me the third quality, *authority*, is the most vexed and the most challenging in the practice of a radically transformative, tropical pedagogy. If, for the purpose of establishing a more democratic, feminist classroom a female professor abdicates the neutrality and objectivity supposedly accruing to the professor in a traditional, hierarchical pedagogy, she risks confirming female stereotypes of woman as emotional, personal, and—horrors—partisan. The woman professor of color must combat an even more insidious set of binary "tropical" stereotypes: volatile, whiny, hot tamale, and so on, or, alternatively, maternal, schoolmarmish, or angelically sweet and forgiving. These stereotypes place the female professor in a nearly impossible double bind: "it is difficult to challenge the androcentric basis of a discipline when you're trying to prove your own authority within it" (Maher and Tetreault 139). Also, students, especially male students, often perceive female professors as less competent than males, and women of color as least competent of all (Karamcheti 142). To counteract this perception, it is often unbearably tempting to maintain an authoritative—if not completely authoritarian—air in the classroom. I have risked this double bind in my classrooms, fluctuating between a self-parodic, "self"-revealing, tropicalized performativity and a more severe, butchy "neutrality," attempting to mediate, constantly, between students' desires, expectations, and fears. Unfortunately, as Michéle Aina Barale has pointed out for queer professors in her provocative essay on "academic erotic zones," "It doesn't much matter what we wear or how we look. No matter what, we symbolize sexuality and transgression" (23). My negotiations with authority have not always produced successful, positive results; in fact, I could say they very nearly cost me my job.[23]

As I observed previously, I have in general, in all my courses, moved away from the lecture format—designed to "prove" and sustain mastery and authority over both disciplinary field and students—and toward a student-centric question and discussion format. Specifically, I have physically decentered myself, requesting classrooms that have one large seminar table rather than the traditional individual desk setup, and even in this less hierarchical format I do not take the accustomed place at the head of the table, moving around it on different days and even within one class session.[24] I also deliberately attempt to invest students with authority. For example, in my course Tropicalizations, Yvette, one of my Latina advisees, pointed out to me that I had erroneously assumed (from my own Chicana-centric bias) that all the students would know who the Virgen de Guadalupe is. In response to this, in my upper-division courses, I have made the students reponsible for telling their own stories. Thus they become coteachers and colearners, they avoid passivity, and I do not have to stand in as the representative Latina, which, as you can see from Yvette's comment, I am not.

As a teacher of literature, my goal, conceptualized under the category of authority, is to empower students as readers of literary texts, to develop collective models for arriving at possible interpretations. Although it is time-consuming, I have found it effective to request that students share with the class the embryonic working out of their paper topics, even while they are still in process. We circulate a sheet of paper well before the essays are due, and the students write down and briefly describe their topics to the class; the other students critique and brainstorm around the topic. This way, value judgments—especially mine—are generally avoided, and students can test out their ideas before submitting them for a grade in the form of a completed paper. If a student cannot articulate a topic in public at the particular moment of this activity, he or she is not compelled to do so. Nevertheless, my students have been extremely enthusiastic about this activity, and generally, the peer pressure of having almost the entire class submit ideas to the group critique encourages even the shier and less articulate students to seek the help of the group rather than go it alone. Conveniently, this strategy also discourages procrastination.

Finally, another strategy I use to decenter traditional authority is to circulate in all my classes manila folders containing magazine, newspaper, and journal articles, announcements, and advertisements that in any way pertain to the course at hand or to my interests and those of my students. Naturally, this activity is extremely time-consuming for me. But I conceive of Los Angeles, where we live, as the ultimate tropical classroom. ¡*Ojo!* Nerves of steel are required to carry out this activity. Even in the least traditional, most ardently decentralized feminist classroom, it can be unsettling to see students completely engrossed in a "subversive" magazine article that may have little to do with the text the class is "officially" discussing.

The students check out articles for one class period, signing for them on the folders. The cultural documents include serious, popular, or journalistic articles on bisexuality, *la vida loca*, bulimia in the Latino versus Anglo cultures, the many Chicano and Latino authors, actors, and musicians appearing in the Los Angeles area, film and theater announcements and reviews, and current events affecting Los Angeles, California, women, and Latinos/Latinas. In this way, my commitments and positions on a wide range of often very explosive and controversial issues are subtly transmitted to the students. From these manila folders, students glean ideas for paper topics and once even organized a class trip to Los Angeles's theater district to see the Chicano performance art group Culture Clash, enjoying a private question and answer session afterward that I arranged with the group's manager. Students are invited to submit their own articles and announcements to the folders as well, and frequently campus-wide events of interest to women, to gay, lesbian, or bisexual students, or to students of color are publicized anonymously through this unorthodox forum.

Things do not always run smoothly in the tropical classroom. Students who have been socialized within and toward conventional models of success—competitiveness, winning, one "right" answer, hierarchies of knowledge and power—sometimes have considerable trouble with my attempts to divest myself of institutional authority. They seem lost, adrift; yearning for the old days, the old ways, for more combative discourse. In the absence (or deferral) of central professorial authority, the older, more sophisticated, or simply more aggressive students can exercise excessive authority and intimidate or completely silence others. This problem has played itself out according to several scenarios in my upper-division courses. For example, in Woman as Sign and Subject and Introduction to Literary Analysis, two extraordinarily bright, completely bilingual, poised, articulate Chicanas—in classrooms with a majority of Latina women—dominated the classroom absolutely, creating a sense of frustration, repressed anger, and resentment among the other students. To attempt to rectify this situation—without destroying the egos of the two female students in question—I did a mid-semester collective evaluation of the course and anonymously transmitted the information to the class as a whole. In addition, I changed the format to focus on more small-group activities, with different individuals assigned to lead discussions. Ironically, by my temporarily claiming more author-ity than I generally am comfortable with, only to disperse it again in a reorganized fashion, my students began to assume a more collective sense of authority, and both the passivity and the resentment were di-minished.

There are other problems for which I do not have any ready solu-tions. For example, one type of critique occasionally occurs in which a student (usually post facto, in the course evaluation) voices a com-plaint that the course has not been "challenging," "structured," or "dis-ciplined" enough. Another generic complaint, to which I am growing accustomed (but which still disturbs me profoundly), is the accusa-tion of "unfairness" in reference to other students' (cultural, ethnic, linguistic, or gender) "advantages" over the complainer. In both in-stances, I detect a reenactment of gender, class, or race privilege.

In the first example, which occured several years ago, the com-plaining student was, ironically, an advisee of mine, a female student who I believe admired and respected me. She was an out-of-state Anglo student from an upper-class background who had attended an exclusive private prep school. Her complaints about the course not being challenging or structured enough masked her own class privi-lege and her expectations of hierarchical, competitive learning as well as her anxiety at feeling displaced in a classroom that seemed to re-pudiate the learning style she had been conditioned to adopt in high school and, possibly, in other Pomona College classrooms. The sec-ond example is an instance of projection. I read at least one or two of these evaluations—invariably from disgruntled "nonnative" students —every semester. In this type of complaint, students disavow their own class and race privilege, projecting onto Chicano/Chicana and Latino/Latina students prodigious linguistic powers that these stu-dents only rarely actually possess, thus rhetorically endowing them with an unfair "advantage" in studying "their own language."[25]

The final category considered crucial in the elaboration of a fem-inist pedagogy is *positionality*. Here, the authors of *The Feminist Classroom* are referencing postmodern theories of subjectivity and performativity in general and theorists like Joan Scott, Linda Alcoff, Gayatri Chakravorty Spivak, and Judith Butler in particular. For me, positional pedagogy in the tropical classroom implies, above all, that there is no one text. In 1995, for example, my Latin American literature survey students read the hypercanonical novel *María* by

Jorge Isaacs as, variously, the quintessential Romantic autobiography; a tragic, chaste love story; a specifically Colombian meditation on pathetic fallacy; a racist, sexist, tropicalizing exoticization of the woman of color; and the narrative staging of the oedipal conflict and suppressed incestuous desire between María and her adoptive father. This is what undergraduates are capable of in a classroom that privileges the coproduction of knowledge and foregrounds students' textual questions rather than lectures them about Isaacs's position in Latin American Romanticism from some moth-eaten *Historia de la literatura*.

Positionality also implies foregrounding a performative, hybrid version of my self-as-teacher, a self that defers closure and celebrates ambiguity and solicits, thus, an analogous positionality from my students. "Live with the question," I often tell them, quoting the loopy New Age guru from the brilliant, underrated movie *The New Age*. Thus, I try to model for my students, in the words of Mexican poet Rosario Castellanos, *"otro modo de ser, más humano y libre"* ("another way of being, more human and free"): a radical, situated way of embodying and dealing with difference (29).

The risks and pleasures of making and enacting a commitment to a tropical pedagogy—unfortunately even in the liberal arts college, where small, interactive classes are much more central to the institutional culture than they are at research universities—often reveal a vexed relationship between the institution and practitioners of a critical pedagogy as I have been attempting to describe it in this essay. This should come as no surprise: "[I]n most institutions the academic disciplines, as traditionally formulated, still hold sway as modes of structuring and transmitting knowledge" (Maher and Tetreault 208). In addition to the hegemony of the disciplines, the relation between the institution and current political and economic conditions is a strong determinant. As Beverly Guy-Sheftall, of Spelman College and the Ford Foundation, asks, "[C]an overwhelmingly white universities truly embrace multiculturalism so that it exists someplace other than in mission statements and college catalogs?" (qtd. in Maher and Tetreault 243). In the California of the late 1990s, with its budget crisis and its embrace of the reactionary governor Pete Wilson and his racist policies, the answer to this question does not appear affirmative.[26] It is vital to acknowledge that as teachers, "we may aspire to challenge and undermine the social structures [we] inhabit, but [we] cannot completely step outside them" (Maher and Tetreault 203).

outrageous acts and everyday rebellions
—Gloria Steinem

I construct my courses, my pedagogy, and my (teaching) self in opposition to prevailing conceptions of the teaching body in/and the liberal arts college classroom, keenly and painfully aware that, as Pierre Bourdieu and Jean-Claude Passeron have shown, "a pedagogy that disparages hierarchical, institutionalized authority and dreams of [. . .] celebrating [. . .] authority democratically shared with students is only fooling itself" (qtd. in Amirault 71). In other words, as the activist and cultural critic Julio Guerrero has put it, the university expects faculty members of color, queer faculty members, and feminists to come out kicking and screaming; my feminist, tropical pedagogy is always already contained by the institution.[27]

So, ironically, although I have been appointed to the committee on teaching (in charge of the teaching workshop for new faculty members as well as other activities to promote excellent and innovative pedagogy), I doubt I'll ever receive the $6,000. Wig Award for excellence in teaching at Pomona College, the most prestigious award the college offers to its faculty. Nevertheless, I will settle for instances of subversion—*"no estar del todo en cualquiera de las estucturas"* (21), in the words of the inimitable Argentine novelist Julio Cortázar —for embodying the *pícara* (trickster) role, taking pleasure also in Fusco's assertion of the guerrilla-warfare, resistance qualities inherent in "the strategy of taking elements of an established or imposed culture and throwing them back with a different set of meanings" (34).[28] I will settle, in other words, for now, for instances of tropicalizing this beige space.

Notes

This essay is dedicated to Etienne Joseph, my son, and to Gabriela Aparicio, in whose room I wrote the first draft. I would also like to thank Pierre T. Rainville, without whose keenly perceptive readings of me and my work I would never have survived this long in academe. Thanks also to Frances R. Aparicio, one of my most thoughtful readers for the past twenty one years. I am grateful to the following friends and colleagues at Pomona College, who have been staunch supporters of my research and pedagogy, even during the period when the institution itself was not: Michael McGaha, Jack Abecassis, Grace Dávila-López, Deena González, María Donapetry, Miguel Tinker Salas, Sidney Lemelle, Lynn Rapaport, and Margaret Waller. Finally, I wish to thank Genaro Padilla for his thought-provoking editorial comments.

The epigraph from Paul Valéry is quoted in Nancy K. Miller's *Getting Personal* (1). The epigraph from Gloria Steinem is quoted in Martinez Alemán (75).

1. This phrase, the "risk of the autobiographical," is designed to echo Stephen Heath's call to take "the risk of essence" (qtd. in Fuss 18).

2. I am deliberately emptying this term, here, of the derogatory meaning it conveys to some Chicanos/Chicanas and Latinos/Latinas, particularly in the Southwest, in order to embrace its fuller, less loaded etymological significance.

3. Even now, as an adult, brushes with the confusion provoked by my "exotic" but ethnically indeterminate appearance are commonplace. Several years ago, at an ice cream social in Ann Arbor, a woman whispered to my friend, sotto voce, "Um, that woman . . . what *is* she?" My friend replied, "She's half Mexican, half Jewish." In 1997, at a reading by Guillermo Gómez-Peña at a Latino bookstore in Los Angeles, as my dark-eyed *güerito* son, part Cajun *compañero*, and I were leaving, a woman from Gómez-Peña's entourage remarked about us, "Are those people Mexican, or what?"—although we were accompanied by my (visibly) Chicana research assistant and I had conversed in Spanish with the performance artist.

4. I want to thank Elena Tinker Valle, the daughter of my colleague Miguel Tinker Salas and Eva Valle, for the notion of a *"famine* [of visibility]." Elena's term, with its connotation of aching, visceral lack, describes percisely the sense I am trying to get at.

5. I'm thinking, just to cite a few of the most recent examples, not only of Fusco's *English Is Broken Here* but also of Lise Funderberg's *Black, White, Other*, one of the first trade books to focus on biracial Americans and their relationships, of the now classic *Borderlands / La frontera*, by Gloria Anzaldúa, of John Leguizamo's *Mambo Mouth*, of Marjorie Garber's *Vice Versa: Bisexuality and the Eroticism of Everyday Life*, of Emily Hicks's *Border Writing*, and of Guillermo Gómez-Peña's *The New World Border*.

6. Located in Claremont, California, Pomona College has been specifically praised for, and rhetorically positioned in (by our current president in his presidential acceptance address), its important strategic location for the twenty-first century: it is on the edge of the Pacific Rim and Latin America and on the eastern edge, too, of the Los Angeles metropolitan area, that multiculti paradise—or inferno.

7. This situation remained the same from 1989, when I arrived at the college, until recently, despite the college's avowed commitment to diversity in faculty hiring and an articulated "plan for diversity" approved by the faculty, which has been in place for several years. In 1997 I earned tenure, and happily, a junior Chicana came on board that year as well, in a joint appointment with sociology and Chicano studies.

8. In terms of student demographics, as of fall 1996, out of 1,500 admitted stu-

dents, 1,330 provided the college with "ethnicity" data: 36% of these students fall under the "ethnic minority" category; 4.5% are African American; 22% are Asian; 10% are Latino/Latina; 0.59% are Native American. I am grateful to Jeremy Donnelly in the registrar's office and to Margaret Adorno, registrar, for providing me with this information.

In terms of Pomona College students' sexual orientation, the student Thelmo García, director of the Queer Resource Center on campus, estimates that there are approximately 200 gay, lesbian, bisexual, and transgendered active members of the QRC. Of these, however, only about 20 are students of color.

9. The term *extracanonical* is my rewriting of Victoria García Serrano's term *postcanonical*, which she coined in the title of the MLA session she organized and chaired, at which an earlier version of this essay was presented. Thanks to Victoria for a fruitful exchange, by e-mail and on the panel "A Workshop on Teaching the Unknown: Feminist Postcanonical Strategies" (1995), around the notions of canonicity, postcanonicity, and the unknown in the Hispanic literature classroom.

10. I use this term here following its etymological meaning in Afrikaans: "apartness," the state of being apart or separate.

11. Pomona College's publicity literature (such as the student handbook, alumni newsletters, etc.) touts the interactive, student-oriented pedagogy of its faculty, and official administrative bodies—such as the curriculum committee, on which I recently sat for two academic years—offer incentives for faculty development of innovative, interdisciplinary general education courses (I received a grant in spring 1997). However, the hierarchial privileging of science and social science faculty hiring, course development, and equipment funding and the concomitant impoverishment of the humanities—particularly of foreign language and literature courses—reflect, even in the respected private liberal arts institution where I teach, this disturbing national trend. As recently as 1996-97, even faced with the evidence of skyrocketing enrollments in Spanish (in upper-division as well as introductory courses)—again, a reflection of national trends that are even more pronounced given our Southern California location—the chair of the Spanish section had to make an impassioned plea to the dean of faculty not to cut several sections. Needless to say, colleagues in other disciplines, such as psychology and sociology, have reported to me that this wholesale slashing of their curriculum by the administration would be unheard of. Interactivity and innovation, it would seem, is fine in the sciences, but Spanish is widely regarded as a "service" discipline, whose usefulness ends with the third-semester language requirement.

12. I was given a course release in my second year at Pomona College to participate in a faculty seminar, funded by a Pew grant, on gay, lesbian, and bisexual studies. My participation in this seminar afforded me invaluable connections to colleagues working on cutting-edge research in various disciplines (religion, sociology, psychology, geology, and anthropology were represented, as were comparative literature and French). Also, it gave me the inspiration to complete my dissertation in a timely manner and constituted a supportive and challenging space to begin exploring new areas of research. I received another Pew grant to develop my course Tropicalizations in 1992, and in 1997 my colleague Deena González and I were granted a Wig Award to develop

Woman, History, Literature, an interdisciplinary general education course combining our expertise in Latin American and Chicana literature, history, and gender studies.

13. Interestingly, I have encountered much less vigilance—a much greater sense of inclusion—from the Chicano studies department faculty. Perhaps this is because they are not "responsible" for me, nor am I as intimately accountable to them as I am to my "own" department, since I do not have a joint appointment with Chicano studies.

14. Although I was eventually accepted into the literature program, which abolished the English-only rule, there was always some question as to the proper location of my courses, whether they were to be full-fledged "core" or merely "related" courses. The literature program was canceled in 1995, apparently for lack of student interest but also, arguably, because some faculty members who had been drawn to the program years ago have more recently been able to satisfy their theoretical desires doing cultural studies within their own "home" departments.

15. Lest this number of students not sound too impressive, the reader should remember that this was in an upper-division, foreign-language poetry course at a liberal arts college.

16. I did not know that I had the "power" to change the text. In fact, during all my assistant professor years, I received no guidance or mentoring whatsoever from the senior colleague in my field, who protested mightily when I made suggestions about changing to different textbooks for courses we rotated. These protests had to be overridden by other more high-ranking, very senior (Peninsularist) colleagues, from whom I sought curricular and intellectual support.

17. I am a "product" of the California public school system, except for my master's degree, which I obtained at Harvard University (which I attended on a graduate fellowship). I was unprepared for the level of sophistication of the Pomona College undergraduates, and although I had taught at other institutions, I did not begin to feel comfortable in the classroom for a couple of years.

18. This student-centered approach is really for the smaller classroom—or one that at least can be broken up into manageable smaller groups—and a relatively unflappable teacher. To me what I call the "wild zone" is an adrenaline high; by this term I mean that you must be prepared for classroom discussions to take you places you have never been before, to unanswerable questions, far afield from your comfort zone, your sense of mastery of "your" material and "your" classroom, to uncomfortable impasses and the like.

19. I am aware that all these categories are differently inflected by issues of class, race, and so on. However, I am not in the business of invoking quantifiable, atomized oppressions. In my experience, all these groups are historically relatively disempowered in the North American classroom, in terms of voice, some less and some more.

20. It must be acknowledged, as Genaro Padilla pointed out to me, that of course not all Chicano/Chicana and Latino/Latina students are "native" Spanish speakers or even Spanish-dominant. I use this fact to ease the anxiety of the

nonnative students (Anglo and other, non-Latino ethnicities), who invariably perceive the course as a sea of expert native informants. If I can get them to hear the voices of some of the Latino students whose Spanish is not at a native level, I can undermine the essentialism that undergirds the prevailing dominant-culture viewpoint that all Latinos, Chicanos, and Hispanics *hablan español* (in the linguistic as well as the cultural sense).

21. Pomona College faculty members, because of budgetary constraints in California that are trickling down even to private institutions and because of demands from a new set of general education requirements established by the college's curriculum committee (on which I sat from 1995 to 1997), are feeling the pressure to increase class size. Although it has been years since I have been able to keep my enrollments at the 10 to 1 student-faculty ratio touted in Pomona College's publicity literature, in general I do not let my enrollments go much over twenty to twenty-five students.

22. Students became so frustrated by the lack of congruence between the actual content of Spanish 102 and its banal title that I actually held a mock contest to rename the course. Some astounding entries surfaced, such as my student Camille's Spanish Lingo for the Savvy Gringo. In the end, we decided on the bilingual Así se habla: Language, Culture, Writing.

23. In 1994, during my pretenure review, the college administration capitalized on an unfortunate confluence of rumor, gossip (endemic in a small town, small college setting), and my own persona to construct a smear campaign in which I was institutionally represented as a dangerously eroticized, rogue professor. Naively or romantically, I had always believed academe was one of the last bastions of the eccentric, the artsy, the "alternative," particularly in the humanities, and I have dressed accordingly. I'll admit it: I love fashion. It is part of my own self-presentation; women's relation to their bodies and to fashion are aspects of my research as well.

Obviously, the attempt to discredit and get rid of me ultimately failed, but that year, 1994–95, was the worst of my life. I am still here, though, now with tenure. Student support was overwhelming, as was the support of a majority of my colleagues, in my home department (Romance languages and literatures) and at other institutions.

24. As Genero Padilla pointed out to me, all these strategies may in fact just produce the *illusion* of a more egalitarian pedagogy when in the end, it is the professor who gives grades, letters of recommendation, and so forth. This is true, and furthermore I should point out that even the etymological roots of our noble task reinforce a hierarchical praxis. *Educare* means "to lead out" and thus implies that someone will do the leading and someone else will be lead. However, even granting this, what I am really referring to here is the establishment of a less authoritarian classroom setting. I am fully aware that I cannot eradicate the perhaps inevitable power imbalance of undergraduate education, especially since we conduct our enterprise in an institutional setting.

25. Lately I attempt to ease these "nonnative" anxieties by soliciting the students' empathy. California—at least for now—has an enormous immigrant population. I ask the native English speakers to put themselves in the place of their immigrant classmates, especially in an English literature class (any class

would do; all are conducted in English, after all, except the "foreign" language and literature courses). This situation, of course, is far more typical than the reverse one in which the English native speaker may be in the minority for up to an hour a day.

26. As a private college with a generous endowment, however, Pomona College has not been directly affected, as have the University of California and the California State systems, for example, by Proposition 209 or the budget crisis in California.

27. I am grateful to Julio Guerrero for his insightful and committed comments as we read and discussed preliminary drafts of this essay during the winter of 1995 in Ann Arbor, Michigan.

28. I am grateful to my father, the late Joseph H. Silverman, for having read to me from the *Lazarillo de Tormes* when I was at a very young, impressionable age.

Works Cited

Amirault, Chris. "The Good Teacher, the Good Student: Identifications of a Student Teacher." Gallop 64–78.

Aparicio, Frances R., and Susana Chávez Silverman, eds. *Tropicalizations: Transcultural Representations of Latinidad*. Hanover: Dartmouth UP, 1997.

Barale, Michéle Aina. "The Romance of Class and Queers: Academic Erotic Zones." *Tilting the Tower: Lesbians Teaching Queer Subjects*. Ed. Linda Garber. New York: Routledge, 1994. 16–24.

Castellanos, Rosario. *A Rosario Castellanos Reader*. Ed. and intro. Maureen Ahern. Austin: U of Texas P, 1988.

Cisneros, Sandra. *Loose Woman*. New York: Knopf, 1994.

Cortázar, Julio. *La vuelta al día en ochenta mundos*. México: Siglo XXI, 1967.

Fusco, Coco. *English Is Broken Here: Notes on Cultural Fusion in the Americas*. New York: New, 1995.

Fuss, Diana. *Essentially Speaking: Feminism, Nature, and Difference*. New York: Routledge, 1989.

Gallop, Jane, ed. *Pedagogy: The Question of Impersonation*. Bloomington: Indiana UP, 1995.

Gaspar de Alba, Alicia. "Beggar on the Cordoba Bridge." *Three Times a Woman: Chicana Poetry*. Tempe: Bilingual, 1989. 1–50.

Giroux, Henry. *Border Crossings: Cultural Workers and the Politics of Education*. New York: Routledge, 1992.

Gordon, Lewis R. "Critical 'Mixed Race'?" *Social Identities: Journal for the Study of Race, Nation, and Culture* 1.2 (1995): 381–95.

Karamcheti, Indira. "Caliban in the Classroom." Gallop 138–46.

Maher, Frances A., and Mary Kay Thompson Tetreault. *The Feminist Classroom*. New York: Basic, 1994.

Martínez Alemán, Ana M. "Actuando." *The Leaning Ivory Tower: Latino Professors in American Universities*. Ed. Raymond V. Padilla and Rudolfo Chávez Chávez: Albany: State U of New York P, 1995. 67–76.

Miller, Nancy K. *Getting Personal: Feminist Occasions and Other Autobiographical Acts*. New York: Routledge, 1991.

Said, Edward. *Orientalism*. New York: Vintage, 1979.

Spivak, Gayatri C. "Three Women's Texts and a Critique of 'Imperialism.' " *Critical Inquiry* 12.1 (1985): 243–63.

Wolf, Susan. "Comment." *Multiculturalism and "The Politics of Recognition."* Ed. Charles Taylor. Princeton: Princeton UP, 1992. 75–86.

At the Limits of My Feminism

Race, Gender, Class, and the Execution of a Feminist Pedagogy

SHEILA MINN HWANG

Recently, one of my colleagues told me a bleakly humorous story. On the first day of class a student looked at her and exclaimed, "You don't look old enough to be a teacher!" My colleague, a fellow female graduate student in her twenties, asked, "What were you expecting?" "An old man with patches on his jacket" was the immediate reply. The rest of the class nodded their heads. From Disney's endearing absent-minded professor to the sexy, adventurous Indiana Jones, American popular culture has both caricatured and romanticized the university professor. Almost invariably, the professor has been cast by Hollywood as a middle-aged white male. While my colleague and I can aspire to becoming professors, we will never become middle-aged white men.

As a young woman of color, I am not what many students expect from an instructor of (mostly) canonical British literature. Common narratives about young women of color seem diametrically opposed to common narratives about university educators, so much so that we must alter our pedagogical practices in order to respond to these narratives. Since my students in the survey of English literary history at the University of California, Santa Barbara, are English majors ostensibly already adept at making meaning out of small details, I try to discourage any potential misreadings of me by sending specific signals to my students through my behavior and my clothing. I want them to know me as their instructor, not as anything else.

My attempts to forge a professorial identity have been undercut by my pedagogical ideals as well as by my subject position. Wanting students to arrive at a single "correct" reading of my body or of any text conflicts with my feminist pedagogical ideals, which begin with a critique of the notion of a "right answer." For me, teaching in a feminist way requires not a static but a dynamic model of power. I reject the premise that instructors traditionally wield unquestioned power and authority over their students. As an instructor, I must attempt to readjust the balance of power in the classroom through strategies that lessen the degree to which students are force-fed "truths universally acknowledged." Although many students demand that instructors digest the material and give them the "right answer," liberal instructors struggle to help students learn to think in a critical fashion. For people interested in a feminist pedagogy, there is no such thing as a right answer in interpreting literature (though there are certainly better and worse analyses or responses). That is, we teach students methods of literary criticism in class rather than force our own interpretations of literature onto our students. In grading, we place a higher value on originality and critical thinking than on the regurgitation of predigested arguments.

Instructors often experience a shift in power away from themselves when they invite students to participate actively in the learning process. Active learners think critically about how they themselves and their instructors make meaning. Common teaching strategies include having students search for faults in instructors' arguments and having instructors play the devil's advocate so that students learn to work ideas out through debate. Feminist pedagogy involves asking many open-ended questions without settling on a "correct" reading of a text, thereby allowing students to voice their own thoughts. Inviting students to doubt their instructor's interpretations begins the process of student empowerment.

Furthermore, a liberal feminist pedagogy requires that instructors treat students with respect. To that end, it involves responding to papers and exams with intellectual rigor. Barbara Omolade explains that

> a liberal feminist stance should not be used to deny the students an honest appraisal of their learning and skills. I used to err on the side of liberalism and promoted sisterly rapport instead of directly grappling with the difficulty of teaching scholarly writing skills and critical thinking. Such skills can assist Black

women in gaining an overall and coherent way of analyzing the information they receive in the classroom and from the experiences of their lives. (35)

Omolade's justification for intellectual rigor need not be limited to black women. All students can benefit from sensitively conveyed, honest appraisal. As Clare Bright reminds us, "[T]houghtful feedback is a wonderful gift" (131). Teaching student empowerment should consist not of giving false praise but rather of challenging students to push their critical and analytic skills further and further. We achieve success when students transfer skills learned in the classroom to the world around them.

As a young person I want to share common frames of reference so that I can better convey ideas to my students. I try to appeal to common cultural connections that I think will work in my students' minds, thereby demonstrating that pre-1900 British literature is much less alien to them than they might at first expect. To that end, I ask my students to sing poems written in common measure to the tune of a popular ballad: the theme song to *Gilligan's Island*. Sometimes I try to bring temporally distant works closer to my student's experience by using colloquial expressions in my discussions of the literature and by comparing television characters to literary ones so that students can more readily identify with the situations and character types. While my ability to make popular culture connections is often a pedagogical asset, I run the risk of exposing myself as not being so terribly different from my students. Sharing common frames of reference creates a more collegial learning environment, but making ideas more accessible and having fun can lead to students who expect that a more informal atmosphere equals lax grading.

The practical problem I have encountered with my pedagogical ideals is that they have the potential to erode my already tenuous authority. My pedagogical ideals depend on a diffusion of the power and authority students tend to give "naturally" to their instructors. Though challenging "natural" authority can lead to student empowerment, it can also lead to a lack of respect for instructors. When students fail to accord respect to their instructors, feminist pedagogy can not only be ineffective but also be misread as ineptitude, weakness, or inexperience. Conducting an intellectually productive and engaging class demands mutual respect between instructors and students; it is almost impossible when students think, "You don't look old enough to be a teacher!"

The vexing problem of maintaining respect while attempting to relinquish a degree of power and authority becomes even more complicated for young women of color like me. As Ann Ardis notes, "[S]tudents often want to position a teacher as a native informant because that's the easiest way for them to account for a teacher's authority vis-à-vis her subject matter. [. . .] Conversely, if the teacher's relationship to her subject matter cannot be read on the surface of her body, she must work to establish her authority to teach that material" (168). I have found Ardis's observation to be true on more than one occasion.

One particular former student, whom I shall call "Harry," struggled greatly with my authority to teach British literary history. Harry's dissatisfaction with his performance on the midterm and paper, the format of the course (large lecture augmented by small discussion sections), and me as an instructor and grader spurred him to write a long electronic mail letter of complaint to my supervising professor and the chair of my department.[1] In the letter, Harry complained that he and several other students enrolled in my discussion section knew that I was completely incoherent, constantly unprepared, and generally incompetent: in my bumbling way, I tried to teach not only wrong facts but even wrong ideas and opinions. Harry explained that he would have corrected my many mistakes, but as I was so intimidated by him, he could not do so with conscience. Because he feared aggravating my nervous condition, he rarely participated in class.

Faculty members have told me that undergraduates often vent their anger or frustration with courses at teaching assistants in this way. Nevertheless, while these sentiments might often be expressed by undergraduates, they are seldom overtly discussed by graduate students and professors. In this essay, I discuss how my identity as a young woman of color and as a teaching assistant sometimes limits my ability to practice a feminist pedagogy. I hope my case will function as a springboard for others to reflect on the pedagogical problems graduate students of color may experience more generally.

Harry was a Chicano returning student who had transferred to the university from a local community college. He was enrolled in an introductory survey of British literature from *Beowulf* to Milton. Until he wrote his letter of complaint, he had never expressed any dissatisfaction with my teaching or with the course. On the contrary, he was always friendly and even overly deferential to me. As a consequence, I was stunned to find that Harry was the author of such a damning letter.

My own surprise was telling. Since Harry did not fulfill one's typical expectations of a "normal" college student, I mistakenly assumed that he would have greater sympathy for someone else who was not "normal." In other words, I thought that as a returning student of color, Harry was self-reflective enough to avoid making assumptions based on my outward appearance. I assumed that a person who might have faced negative preconceptions or stereotypes—someone whose age, ethnicity, and transfer status might undermine his own abilities to speak in the university classroom—would have been one of my best allies against those who might accuse me of having little authority to speak.

Clearly I made a mistake in presupposing Harry's support and understanding. However, my mistake was not in thinking that Harry would identify with me; rather, it was a mistake in understanding the way in which the identification would affect Harry's attitude toward me. In fact, Harry's letter points to a rather complex identification with me that allowed him to project his own anxieties onto me. His case demonstrates the difficulty some students encounter in avoiding the internalization of stereotypical hierarchies and dominant discourse. I now realize that Harry's insecurities about being a returning student of color led him to believe that my status as a student of color affected my abilities and my authority to speak. In his letter, Harry transfers his fears and anxieties to me and then transposes a reading of my body onto readings of my abilities and intellect. He feels so intimidated that he cannot participate in classroom discussion. However, he resists the notion that he himself is uncomfortable and projects his feelings of intimidation onto me. Rationalizing to himself, Harry believes that by not speaking up in class, he spares me from having to come to terms with my inabilities and insecurities. Ironically, it is Harry himself who needs to come to terms with his inabilities and insecurities. Moreover, Harry makes the same accusations against me that he worries will be made against him when he speaks in class. He makes the transference clear later in the letter when he anticipates one day speaking before a class and duplicating what he characterizes as my incoherent manner. Throughout his letter, Harry's accusations against me are based on his understanding of my race, gender, and class, all of which fail to match Harry's idea of how a person leading a class on medieval and Renaissance English literature should look and act.

Members of various minority groups in the United States are often victims of generalizations about their timidity, stupidity, and general inability to communicate anything of value. Harry relies on such culturally accepted stereotypes, making several unsupported assertions about me throughout the letter that use generalizations and universal truths as his evidence: I was completely incoherent, constantly unprepared, and generally incompetent, and almost everybody in the discussion section saw it. Harry's letter lacks concrete examples (when? what material?); instead Harry chooses to rely on common complaints that one can make against almost anyone but most easily against university educators who do not "look the part." He writes that he often had the opportunity to correct the misinformation I gave to the class yet fails to specify what that misinformation was. The reliance on generalization and stereotype reveals Harry's limited definitions of appropriate pedagogy and what constitutes authority; Harry's point of view is infected by his reliance on stereotypical narratives about lack of knowledge and inabilities to communicate. Of course, Harry is not the only person to have these sorts of difficulties. Some students assume that authority comes in specific packages and that a particular kind of authority is necessary for effective teaching.

Likewise, students tend to make assumptions about correlations between one's ethnic background and one's area of expertise. I find that students come into my class with specific stereotypes about Asian Americans in the university. Because of my Asian face, I must constantly defend my right to talk knowledgeably about British literature. Even here on the West Coast where the Asian American population is significantly higher than in other parts of the country, students of almost all ethnic and racial backgrounds mistake me for a foreign student. In fact, perhaps the most offensive errors have been made by other Asian Americans. One quarter I worked very closely with a recent Vietnamese immigrant, whom I shall call "Jane." Jane had only lived in the United States for a few years and had never learned any English before arriving in the United States, so nineteenth-century

British literature was not easy reading for her. One day when we were finishing up one of our tutorials, Jane asked me about my own studies. I told her that I intended to specialize in late-eighteenth- and early-nineteenth-century British literature. She responded with awe and said that she admired me immensely because reading English literature was enormously difficult for *people like us*. It took me a moment to realize that Jane assumed that I, like she, was not American by birth and that English was a second language for me. Like Harry, Jane projected her own situation onto me. Though I recognized that she was attempting to extend a compliment, I was offended by her logic: that since I do not look "American," I am not. I responded to Jane by signaling my appreciation of her admiration and then explaining that it was undeserved because she had made a mistaken assumption about me.

Whenever I get up in front of a classroom, I know that some of my students make assumptions about my background even before I speak: they generalize that I am a member of the Hong Kong or Taiwan superwealthy elite, a working-class immigrant, or a refugee who spent years performing menial labor in abject conditions. Yet I am none of these. The fact of the matter is that these fictions are extremely far from my experience.

My subject position is not easily identifiable with my field of expertise. As an Asian American woman in the academy, I am often assumed to work in either women's studies or Asian American studies. When I was an undergraduate I told one of my professors that I wanted to specialize in eighteenth-century British literature. He responded that I should also further develop my interests in minority literatures because I was sure to be typecast by search committees as well as by undergraduates. My professor was trying to help me think about what he saw as the realities of the academy. I find it a sad reflection of the inherent prejudices in this profession to think that my face or my skin color allows people to assume that my primary interest is in minority literatures. My academic background has prepared me best to teach eighteenth- and nineteenth-century British literature rather than twentieth-century American literature. Yet since I do not look like the crusty old English professor of popular imagination, students question my authority to teach my field of specialization.

My ethnic background further complicates students' readings of how my gender inflects my ability to teach British literature. Feminist scholars have noted gender's traditional relation to the power dynamics in the classroom. Gender plays an important role in a teacher's ability to execute a feminist pedagogy, for students tend to have rather disparate preconceived notions of the teacher's relation to authority depending on his or her gender. In "The Writing Instructor as Gendered Text: A Collaborative Inquiry," Russ Cunningham and Samantha H. Goldstein examine how students read Cunningham's male body and Goldstein's female body, giving us a comparative view of what it means to be a gendered text for a class. Cunningham and Goldstein write that "we, as teachers, often come to embody the language we speak and how our students, in turn, often read our bodies as they reflect our positionality and discursive authority in (and beyond) the classroom" (31–32). Cunningham notes that it is easier for him to incorporate feminist pedagogy in the classroom than it is for Goldstein because Cunningham has the weight of authority from his sex. That is, students more easily grant him the authority to mandate that classes must be conducted along feminist lines, whereas they do not necessarily grant women instructors the same kind of authority to set the terms of the class. Cunningham and Goldstein's discussion shows that instructors granted greater respect and thereby authority by students find it easier to execute a feminist pedagogy.

Omolade provides insight on alternative ways instructors may find respect from their students. She describes her experience teaching black women returning students who "immediately regarded [her] more as a sister than an instructor" because they shared similarities in age, economic background, and cultural background (32).[2] The natural respect for a "sister" accorded to Omolade allowed her to understand that "[t]hey wanted me to teach them, not just to be sisterly and befriend or rant politics at them. They gave me automatic deference and respect, and in fact, were too respectful to question me closely" (32). This parallels Cunningham's remark that his "writing courses have been informed by a widespread docility and complacency" (34). Cunningham says of his writing students: "All too often, they resign themselves to being the proverbial empty vessels in the classroom, waiting quietly to serve as repositories for my teacherly insights" (34). Cunningham's maleness gains him automatic respect, and Omolade's black womanhood performs the same function for those who share her race and gender. That is, Omolade's ability to practice a feminist pedagogy in the classroom is dictated by the safe environment of sameness; Cunningham relies on an authority of difference. Yet as a young female graduate student of color, I can rely neither on my ethnicity nor on my gender as automatic aides in my teaching. Instead, graduate students of color tend at once to be much too different and much too similar to their undergraduate students.

As a consequence, we must play a game of claiming respect and refusing authority at the same time. Because I have been the target of undergraduate criticisms, I sometimes fall into a role that I do not enjoy playing. Forced to the limits of my feminist pedagogy, I willingly assume authority by acting as an attendance cop, taking roll, giving quizzes, being very strict with due dates, and allowing students to believe that I am rather inflexible about my course policies. Sometimes I must use an aggressively Socratic method of teaching, and occasionally I lecture in discussion sections. Other graduate students and I have regularly discussed how our classroom personas seem to conflict with our pedagogical ideals. One way we compensate for this gap is to restrict our more overtly feminist pedagogical stance to one-on-one meetings with students. Feminist pedagogy cannot be applied equally to every teaching situation. Our profession, I now know, is a profession of constant positioning, adjusting, and repositioning.

Our illegitimate authority is not only falsely imagined to be illegitimate on the basis of readings of gender and race; unfortunately our authority is "illegitimate" given the structure of the university. In the university's hierarchy, graduate students stand awkwardly positioned in the both powerful and powerless place accorded to the teaching assistant. Before I discuss teaching assistantship directly, I want to address one last problem related to bodies that many teaching assistants experience. Many graduate students are closer in age to their students than tenure-track professors are, and relative youth can encourage undergraduates to lack respect for their teaching assistants. Age discrimination is not limited to discrimination against the elderly. Harry points out in his letter that he is a man of thirty who works to pay for his education, not a teenager who has come to the university to party with his parents' hard-earned money. Harry unfairly denigrates most of my students and perhaps even me, using his age as evidence for his commitment to education and associating youth with frivolity. His views reflect an alienation from campus life that older students can experience. In assuming that younger students neither pay for nor appreciate their education, returning students can be somewhat impatient with seventeen- to twenty-three-year-olds. And because I not only look but also am younger than thirty, Harry can subtly indict me too. His assumption that one's age indicates one's commitment to education insults his fellow classmates as well as me.[3]

Harry links me even more closely to "uncommitted" younger students by accusing me of speaking in a teen dialect; he reaffirms the stereotypical image of brainless California girls. Because I was born in Minnesota and raised in California, I speak what might be considered fairly standard American English.[4] Yet Harry uses my California background against me to assert that I can only communicate in incomprehensible "Valley Girl" speak. He explains that he wants to learn the course material well so that he will be able to teach it when he becomes a teaching assistant, but he cannot when every other word I say is "like" or "do you know what I mean." Using quotation marks as if he had written down exactly what I said, Harry cites a question about blood that I posed to the discussion section as an example of my incoherence. Harry has evidently already built up such misconceptions about me that he not only misreads but also mishears me, for his Valley Girl rendition of the question misses the mark entirely.

Since this is the only specific incident in our discussion section that Harry cites, I will respond minutely. Certainly, I did ask my students, "When is she like blood?" and I probably asked them if they understood the question, but I reject Harry's reading of the exchange. I was leading a discussion on the autobiography of the medieval mystic and author Margery Kempe and her relation to the four humours (blood, phlegm, choler, and melancholy or black choler), something that was presented during the week's lecture. Ultimately my question was comparative: at what points in the text does Kempe display humoural characteristics associated with blood? However, Harry turns a comparative "like" into a Valley Girl "like" and claims that my very delivery of the question is unintelligible. Harry presents my solicitation of feedback as my not knowing the material well enough to tell my students when Kempe resembles which humour.[5] He misreads my strategically open-ended question as my inability to give students the "correct" interpretation.

Even when a student is not older than the teaching assistant by several years, some graduate students' relative youth still poses a problem; undergraduates sometimes try to transgress instructor-student boundaries. I remember meeting with a student, "Sally," to discuss her plans to write a paper. When we were almost finished, Sally said that she needed one more bit of advice. She then asked me what strategies I would suggest in attaining some guy's attention and affection. I appreciated that Sally felt comfortable enough with me to confide details of her personal life and that she felt that I possessed some form of wisdom or authority, but I was also disturbed by the idea that Sally saw our relationship more as girlfriends than as teacher and student. For better or worse, I answered Sally's question with bland generalizations about success and intelligence being attractive. Then I brought her back to the paper topic. I still feel awkward in situations such as this one, for I do not want to cross the line between teacher and student, even with the best, brightest, and most interesting of my students. Becoming friends with students undermines learning; it is hard enough to evaluate a student's performance without having to worry about jeopardizing a growing friendship.[6] To avoid accusations of betrayal, I prefer to have the teaching assistant– student barrier in place and clearly marked. The military's rules against fraternization between officers and the enlisted seems almost sensible once I realize the dangers of crossing hierarchical boundaries.[7]

Nevertheless, I have read many undergraduate evaluations of my teaching that fantasize about friendships or other inappropriate relationships between student and instructor. Students have written comments such as "Sheila is someone I would want to meet at a bar and have a beer with." One former student even went as far as to suggest that I would be the ideal date for a romantic weekend getaway. Although such remarks are ostensibly meant to flatter, I have become extremely irritated with them because they constitute a particular kind of sexual harassment that is not actionable. I want students to evaluate me on my teaching, not on some social fantasy they may have about me. Many graduate students I have met share similar stories, but few have been able to provide solutions to inappropriately personal comments on undergraduate evaluations.

The danger in seeing teaching assistants as peers intensifies when students earn poor grades. A poor grade can be read as an "older sister" unfairly punishing a "younger sibling." Students then appeal to the parent figure, the professor, to point out that I am not yet a "grown up" and that I should have no authority to judge or grade them. For example, one quarter a young female student, whom I shall call "Phyllis," repeatedly "informed" me that the previous quarter she had had a professor who adored her ideas and a TA who always gave her C's on her papers. Phyllis blamed the poor grade on the teaching assistant by implying that his thinking was much less sophisticated than her own or the professor's: he just was not smart enough to understand her argument. She did not (or refused to) recognize that the difference in assessment could reside in the transition from abstract thoughts to actual writing and that she needed to push her interesting ideas further to form a coherent and convincing paper. The story made me wary of Phyllis, so I tried especially hard to work with her individually. Yet she steadfastly refused to take my advice on strategies for improving her papers. In fact, she even refused to agree on the basis of grading close-reading exercises; she would respond that she thought that my interest in close reading was off base and that to address one theme or to trace one image in a text was inherently wrong. Phyllis said that English papers ought to be exercises in creative writing rather than critical thinking. I too gave her a C. I later learned that she also complained to the professor about my "wrong" expectations. The professor, quite admirably, told Phyllis that she would first have to contest the grade to me before the professor would be willing to interfere.[8] I was fortunate enough to be working with a professor who showed respect for my position in the classroom by allowing me a great deal of autonomy and by deferring to many of my decisions. All undergraduates know that teaching assistants assign grades, yet they also know that the teaching assistant assigns grades only on a provisional basis; it is the tenure-track professor who actually signs off on final grade sheets.

As a teaching assistant for a large lecture course, I am not the instructor of record.[9] In the term "teaching assistant," the critical word is *assistant* — that is, not the source of knowledge or instruction but merely an apprentice who assists the master-professor. Joseph Litvak has noted that

> the unhappiness of grad students, their feelings of powerlessness, of abjectness [is] something that people don't talk about very much in the academy, but it's as much a force as some of the other things we're starting to talk about, like sexuality. I

guess you could call it the class issue, and it's the last taboo.
(qtd. in Talbot 39)[10]

Graduate students feel powerless because they really are powerless in the classroom and in the university more generally. The main function of the teaching assistants is to grade, which is perhaps the most inglorious aspect of teaching and typically the point of friction between instructors and students. Grading lays one open to attack, especially when the teaching assistant as grader does not create the initial assignments or syllabus. And despite a teaching assistant's role as primary grader of course material, the professor earns the greater compensation, fame, and glory. The university has created an underclass of graduate students, and undergraduates carefully exploit that fact.

Undergraduates commonly complain that they are not getting their money's worth when instructed by graduate students. In his letter, Harry explains that he dropped my class because he felt cheated by having people like me teach him. He claims that all his hard work had been invalidated by someone who herself is incompetent to judge his efforts. This line of argumentation accurately identifies graduate students as the underclass of the university. Although Harry confuses effort with performance, the passage possesses an important underlying premise. Harry seems to think there is a distinct division between a professor's abilities to grade work and a teaching assistant's—that as a teaching assistant I have not yet learned proper discernment. Once one has received a degree, it seems, according to the logic of Harry's letter, one magically learns how to grade objectively. Indeed, at one point in his letter, Harry wonders whether *any* teaching assistant can construct and implement a fair system of grading. In short, Harry's anger with the structure of the university is as much behind his hostility as his personal frustration with me.

The teaching assistant's unresolved relation to power worsens when his or her relative authority in the classroom may change each term. Because graduate students do not choose the professor for whom they assist, they cannot tell whether or not specific professors will support pedagogical styles different from their own. There seems to be little uniformity in the expectations professors have of their teaching assistants or in the authority or autonomy professors are willing to grant them. To make matters worse, if a teaching assistant's pedagogical practices differ from the supervising professor's practices, that teaching assistant must follow the professor's lead. Although teaching assistants, as apprentices, should be open to a variety of teaching styles, it is no secret that what works for one person may utterly fail for another. The differences in power between the subject position of faculty members and that of many teaching assistants exacerbates that fact. Furthermore, teaching assistants do not choose the texts and cannot control the primary interpretations of texts conveyed to students. As a teaching assistant, I can only react to a professor's choices and interpretation of texts. Although I sometimes openly disagree with a professor's lectures in my discussion sections, some students resist my resistance because they want to have the "right answer." Any ideas that run contrary to the professor's may seem like wrong answers to undergraduates who wish to memorize rather than truly engage with particular bodies of knowledge.

I have drawn on my experiences to show the difficulties I have encountered in employing a feminist pedagogy. Some of the resistances have resulted from the uncertainty undergraduates feel when granted more power than they are accustomed to. Some result from misreadings of me as an instructor. And yet, as my colleague's story about old men with jacket patches demonstrates, part of the problem can be traced to stereotyped notions of authority and the teaching assistant's always "almost but not quite" professorial status in the university hierarchy. The latter problem is the easiest for departments to address.

It might be argued that the pedagogical problems I and other graduate students experience by virtue of our status as teaching assistants are only temporary and therefore not urgent. Even so, five or more years is a long time to be without a practical pedagogy. Professors and graduate students need to push themselves to think critically about the ambiguous place of the teaching assistant and explore ways to minimize that position's vulnerability. Although some individual departments and universities provide practical in-house guides on how to teach discussion sections (mostly directed at first-time instructors), teaching assistants need more. We need more theoretically nuanced approaches to our always negotiated and challenging pedagogical position. Perhaps an interesting and productive way to begin an open discussion of the teaching assistant's position would be for faculty members to share stories of their own teaching failures as well as successes, from their graduate student days to the present. By collecting these stories, we may be able to discover ways in which teaching assistants may practice liberal pedagogies without laying themselves open to attack by undergraduates.

Many problems can be avoided easily if professors treat their teaching assistants as colleagues rather than subordinates in training. To that end, it would be helpful if professors asked for teaching assistant input on the content of the course and the format of graded material. Inviting teaching assistants to give guest lectures forces undergraduates to realize that graduate students are junior members of the profession. Greater input into the material taught and greater visibility boost undergraduates' confidence in their teaching assistants.[11] In addition, it would be helpful if professors did not discuss grades with undergraduates until a discussion of the grade has taken place between teaching assistant and student, as well as between teaching assistant and professor. Faculty members should feel free to think of their relationships with teaching assistants less as supervisory ones than as collaborative teaching endeavors in which all participants may learn from one another.

Many graduate students will never become the stereotypical "old man with patches on his jacket," but we do not aspire to that model. In my view, the traditional, authoritarian way of teaching does not promote the best environment for learning, because students sometimes openly, sometimes covertly, rebel against this imposition of power. From *Ferris Bueller's Day Off* to *The Mirror Has Two Faces*, American popular culture reflects how ineffective the old model of teaching seems for today's students. The power and authority of the stereotypical middle-aged white male professor is potentially as dispersed as mine, as a young woman of color; however, I consciously shift power and authority away from myself. I hope to become the kind of professor who creates a learning environment in which students feel comfortable voicing their thoughts, ideas, and intellectual concerns. Because of the inevitably varied subject positions of our students, our pedagogical strategies will always have uneven results. Some students will embrace the feminist pedagogical model, while others will resist; but even open opposition from students indicates their engagement.

Notes

Without my colleagues, I would not have been able to complete this paper. I wish to thank the members of Shirley Lim's graduate seminar on feminist epistemologies (winter 1996) for helping to shape my understanding of feminist pedagogy. In addition, I am grateful to Jennifer Jones, Noelle Williams, Vince Willoughby, Lisa Wilson, and Rebecca Wood for providing many useful comments on various drafts of this essay.

1. In earlier versions of this paper, I quoted directly from Harry's letter of complaint, for I found much to say about the words he used. Unfortunately, I cannot quote directly from the electronic mail letter because I have not obtained explicit permission from Harry to do so.

2. At the 1998 San Francisco MLA convention, Rachel Lee and Caren Caplan chaired a fascinating session, entitled "Feminist Pedagogy, Theory, Practice: Teaching and Reading 'Women of Color,' " on women of color teaching women of color courses. Speakers included Minoo Moallem, Laura Hyun Yi Kang, Rachel Lee, and Daphne Ann Brooks.

3. Of course, not all returning students feel this way. My first and one of my best university teaching experiences was a night course offered by university extension, in which the majority of my students were much older than my own twenty-two years. This environment was an excellent one in which to practice a feminist pedagogy based on the twin ideals of mutual respect and rigor.

4. That is, I speak "Hollywood" English just as certain Britons speak BBC English rather than some other regional dialect that is not so widely disseminated.

5. In fact, the class Harry criticizes was a *discussion* section. The aim of a discussion section for a large lecture is to provide students with the opportunity to discuss the issues raised in their readings and in lecture. A discussion section, as I understand it, provides students in a large lecture course with a forum to exchange ideas and a place for the teaching assistant to clarify or expand on what was said in lecture. The discussion section offers a change for students to ask questions, test their own knowledge, and exchange opinions; it neither claims nor desires to be yet another lecture. My pedagogical practice is not only feminist but also integral to the concept of a discussion section.

6. In thinking about the professors who befriended me when I was an undergraduate, I realize that most of them were already well-established, happily married, middle-aged, white men who were tenured. I am envious of their freedom in forming friendships with students, for their naturalized authority remains steadfast. By contrast, my hard-fought authority is always in jeopardy of being compromised. Margaret Talbot quotes Jane Gallop on informality: Gallop explains, "[O]ne of the reasons I can't undercut my authority with students by being shockingly informal is that my authority is based on an authorial persona or a theoretical persona that is itself shockingly informal — that's part of its authority" (30). There is authority in freely leaving one's authority behind.

7. Again, my first teaching experience in university extension courses seems to support this notion. An unusually large proportion of my students in that class were former military and therefore accustomed to granting authority to whoever was ostensibly in charge. Because I was granted so much "natural" authority, I found it easy to practice a feminist pedagogy.

8. I have been lucky enough to have always been supported in my grading and evaluation of students by my supervising professors. However, I know of many other teaching assistants who have been overruled with disastrous results. The undergraduate can tell other classmates of the advantages of complaining to the professor, and then the teaching assistant is under constant attack from the entire class. In fact, if students in a current class spread rumors about a particular teaching assistant, then her or his ability to run an effective class may be adversely affected for several terms.

9. Some of the problems I discuss do not occur as frequently in composition courses because even though a teaching assistant may not be the instructor of record for those courses either, the students rarely see anyone else at the head of the class. The physical absence of a supervising professor endows teaching assistants with greater authority.

10. I find it significant that this subject comes up in an article about Jane Gallop's radical feminist pedagogy. Even her radical approach relies on the university's validation of her position as a professor. Graduate students have no recourse to such validation in their pedagogy.

11. I argue that this is generally true, though Harry expressed the most anxiety on my specific topic of expertise—the material covered in my guest lecture on Margery Kempe.

Works Cited

Ardis, Ann. "Presence of Mind, Presence of Body: Embodying Positionality in the Classroom." *Hypatia* 7.2 (1992): 166–76.

Bright, Clare. "Teaching Feminist Pedagogy: An Undergraduate Course." *Women's Studies Quarterly* 21.3–4 (1993): 128–32.

Cunningham, Russ. "Struggling with(in) Patriarchy: Reconciling Masculine Presence with 'Feminist Style' in a College Writing Course." *Composition Forum* 7.1 (1996): 32–39.

Cunningham, Russ, and Samantha H. Goldstein. "The Writing Instructor as Gendered Text: A Collaborative Inquiry." *Composition Forum* 7.1 (1996): 31–32.

Omolade, Barbara. "A Black Feminist Pedagogy." *Women's Studies Quarterly* 21.3–4 (1993): 31–38.

Talbot, Margaret. "A Most Dangerous Method." *Lingua Franca* Jan.-Feb. 1994: 24–40.

Now That They Have Us, What's the Point?

The Challenge of Hiring to Create Diversity

SANDRA GUNNING

On the bus to work one morning, early in my career at the public midwestern university where I'm currently employed, I remember overhearing a local resident telling some tourists about our campus: "And you'll know the professors when you see 'em," he said. "They're the old men with the bow ties and suits." Since I was hoping to have a good day, I chose to laugh off this inadvertent erasure of my own identity, especially since the crack about "old men in bow ties" falsely homogenized the very white male faculty to which it seemingly referred. And besides, if I was invisible to those outside the academy, I knew I was certainly "visible" to my own English department.

Indeed, our chair had attracted some notoriety by building, in a short space of time, a cohort of feminist scholars, African Americanists, Africanists, and an Asian Americanist. Many of us were junior, but as a group we provided the department with courses in postcolonial studies, feminist theory, Caribbean literature, Asian American literature, Victorian women writers, and the literature of the Harlem Renaissance, to name a few. Although we hadn't yet made much progress in Chicano/Chicana or Native American literature, it was assumed that those hires would eventually come, given the apparent commitment to reimagining the constituency of the department. My senior white colleagues had even made some important steps toward ensuring that we were visible in the undergraduate curriculum, by adding a "new traditions" requirement to the major — "new traditions" being defined by the department administration as any course that didn't cover dead white male writers. And, of course, when I started teaching my freshman- and sophomore-level courses that year, I was certainly visible in classes where you had to hunt around the room to find a single student of color.

Judging from my own experience and from conversations I've had with colleagues over the past six years, I believe that most of us could claim to be personally well treated, and most of us were enthusiastically confident that our presence was the start of something new in the department. This was certainly heartening, compared with what I'd experienced previously in a graduate setting where a person of color was rarely seen: for the first three years of course work and examinations in my PhD program, some fellow students and faculty members persisted in asking me if I was a visitor who was planning to apply to be a real graduate student some day. And while I was writing a dissertation on late-nineteenth-century Anglo-American and African American literature, other people kept inquiring how my dissertation on Toni Morrison was going. So, it *was* an initial relief to be in the new job where people seemed genuinely glad to see me as a colleague and where those Americanists who did read my work seemed really interested in what I had to contribute to the field. But it was on this same point that things seemed to unravel: even as we seemed to become visible, individual examples of the department's willingness to be inclusive, the full meaning and consequence of those hirings—especially for junior faculty members of color—seemed never to get a great deal of attention. Pragmatically, how was our presence making an impact?

Any attempt to unite a department under a single definition of diversity is a lost cause, but for a department that was hiring people of color so fast and furiously, I was (and still am) more than a little concerned that a lot of basic questions were not being asked. Did my department think of diversity as a philosophical refiguration from inside, as, for instance, when a literature department shifts from a traditional field emphasis on the "great books" of British and American literature to offering subconcentrations in feminist theory, African American literature, film studies, or cultural studies? What was the relation between this kind of field diversification and the desire for numerical diversity, defined as the hiring of persons traditionally underrepresented in the university setting? How was the diversity of the department's faculty to be seen in relation to the diversity of its student body? Some senior faculty members seemed to collapse the above questions by assuming that diversity hiring dramatically ushered in a visibly different set of junior colleagues who presumably would relate to white female students and students of color more effectively than white male professors did and who would be interested in a different kind of scholarship not practiced by their senior counterparts. When my department expressed a commitment to increasing minority or female faculty representation and then hired to achieve visible difference, exactly what ambiguities existed behind both the disciplinary and the pedagogical roles the new hire was expected to play? That these questions were unaddressed betrayed a lack of attention to affirmative action (that is, the question of equal access to opportunity) as related to but separate from questions of field reorganization and teaching. In other words, what was missing from the equation was the senior faculty's programmatic attention to the recontextualization of department life that we all had to face in the wake of such hiring. Unfortunately, by collapsing these issues, many of my senior colleagues had set into place the conditions that would ensure a dysfunctional, deeply alienating experience for the very persons they had worked so hard to recruit.

Instead, what was getting all the attention was recruitment of faculty members of color, as if the answer to questions of diversity rested merely on the achievement of recruitment goals. Though not without its particular challenges, recruitment of faculty members of color was more clearly and cleanly definable in both its goals (to identify and successfully hire candidates) and immediate obstacles (obtaining funding, competing with other schools for the same pool of candidates). In contrast, with the exception of new faces and new courses listed in the student guide to department offerings, the aftereffects of recruitment were more difficult to pin down, especially because they provoked a range of difficult ideological and social questions that could never be adequately answered to everyone's satisfaction. And yet, in any department, confrontation of these questions is vital if that department truly seeks to enhance the quality of life for (and finally retain) white women and people of color hired at the junior level, especially if their hiring is meant to signal a shift in a department's vision of itself. In other words, to paraphrase one of my former professors from graduate school, it wasn't simply a matter of adding women and people of color to the pot and giving the whole mixture a good stir.

Clearly the dilemma here is how much, even before the arrival of the new hires, did my department work through the conceptual challenges posed by postcolonialism, feminist theory, cultural studies, multiculturalism, and so forth to traditional definitions of literary studies. Despite the first wave of euphoria generated by the presence of all the newly hired faculty members, I started to wonder whether some of my colleagues and I—especially those of us who were junior —would find ourselves operating as disempowered symbols of a stalled debate rather than as full participants in a process of change. My department made matters worse by invariably using affirmative action funding lines to fund ethnic or world literature, postcolonial theory, or feminist theory positions. In this practice, my department acted within the norm of most academic units nationwide: from a bureaucratic point of view, the merger of bodies and fields is a convenient way to achieve two distinct goals. But such a funding structure promoted and naturalized the troubling but all too familiar vision of dual essentialism on the part of hiring departments, where a job in African American literature would be filled by a black candidate, while jobs in literary theory would be filled by white candidates.

Such an overdetermined reading of race, gender, and scholarship meant that junior faculty members of color were publicly identified as working outside the tradition of the "dead white males" and therefore somehow completely separate from their white male colleagues, regardless of rank. But what was lost here is the reality that the academic work of "target of opportunity" or affirmative action hires (often persons who are themselves products of traditional literature departments) emerges out of and always in conversation with the recognized canon. In some cases their work might call into question certain assumptions and cherished notions about that canon. Therefore, while hiring to introduce difference is important, just as crucial are the ways in which a department chooses to categorize the scholarship and teaching of specifically these junior members. In our department in particular, while the new traditions requirement for the major seemed to have been an excellent start in department refiguration, senior faculty members seemed to see the requirement as the end of the process rather than as a necessary first step from which more meaningful integrations might be launched.

In any number of ways, the slippage between individual identity and the politics of field was guaranteed to surface in the context of teaching, since the visibility of the junior faculty member in the classroom as different from his or her senior colleagues contextualizes his or her claims to authority as a teacher and scholar. It should come as no surprise that some students at both the graduate and the undergraduate levels evaluate the performance of their professors on the basis of assumptions about the latter's assumed right to expertise in particular fields. Few departments—including my own—seem to pay much attention to this fact, despite seemingly endless discussions on pedagogy. Meanwhile, I couldn't help thinking that the linking of research topic and personal identity (something I experienced in graduate school) was being perpetuated for a new generation of scholars every time white faculty members accepted unquestioningly the collapse of bodies and fields, tracking graduate students and undergraduates into specializations such as feminist theory or Asian American or Chicano/Chicana studies, depending on the students' race or gender identification.

Do students in fact expect the same rigor from an Asian American female professor teaching Chaucer as they would from a white male professor? Do students expect a feminist line from a woman professor, as well as more nurturing, and lower grading standards, because she's a woman? What is the effect on junior faculty members when students assume (as one of my white students did) that a class on African American literature will be less rigorous than a class on something more traditional? What does it mean to students who have this same assumption that (because of department hiring patterns) they can count on having black faculty members teach these courses? When graduate students ask senior male specialists in their fields to direct the dissertation and then also ask junior white women to join the committee to cover the gender side of things, are they really opting for the benefit of seniority in a director, while also putting together a balanced committee, or are they simply reproducing existing department patterns of diversification without inclusion or integration? While clearly these questions are not indicative of hard-and-fast rules of the relationship between students and faculty members of color, neither can they be read as the insecure imaginings of faculty members of color, since questions of and prejudices toward class, race, gender, sexual orientation, and national identity inform social relations within the university, as they do in every other aspect of our lives. It is ironic, however, that so few people, at least among my colleagues anyway, cared to look at how closely we mirrored the larger world.

Instead, my colleagues seemed eternally impressed with reading the teacher-student relationship as in fact the model of a parent-child relationship, given the assumed balance of power that resided between the adult professor of knowledge, dispensing grades and instruction, and the rows and rows of relatively powerless students who were presumably going to soak up knowledge and expand like so many sponges. Indeed, with the face of our department changing so rapidly, in public meetings my colleagues seemed to retreat again and again to teaching as the seemingly only stable social relationship in the academy one could take for granted. But even this illusion would have been shattered if, in disentangling the politics of affirmative action, the politics of literary study, and the politics of the classroom, the specificity of experience for junior faculty members of color—and especially junior women—came to the forefront.

For many tenured white faculty members, the issue was how much independence we as teachers should dole out to students, to achieve the so-called teachable moment. If my senior colleagues' views on pedagogy had moments of value (and they probably did), I was unable to appreciate them. Increasingly, these discussions seemed to be so wholly separate from my classroom reality and, as conversation with other junior women soon revealed, the reality of many others. What I did come to realize in very personal ways, however, was that one very real effect of prefiguring a department's population in terms of gender is the increased likelihood of sexual harassment, especially harassment perpetuated against junior women by male students. Still in quest of some forum to address my teaching needs, one fateful winter term I attended a workshop for junior faculty members entitled Teaching in the Multicultural Classroom, run by an extradepartmental campus organization. Its attendees turned out overwhelmingly to be junior women from all across campus (and why virtually no men showed up is still a mystery to me, since the workshop was advertised as rank, not gender, specific). What I thought was going to be a workshop on how to handle student anxieties in a multiracial setting turned into an impromptu airing by junior women of their experiences of sexual and other harassment in the classroom. For all participants, the workshop was cathartic, but I was still bothered by the fact that I had to go outside my department for any acknowledgment of the particular working conditions that affected how I did my job. Eventually the organizers issued a report on and summary of the workshop, complete with a bibliography of further readings on gender and race dynamics in the classroom. Though these materials were distributed to chairs and program heads, there was never a word about it in my department. Around the same time, by coincidence, the department administration did distribute a series of guidelines—produced from the university human resources office— to help female office workers identify and deal with sexual or other types of harassment from students or members of the public visiting the department offices.

Clearly, most universities have policies against the harassment of female employees by male coworkers, but junior women are assumed to be protected from student harassment by virtue of their status as faculty members. However, their experience as women and the fact that some male students register that difference as sexual vulnerability have been completely ignored in the current debates over sexual harassment on campus. Ironically, as the battle over who can claim victim status heats up, neither those who fight for sanctions against the sexual harassment of female students by their male professors nor those who claim that male faculty members' careers are ruined every time a female student makes a rash accusation question the increasingly false analogy that faculty member is to student as male is to female. To counteract this particular denial of the specificity of junior women's experiences, departments are even more closely challenged to recognize that faculty authority is structured through— rather than in spite of—race, class, gender, and sexuality and that this authority is still perceived by those within and outside academia as essentially male.

In tandem with the marginalization of the female or minority faculty members in terms of field and the unrecognized politics of the classroom comes an increased faith in their ability to serve as mentors or positive role models, especially for students of color at the university. According to this argument (sometimes made by students themselves and often used by university administrators arguing for affirmative action funding), white female students and students of color will naturally identify with role models from their own group, thereby counteracting the alienation they feel when working with white male instructors. While some students' sense of exclusion from the university is directly related to the presence in class after class of only white men at the podium, we cannot assume that by definition white male instructors are therefore incapable of learning and understanding how to be highly effective mentors to students who are not also white and male. Such a belief expects too little of the white male instructor and oversimplifies the faculty-student relationship, while at the same time fostering naive (and some would say sexist or racist) assumptions about a junior white woman or person of color's supposed affinity for certain students. In its extreme conditions, this situation perpetuates what an East Coast colleague calls the "black mammy complex," since the junior woman or person of color is suddenly naturalized as the "caretaker," while her or his white male colleagues are given the option of opting out. (Since I only had one black woman mentor for my entire graduate and undergraduate career, I count myself lucky in having had a few—but very key—male professors who didn't feel that their race or their maleness got in the way of their mentoring.)

Even when a white female or Native American or Chicano/Chicana assistant professor does have a strong mentoring relationship with students in that faculty's identity group, we need to acknowledge that those students, precisely because their feelings of alienation encourage a sense of entitlement to that faculty person's attention, will demand vastly different things of their mentors than they would from white men. By now, almost everyone has heard at least one story of the junior faculty white woman or person of color who seems to spend an inordinate amount of time in office hours; this same individual is often besieged as well with requests from students to take part in any number of undergraduate activities. Less discernible complications arise when some students use their relationship with the faculty person to consciously or unconsciously act out conflicts about their own perceived disempowerment within the university structure: these incidents are difficult to explain even to the most well-meaning white male colleague, because they reference a tangle of ambivalent feelings and experiences that create a powerful yet not always positive link between the junior faculty member and the student. Ironically, this link is forged not because of any *natural* affinity due to race, gender, or class but because both individuals have had to negotiate the experience and alienation of the university's pronouncement of them as "different" from the mainstream, as emblems of whole populations rather than as individuals unto themselves.

Because my department had been so successful in hiring black faculty members, the challenge of mentoring black students seemed to be tolerably distributed as long as those faculty members remained in the department. But what about junior faculty members who were isolated by being the "only one" (that is, the only Native American or Chicano, etc.) hired? They presumably had to "service" particular student populations all on their own, a strain that could often be emotionally and professionally debilitating if these faculty members were not careful. Yet whatever our teaching burdens, by virtue of our symbolic currency as faculty members of color, we all had to deal with the administrative call to officiate at Martin Luther King Day events or on task forces about campus multiculturalism. Our visibility in the classroom and on committees was meant to testify to the institution's sensitivity to and embrace of difference, but when individual faculty members were repeatedly put into the impossible position of becoming group representatives, the lines between inclusion and mere tokenism were effectively blurred.

In my department, the difficulty of achieving a public airing of these issues arose because marginalization, sometimes by field but certainly by race or gender, unreasonable expectations about one's ability to bond with students, and the experience of sexual harassment fell outside the experience of many senior faculty members. As a result, even in a unit where senior colleagues were well-meaning and believed themselves to be empathetic, junior women and people of color found themselves irritatingly visible as important numbers in statistical reports on affirmative action circulated among university officials and as visible bodies at department meetings, on administrative and dissertation committees, and in classrooms. At the same time they seemed to undergo a simultaneous institutional erasure when it came to how administrators and colleagues acknowledged their very different negotiation of the professorship. Where and under what conditions could the difference in experiences, the differences in perceptions, be addressed?

Clearly, getting the testimony of junior faculty members is one step toward the establishment of a forum. But in what ways might a department respond to such testimony? If we set aside the inevitable variances among individual cases, the general problems that arise from diversity hiring have to be perceived as symptoms of larger departmental issues rather than as specific conditions of experience within which junior women and faculty members of color are hopelessly trapped because they are junior women and faculty members of color. Many of the situations I've experienced could not be solved entirely, but they could have been managed more effectively in a professional environment where senior and junior colleagues came to terms with the social conditions of their workplace.

Certainly, mentoring has traditionally been the one site for one-on-one negotiation of junior-senior politics. But, as many colleagues continually remind me, mentoring is one method by which departments reproduce themselves, where the difference between senior and junior faculty members is perceived to be simply that of generation or, at least, time logged in the profession. Under these conditions, how effective are current models of mentoring for promoting constructive dialogue? Clearly, the practical goals of mentoring (for example, advising a junior faculty person on how to turn a dissertation into a book and concrete information about general career development, etc.) are crucial and therefore should be part of a department's overall commitment to any junior person hired. But, in addition, all senior faculty members need to think carefully about how their own positions are necessarily reoriented because of the entry of junior women and people of color.

Another colleague recently reminded me that political hierarchy by definition must structure the mentoring process. Yet, if senior and junior colleagues see themselves sharing research rather than merely inhabiting another version of the parent-child pedagogy model, what possibilities for constructive reciprocity might ensue? Even the greenest junior faculty person will have some research questions that a department would find new and challenging; otherwise, why would that person be hired in the first place? But equally important, what if mentoring were conceived not just as the dispensing of advice or as empathetic listening but also as the reimagining of self and place in a new context? That is, what if the mentor used that moment to think about what junior faculty experiences—especially the experiences of women and people of color—reveal about the culture of a department? In the words of yet another thoughtful colleague, while one makes room for individual differences, certain kinds of junior faculty experiences do add up to more than just a long series of individual exceptions.

Especially in terms of the classroom, what does it mean that the experience of white female and minority faculty members foregrounds the experience of white male faculty members as nonstandard and nonnormative? In other words, what does it mean that the professional identity of "professor" is destabilized as a fixed class or gendered or raced category if we move beyond the stereotypes invoked in the conversation on the bus that I referred to at the beginning of this essay? Can difference really be perceived as entering a department only on the hiring of a person of color or a white woman? Such an assumption solidifies the stereotype of homogeneity among white male faculty members in age, class, national origin, sexuality, scholarly commitment, and cultural affiliation. And what about the slippage between white male power versus senior faculty power, a distinction that becomes visible in the few departments where one actually finds senior faculty members who are not white or male? Just as one cannot assume an affinity between, for example, female faculty members and students, one cannot assume an analogous affinity between junior and senior women. Rank has a structuring power all its own, and so the responsibility for creating a workable atmosphere for junior women and people of color belongs to every senior member of a department, and not just to particular designated members.

Some final concerns remain about how a department comes to terms with the experiences of those hired under affirmative action politics: How might the arrival of newcomers challenge codes of behavior, ideas about departmental mission, and naturalized assumptions about power and pedagogy, for men as well as women, for whites as well as people of color, for senior as well as junior faculty members? How can senior members become more sensitive to the lived experiences of junior faculty members hired to achieve diversity, until and unless these senior faculty members recognize that their naturalized access to authority and, indeed, the very construction of knowledge and research methodology they have often taken for granted are distinct, historicized products forged in earlier moments of exclusion within the profession? It is too often assumed that these questions can be raised only when junior women and people of color arrive on the scene. And yet so much of the reconceptualization toward change—if change is what a department actually desires—has to occur *before* the arrival of these new hires, since prevailing department structures and the attitude of senior faculty members themselves will negatively or positively affect the conditions of work for those hires. When a department fails to confront these problems, junior faculty members are left to bear the burden of a cosmetic departmental effort toward transformation, sometimes to the detriment of their professional lives. Meanwhile, their presence will provide little or no impact on the very department that professes a commitment to them.

"Where's Oz, Toto?"

Idealism and the Politics of Gender and Race in Academe

RUTH Y. HSU

> For many, displacement is the factor that defines a colonized or
> expropriated place. And even if we can locate ourselves, we
> haven't necessarily examined our place in, or our actual rela-
> tionship to, that place. Yet our personal relationships to history
> and place form us, as individuals and groups, and in reciprocal
> ways we form them.
>
> —Lucy Lippard, *The Lure of the Local*

In the past decade, the popular press has devoted much attention
to the economic crisis and the culture wars within the academy.
The public appears to have little interest in seemingly unimportant,
internecine squabbles about which books to teach; rather, as con-
sumers, they have been concerned with increasing tuition and class
sizes and diplomas that take longer and longer to obtain. Within the
academy, however, the view is different. Academics seem most concerned about the culture wars. Economic woes are barely discussed,
partly because scholars operate under the liberal humanist assumption that we and our work are above such mundane matters as fi-
nances. Accordingly, we seem capable of only a vague sense of
anxiety at the fundamental changes sweeping through higher education: shrinking undergraduate enrollment, expanding class sizes, the
emergence of an underclass of lecturers and instructors, the erosion
of full-time faculty positions, and the bottom dropping out of the job
market. However, these two arenas—financial exigencies and what
we profess—are intimately linked. A shrinking budget means not
only a loss of tenured positions but also, inevitably, battles over who

gets hired and in which fields of research. The economic rationale that structures the academy is imbricated in "purely" intellectual issues.

Women and people of color in higher education are only too aware of the relation between material reality and intellectual concerns, having experienced the difficulty of obtaining funding, for example, to hire more minority scholars. The financial state of tertiary education affects every aspect of the lived experiences of raced and gendered academics, yet very little attention has been given to budgetary practices and the recent financial crisis as they affect the status of minority academics. Even less attention has been devoted to the implications of the status of minorities for academe as a whole. The way minority laborers fare in hiring, tenure and promotion, retention, and real access to decision making is indicative of the state of academic culture and, specifically, of the extent to which academe is democratic and progressive. The culture wars are ultimately a struggle to reconceptualize the present cultural paradigm. Yet the foci of these debates, whether clustered around definitions of great books or America, have remained mainly philosophical, confined to theoretical exchanges in journals or at conferences. There is an unwillingness to engage the issues discussed in the culture wars in terms of the larger community outside the ivory tower or in terms of the people of color in academe who embody those issues. They have become a theoretical debate over taxonomy: What is a real American? What is literature? It is a debate that elides the connection between ideas and actual people, enabled by the scholarly predilection for abstractions. In the midst of swirling philosophical arguments and the flinging of terminology, women and people of color and the communities that they represent undergo further silencing, a dis(re)membering, as we give ideas a trajectory divorced from the lived experiences of actual people, and skin color, hair, and eyes become objects of theorizing and are redistributed into academic categories of discussion. Minority faculty members, students, and administrators today—thirty years after the civil rights and various ethnic renaissance movements and over twenty years after the initiation of affirmative action policies— are still underrepresented, and the academy is still a fundamentally conservative, Eurocentric, and masculinist institution in its hierarchical structure, modus operandi, and cultural assumptions.

For women and racial minorities to gain entrance into the academy is merely the first step in decolonizing the institution. What is then required is a continual critique of the place that we want to enter, particularly "our actual relationship [. . .] to that place" (Lippard 9). This essay examines the ways in which the existing academic structure—both the economics of higher education and its belief system—limits and undermines the effectiveness of minority faculty members and liberatory agendas. The place of minorities in academe is fraught with undesirable compromises and battles, in which we are routinely devalued, erased, and attacked, in which almost every aspect of our daily experiences with students, scholars, and administrators is embroiled in a hierarchical power structure constructed along axes of race, gender, sexuality, class, and age. Success in scaling the walls of the ivory tower does not mean that minorities have found the tower to be habitable. The ultimate goal, therefore, is not simply to unlock the gates of academe but also to transform this place and change all of us.[1]

This essay comes from my experiences as a graduate student in the English department at the University of Southern California, which has an overwhelmingly white faculty, and from the past six years that I have spent as an Asian Americanist in the Department of English at the University of Hawai'i, Manoa, and from my numerous conversations with colleagues in Hawai'i and elsewhere on the role and status of minorities in academe. Two key concerns inform this analysis. The first one is that any analysis of the experiences of people of color and women in academe needs to be grounded within the larger, national socioeconomic and cultural context in which American universities and colleges exist. Yet the past six years in Hawai'i have also made me realize that any national analysis of the ways that minority scholars, students, and administrators negotiate economic realities and prevailing dominant discourses on "America" and "American" must also pay careful attention to regional specificities and local cultural and social contexts—interacting in complex and at times contestatory ways in relation to dominant national discourses —that inform the position of women and other minority groups in individual institutions.

The second concern has to do with the need to distinguish between the experiences of white women in higher education and those of people of color. Moreover, significant differences exist in the ways that women of color and men of color experience institutional power structures. The point is not to minimize the ongoing marginalization of white women in the academy. Rather, the point is that the concerns of people of color have been neglected or subsumed under white female liberal agendas that fail to address needs specific to racial minorities. The 1997 *Chronicle of Higher Education Almanac* shows 86.8% of all faculty members to be white. White women account for 27.9% of all faculty members, while people of color, men and women, constitute 13.2%. The figure for male faculty members of color is given at 8.6%, and that for female faculty members of color is 4.6% (26) (see app. A). Therefore, only one out of every seven female faculty members is a woman of color. The lack of adequate representation of people of color in academe prompted the MLA's Committee on the Status of Women in the Profession to publish a special report that noted, "In the current climate there is a real danger that, when faculties and programs are trimmed to deal with new financial, political, and technological realities, the gains made by people of color in the modern languages during the last twenty years will be lost." Figures from the 1997 *Chronicle Almanac* are borne out by statistics in *Minorities in Higher Education: 1996–1997, Fifteenth Annual Status Report,* put out by the American Council on Education (Carter and Wilson). The report notes that large gender gaps are evident for the four major racial groups but that this gap is particularly true for Asian Pacific Americans. According to Shirley Hune and Kenyon S. Chan's special section on Asian Pacific Americans, "APA men still represent three-quarters of all APA faculty. APAs have the largest gender gap of any racial-ethnic group" (57). The report also notes that "whites have the highest [tenure] rate of all racial-ethnic groups and men are tenured at higher rates than women in each of the major racial/ethnic groups [. . .]. APA women have actually lost ground over the past decade" (58).[2]

While people of color do have common interests with white women in academe, possible alliances are undercut by the differences in the experiences of white women and racial minorities in higher education and the inability of most white female academics to comprehend with any depth the lived reality of people of color beyond what has been theorized and written about. Undoubtedly, the absence of effective alliances between white women and people of color has negatively affected the status of both.

The economic nature of higher education affects the status of minorities in such areas as hiring and retention, both of which in turn affect the ability of faculty members and administrators to undertake meaningful changes to the existing institution. In contrast to the popular notion of the university as a sanitized space, purely devoted to the pursuit of knowledge and untrammeled by such mundane concerns as money, the academy is subject to market forces much like any other organization in a capitalist and consumer economy. As such, colleges and universities must continuously adjust what they produce in response to the expectations of the larger society in terms of both labor and know-how.

The experiences of minorities in universities need to be placed within the context of the larger society and culture in which colleges and universities exist. On the most basic level, academic policies follow, and are very much affected by, dominant social (including economic) and cultural trends or movements. The most recent example is the successful grassroots movement to do away with affirmative action policies in California schools (among other sectors of society).[3] With the passage of Proposition 209 in the 1996 California elections, schools by law are no longer able to consider race, gender, ethnicity, and so on in faculty and staff hiring, student admission, or financial aid. The effect of this roll-back in antidiscriminatory practices has already been felt in undergraduate admission figures. Whatever the exact effects may be on minority academics, the result of this latest form of conservative backlash will be significant (see also the MLA committee's report). Recent attacks on affirmative action and other "ideological" (defined in the most narrow, conventional sense) flashpoints in the last two decades are part of a serious anti-nonwhite, anti-immigration backlash. A number of grass-roots movements are motivated by fear and hostility toward women and people of color, citizens and noncitizens alike, but particularly toward people of color. In the 1996 election, the following issues were highly visible in the media: English-only schools, a much tougher approach toward crime, reform of a welfare system said to be too "liberal," disallowing welfare for *all* immigrants and Supplemental Security Income for United States residents, as well as much more stringent immigration laws and quotas. As others have noted, the public outcry against crime, although typically constructed in terms of criminality and not race, actually contains a racist subtext that usually targets African Americans, Chicanos/Chicanas, and other racial groups depending on the specific region. Similarly, the furor over the welfare system, the English-only issue, and immigration may be played out in discourse that, at times, markedly and self-consciously deracializes the issues and instead constructs them in language to do with fair play or legality. Our present desire to examine the place and effectiveness of a "liberal" agenda in academe gains even more urgency when contextualized within this larger social and cultural environment. "Liberal" academics so far have been unable to undercut the conservative discourse being played out in various socioideological arenas.

The issue goes beyond the effect of social trends on universities. The ineffectiveness of a supposedly liberal academe in the face of this national swing toward the conservative reveals the conservative nature of higher education itself, the marginalized status of "liberal" groups, and most important, how deeply the dominant worldview permeates academic thinking and practice. The crucial issue is that much of academic culture validates, reproduces, and perpetuates the prevailing paradigm. We need to interrogate much more critically, for instance, the idea that the acquisition of knowledge is not politicized in any way, that we have the right to "map out," to "acquire," to become "authorities" in any field of knowledge, that the academy operates as a meritocracy, and that masculinist competitiveness, ambition, and desire for power are not the primary motivating force behind much of what we do. That is, we must examine the ways in which higher education—residing as it does in a larger economic and socioideological environment, national and local—is an institution that both constitutes social and cultural discourse and, more centrally, is itself constituted by the discursive practices it produces and participates in. The academy not only responds to obvious social trends but also is undergirded and operates according to hidden hegemonic agendas masked in a plethora of academic discourses that maintain academe as a socioideological state apparatus (the concept of socioideological state is from Althusser).

In responding to and, indeed, in perpetuating the existing socioeconomic and cultural structure, the academy has a direct effect on the hiring of women and people of color and on the birth, development, and longevity of women's studies and ethnic studies departments. In the economics of higher education, the amount of funding allocated to departments is tied to student demand for what departments can offer them. And what students desire in a college diploma is in turn driven by the exigencies of the job market and related concerns over social status and so on. Therefore, the amount of money distributed to "popular" undergraduate majors such as business administration and computer science is far more than has been given to the arts and humanities. As Simon During recently wrote:

> Academic departments are increasingly funded per capita based not just on "quality" but on student enrollments or other measurements of student demand or academic labor productivity— ironically enough, this is done in the effort to "reform" education so as to increase national competitiveness in the global economy.[4] That need to increase competitiveness also shifts student enrollments out of the humanities into more vocational disciplines; even in the U.S., between the late seventies and the mid-eighties, degrees given in English, for instance, fell from 7.6 percent of the total to 2.6 percent.   (822)

The economic rationale of supply and demand is one easy way for a university administration to resist establishing ethnic or women's studies programs or to resist hiring minorities. In the 1970s, even when universities were induced by intense pressure from students, community activists, and liberal faculty members to establish minority programs, the smallest budgets possible were designated. These programs were (and still are) often understaffed and neglected by the administration. Not only do they constantly have to fight for academic legitimacy, funding, and often actual survival, they are also faced with the Herculean task of trying to reform the college curriculum so that their courses reside more centrally in the university experience rather than along the margins as electives. One of the problems of trying to push through such curricular reforms is the labyrinthine and resistant nature of academic bureaucracy. Often, minority faculty members find themselves having to restage the arguments for a Chicano/Chicana studies program to an administrator who cannot comprehend the importance of establishing a particular program and who is also unable to see why that program cannot make do with the two faculty members already hired. In matters of curriculum, classes having to do with issues of race, gender, and ethnicity are often perceived as "special interest" courses, designed for only a small student population. This perception of special interest status allows such classes to be safely tucked away in the electives category. Such a designation undercuts the endeavor to liberalize the academy in that it ghettoizes crucial discussions about the dominant discourse that bespeak this country as well as the faculty members identified with those discussions and hired to teach so-called minority courses. This special interest, elective status may account for relatively low enrollment for these classes, which in turn serves as justification for the administration's denying funds for research support or additional faculty or staff hiring. In a sense, newly established minority departments or programs often find themselves in a catch-22 situation: to expand a fledgling program, more faculty members need to be hired; yet, to be able to do more hiring, programs have to be able to argue that enrollment figures warrant an increase in the number of faculty members, which may not be possible since the status of these classes as electives tends to make them less attractive to students already under pressure (due to the rising cost of tuition and books) to finish college expediently. In sum, the goal of liberalizing the academy, although most visibly played out as debates about the great books (or in the register of theory or methodology), has to do basically with the material reality of the academy and in which the academy exists.[5]

We must also take into account other scenarios in which the economics of higher education significantly affect people of color and women in academe. Universities, for example, often decide to bring about minority hiring by creating joint appointments, say, half-time between an English department and an ethnic studies program. An alternative possibility is for a minority scholar to be hired solely by an individual department. Both options, from the perspective of administrators who apportion funds and decide on the budget, shelter the university from intense criticism, and both options do so in a way that also saves money. In other words, hiring a minority scholar here and there among various already established programs and departments costs much less than establishing a new and discrete program. These hiring strategies are seen as quite attractive—rational—in the light of the economic crisis in the United States in the past decade.

Such strategies create at least two main areas of concern for people of color and women in academe. Most immediately, junior faculty members, hired either by a department or jointly with a minority program, are often the lone representative of their area in departments that are usually still reactionary. It is common for such faculty members to have to deal with colleagues who either do not have a very good idea about their area or who are hostile to their beliefs. Indeed, it seems that such departments often hire in, say, women's or ethnic studies without having thoroughly worked out the various philosophical implications of recruiting in those fields. Minority faculty members in these situations may find themselves marginalized in their departments. The second area of concern arises when scholars, hired to fill joint appointments, say, in Asian American studies and English, apply for contract renewal and tenure and promotion. These scholars must meet the demands of both academic locations, which may espouse ideas, beliefs, and critical approaches that are in certain respects fundamentally opposed. These faculty members may well find themselves having to defend not just the quality and the significance of their work but also its very legitimacy and relevance. For the Chicano/Chicana scholar, say, housed solely in a traditional English department, the process of professional evaluation can prove to be a troubling issue for similar reasons.

The ability to effect significant changes in the academy is contingent on the ability to gain access to and to influence people who make budgetary decisions, both within the university and in the legislature. Indeed, any gains in pushing through a liberal agenda will be minimal ones until we recognize that the lack of control minorities have over funding priorities continues to negatively affect many aspects of our position in academe. Figures from the 1997 *Chronicle Almanac* show the underrepresentation of racial minorities in administrative positions (see app. B). Presently, most of us in the humanities seem willing to deal with issues of hiring and curricular reform only as philosophical debates. These debates about the canon are not "false" issues, for how we come down on these matters makes a crucial statement about who we are and where we think the profession ought to be headed. The issue, rather, is that the academy cannot be understood apart from the material reality and the discursive practices of the larger world in which it exists. Somewhere in our awareness, we do recognize the economic (and socioideological) function of the academy and its oppressive nature. The note of desperation that creeps into raised voices during departmental curriculum debates about the great books comes not only from the sense that one's cultural heritage is being challenged but also from the half-realized and unacknowledged feeling that the profession has been devalued, as revealed in the continually shrinking number of faculty positions and undergraduate majors in the humanities. Each faculty position that is retained or obtained is therefore precious, with great importance placed on whether a position should go for an eighteenth-century or a postcolonial scholar. Unfortunately, it has been my experience that the reluctance of faculty members to see where one crucial axis of power—the economics of higher education—really resides results in rancorous arguments during which junior, untenured faculty members, who are often women and people of color, are indiscriminately constructed as homogeneous "radicals" (anticulture, anti-American, antiliterature) and made into scapegoats for the larger economic and socioideological processes that are dominating events in the academy.

To reiterate, for us to engage each other solely along the axis of philosophy is to misrecognize the fundamental drives operating in academe; it is willfully to misrecognize the economic nature of this institution. For us to think that the battle for the academy is going to come down simply to a question of which ideas have "merit," that is, more truth to them, is to abrogate our responsibilities in exchange for the self-indulgence of a utopic ideal. Ideas do not exist in a vacuum, outside the socioideological environment, but are constituted in part by the material conditions of that society. We will become increasingly frustrated with debates about whether, for instance, queer theory is a legitimate form of literary criticism, if these debates are not also accompanied by actual political and economic will and clout. For us to go where we want to go, we first have to see with great clarity where we are. We need to see that whoever decides how money is to be spent has the power to order, to define the lived experiences of that institution and the people who work in it, not just in hiring but also in other aspects of academic life that create the conditions for success in a career, such as access to grants, travel subsidies, book and journal acquisitions, and so on. Essentially, ultimate power in the academy does not reside in the strength of ideas; it is found either in the ability to affect or to control the economics of higher education or in the ability to revise the ways in which we fund those institutions.

The way money is apportioned is fundamentally a political-ideological issue. The power to distribute funds is the power to include or to exclude certain bodies, the power to distribute those bodies and the knowledge associated with those bodies to where they "truly" belong. Today, as before, the challenge is to ensure that these "bodies" are not marginalized in academe or excluded from higher education altogether. Therefore, the allocation of funds or funding priorities is one crucial site of privilege and power that must be contested, along with others. Unless we scholars are willing to educate ourselves about the ways in which money is distributed to and within universities, we will never be able to achieve our desired goals. If we wish to see significant changes, minority faculty members and administrators must gain more control over the budgetary process and the administration of the university, including the selection and appointment of deans, program directors, presidents, and chancellors and the development of strong faculty unions and senates committed to diversifying and liberalizing the institution.

I turn now to some of the fundamental beliefs and values in academe that affect the position of minority scholars and administrators. According to Lippard, "Space defines landscape, where space combined with memory defines place" (9). The memory that we hold of the hallowed landscape of academe before the last thirty years is indeed that it was a place, an arena, exclusively reserved for white, Anglo-Saxon males. In the light of such a *his*tory, the university has made some progress in the hiring of women and people of color. Yet contained in Lippard's articulation of space, memory, and place is not just the issue of surface features but also the question of what forms give rise to or condition those features.

While it may be true that more space than ever before has been carved out for women and people of color as scholars and administrators, numerical progress does not appear to denote a meaningful metamorphosis of fundamental academic attitudes. This last statement is not meant to imply that those thirty years have been a failure. The intention, rather, is to focus our attention on the need to undertake an even more thorough interrogation than has yet occurred of the deeply embedded impulses that continue to undergird, to order, and to define this institution. Unless the basic academic worldview as we know it today undergoes extensive revisioning, the effort to push forward any progressive agenda will be restricted and will continue to be undermined.

A basic problem has to do with the limit that the present socioideological and economic structure places on the possibilities of inventing one's own identity and roles and places in life. Many of us were attracted to academe as a place that enables a measure of self-determination, an alternative to a uniform corporate identity that is late capitalist peonage. Academe, in other words, allows us to pay the bills as well as gives us the chance to think and write about and say what we strongly believe in. And the value of what we do does not depend on the trading of stocks or futures or any such "external" variables. Instead, what wins out in our world, we are wont to believe, is the merit contained in hard work, in painstaking research, in writing according to one's conscience, in teaching, in the well-constructed idea or theory. One of our fondest imaginings (closet remnants of Leavism?) is that, as intellectuals, we lead the rest of society in envisioning the future—after all, do we not see more astutely than anyone else? The trouble with this idea(l) of the university lies in the thinking that research and teaching can be unaffected by academe as a state apparatus. That is, the work we do is always part of a structure of economic and cultural or, more accurately, socioideological drives that maintain the dominant culture. While we may have made progress in eroding explicitly classist, racist, and sexist attitudes in higher education, the endeavor to dismantle the enabling hegemonic impulses underlying such attitudes has not been dealt with effectively. Such an endeavor is difficult because many of us continue to hold some of the institutional myths undergirded by these hegemonic impulses. We have chosen an identity that supposedly affords us more freedom, relatively speaking, than other roles in society would but that actually still positions us as *subjects* of a hegemonic agenda. And in that sense, we are no different from the rest of society. We inhabit specific positions in a matrix of ideologically constructed identities that obstruct and restrict the possibilities of whom we could even imagine ourselves to be and where we believe we may "rightfully" belong.

Our reluctance to face the political nature of academe allows for the continued marginalization of minorities in both our status and our ability to change academic culture. As I have mentioned previously, the economics of higher education create situations in which minority faculty members, particularly racial minorities, find themselves outnumbered in a traditional department. In my experience, it is quite difficult under those circumstances to effect any meaningful reform since the votes in favor of implementing change are insufficient. Faculty members' chances of pushing through reform are also constrained because of what Gerald Graff has termed "compartmentalization" (3), in which courses with the most disparate assumptions and methodologies are offered alongside one another, with no attempt to bring opposing perspectives of a discipline into critical exchange. Ostensibly, the motivation there is to avoid possibly rancorous relationships among people who work in close proximity with one another. After all, we all know of a department or two in which colleagues have ceased talking to one another precisely over issues of canonicity and methodology.

A "compartmentalized" or "pluralistic" departmental structure is partly enabled by the belief that the political is an interloper into scholarly work. Such a departmental structure also comes from a vague and diffuse allegiance within the academy to liberalism, manifested in one way as a "live and let live" attitude that enables some diversification of curricula, which in turn makes departments more economically viable. Often, departments hire in "radical" areas of scholarship because they do not want to be perceived as reactionary or because they need to improve enrollment. The motivation is one of practical necessity rather than of conviction in the need, say, for English studies to be reconstituted. The trouble with both these attitudes and a pluralistic departmental structure is that we are refusing to do the hard work of reexamining our own fundamental beliefs and cultural assumptions, including liberalism, not to mention the role of academics and administrators. Such self-scrutiny is too threatening for us, because it will likely lead to the dismantling of the existing worldview that many still adhere to.

Such self-scrutiny would force us to rethink and remold our roles as teachers and researchers. We would need to recognize, foremost, that academe is a politicized state apparatus and that the work we do is inherently political.[6] Doing so would engender a paradigm change. No longer would we write on topics because they have so-called inherent merit as we presently define *merit* but because the research could possibly effect constructive social change. The point of publishing, then, would certainly not be to get into prestigious journals and to obtain the reward of individual status enhancement that comes from having done so. The aim, instead, would be to engage in debates that might in turn result in meaningful revisions of academe and beyond. This perspective on research and writing could go far toward dismantling the "star" system (I am thinking principally of the one operating in literary studies), which is one way that the academic version of the corporate ladder is kept in place. Such a perspective would, we hope, recalibrate our ambitions from the focus on self—in relation to that ladder—to the need to make our work more relevant to the larger community and to undertake such a re-visioning not as intellectuals standing outside and above the group but as a part of that community. The reasons we write, teach, and administer would be informed by goals other than the ones that presently drive academe. Reconstituting academic subjectivity is central to the goal of re-visioning higher education.

The scope of what needs to be achieved consists of more than changing pedagogy, research objectives, and curricula. It also requires conceptualizing anew the professorate, to recognize, for instance, that academic rank, enabled by a discourse of meritocracy and a "star" system, is fundamentally a class structure, a hierarchical and exploitative system built on inequality and notions of worth that benefit a few. Equally crucial is the need to look beyond the class separation now operating between the professorate and other teachers in higher education, namely, faculty members in two-year colleges, as well as graduate students and instructors at all institutions (see Nelson, *Will Teach for Food*). These teachers are the ones who do most of the grunt work. It is because instructors teach lower-division courses that professors have more flexibility in the courses they teach and that they have some time to undertake research. It is a mistake for minority faculty members to think that our allies are to be found only among our own rank and among the professorate. If we examine the landscape of higher education as a whole, and if we consider the issue of who is marginalized by placing that issue within the overall academy, then we will see that the disenfranchised consist also of instructors, graduate students, and staff members. According to statistics published in fall 1995 by the Office of Women's Research at the University of Hawai'i, between 1985 and 1995, nationally, women gained in numbers mostly in the ranks of instructor and assistant professor. Universities and colleges nationally employed more male than female instructors; at the University of Hawai'i, the only rank that acquired more women than men in those years was instructorships. These figures also reveal that, nationally, over the same time span, only 13% of full professors were women, which means that of all the female PhDs who started out as tenure-track assistant professors, only approximately 25% reached the full professor rank.

The ways in which the existing academic culture perpetuates a continuing conservatism have a negative effect on the lives of minority scholars in key areas of departmental governance, such as hiring, committee assignments, and tenure and promotion, as well as in everyday interactions with colleagues. For example, in my experience in literary studies, senior faculty members (who are typically white) attempt to devalue the work of minority faculty members in a number of ways, one of which is to suggest that "contemporary literary theory" is merely a passing fad. Such pronouncements, ostensibly directed toward the issue of methodology, are actually a coded way of expressing their hostility, say, to feminist scholarship, for in the academic cosmology of many senior or more mainstream faculty members, contemporary literary theory is synonymous with the "radical" —that is, minority—fringe in universities. The opinion that contemporary literary theory is merely a passing fad (despite all the indications otherwise) clearly stems from the desire to have things back to the way they were. This suspicion of, and hostility toward, theory is accorded to American ethnic and postcolonial literatures as well, since these areas are often conflated with contemporary theory. Other manifestations of the ongoing marginalization of minority faculty members reveal themselves, for instance, in the inability of some senior faculty members to conceive of Asian American literature as part of American literature. Although Asian American cultural production has been an area of scholarly attention since at least the late 1970s, a colleague recently asked me why I do not include *The Tale of Genji* in my classes. This construction of Asian American literature attempts to maintain its status as the other. Even when faculty members incorporate an "ethnic" text or two in a course on, say, American fiction, the ways in which those texts are analyzed reveal that many faculty members still consider ethnic writing as belonging to the margins of the real canon, the Heath anthology notwithstanding. In discussions with white colleagues who wish to incorporate into their syllabi literature by people of color, it is disturbing to me that they insist on dealing with "ethnic" literature when many of them have a very limited understanding of the fundamental issues that frame writing by people of color. White male colleagues, for example, have told me that they present Maxine Hong Kingston's *Woman Warrior* to their students as an immigrant, culture clash story. I point out to them that the text needs to be contextualized in current debates concerning race, gender, and class and in dialogue with other texts such as Louis Chu's *Eat a Bowl of Tea*—advice that is not understood much less followed. Writings by people of color are often token presences on syllabi; they diversify what would otherwise be an all-white list of authors, and they are a means for white faculty members to legitimate their presence in multiracial and multicultural classrooms. However, faculty members who include writing by people of color without really understanding that writing are exploiting people of color and doing violence to the literature. The solution is not for white faculty members to stop studying "ethnic" literature but for them to do so with a heightened awareness of their own limitations in the face of this writing and of their responsibility to get it "right."

The foregoing examples of academic solipsism are especially lamentable because they occurred in Hawai'i. These islands had been inhabited by Polynesian people for two thousand years before Western "discovery" in the form of Captain James Cook and subsequent annexation by the United States in 1898. Western colonialism resulted in the decimation of the indigenous Hawaiians and their culture. The islands were harnessed by Western commerce largely through the importation of Japanese, Chinese, Korean, Filipino, Portuguese, and Puerto Rican laborers who worked under terrible conditions of indentured servitude on plantations. According to 1990 census figures, Hawaiians make up only 12.5% of the total population (1,108,229), while Asians account for 49.3%, Caucasians 33.4%, and blacks 2.5%.[7] This essay can merely hint at the detrimental effect of Western colonialism on native Hawaiians. Today, they are the most disenfranchised ethnic group in the state, as reflected in statistics on health, literacy, crime, the prison population, drug abuse. The importation of English and the Western education system was a powerful means of colonizing Hawai'i. In the nineteenth century, for example, missionaries irrevocably changed Hawaiian culture with the introduction of the Bible and schools. And in the twentieth century, as Eileen Tamura writes, the "English-only effort was an integral part of the Americanization crusade that swept the nation during and after World War I. Underlying the crusade was the doctrine of Anglo-Saxon superiority [. . .]" (37).

Although Hawai'i is in many ways a multicultural society, most University of Hawai'i faculty members, who are typically white, are isolated from local communities. Most academics, both faculty members and administrators, evince only a limited commitment to the community from which the majority of their students originate and identify with. A colleague who has resided in Hawai'i for over thirty years recently decried to me the behavior of those of her (white) "tribe." She noted that many "mainland" faculty members (typically white) come to Hawai'i with the unquestioned assumption that it is their right to take any aspect of Hawai'i's culture as an object of research. Many faculty members fail to adequately critique their own privileged position in relation to the members of the local population, the vast majority of whom are nonwhite, and in fact work to establish their academic credentials by constructing as the other various aspects of Hawai'i and the Asian and Pacific regions and by writing about those aspects of the other. It is especially troubling when white female academics engage in such orientalist behavior.

Aside from the efforts of a small group of relatively more progressive faculty members, university curricula, pedagogy, and hiring practices do not reflect a sense of responsibility toward critiquing Hawaii's colonial history or exposing and rectifying the results, evident today, of that past. It is worth noting at this juncture that the English department hired its first "ethnic" literature specialist only six years ago. Since then, the department has been attempting to further diversify its faculty and course offerings. (A previous tenure-track assistant professor in Asian American literature left after three years, supposedly because of a change in circumstance in her personal life.) Such efforts, however, when placed in the context of the university as a whole have little effect on an institution that is very much an arm of Western imperialism and hegemony. A brief account of the ethnic makeup of the faculty and students at the university reinforces this point. In fall 1993, the population at the University of Hawai'i consisted of 76.4% Asian and Pacific Islander students, including Hawaiians at 7%, and 21.8% caucasian students.[8] However, even though the overwhelming majority of the students are people of color, only 30.4% of the faculty members at the university are nonwhite. And even though 76.4% of students are Asian and Pacific Islanders, only 29% of faculty members are in that category.[9] In addition, the university has a very poor retention rate for female faculty members, especially junior faculty members. Much like universities in the contiguous United States, the University of Hawai'i is a hostile place for women, but more so for people of color (Hippensteele).

One academic structure that could offer protection to minority faculty members has evolved, unfortunately, into a series of obstacles that hinder their advancement. Tenure and promotion were originally intended to nurture revolutionary thinking. Yet in the existing academic culture this process is often a means to weed out scholars deemed too radical in thought or too different in some other way from a professorate that continues to perpetuate the dominant values of mainstream "America." It is not unusual for untenured minority faculty members to feel constrained about what they write or teach because their tenure application will be judged by conservative colleagues. Sometimes minority faculty members are also undermined because they teach courses designated as electives and not as part of the requirements for the major. "Poor" enrollment figures in these elective classes can be interpreted as an indication that the faculty member is a poor scholar or teacher or that there is really no need for the course. In addition, because African American or queer studies, for example, deals with controversial issues, it is not unusual for minority faculty members to receive complaints from students regarding course content. Those complaints can be turned into a reason to deny tenure or promotion. Also, tenure and promotion review committees often do not understand about the additional workload that minority faculty members bear. Since there are only a few, say, Chicano/Chicana scholars on a particular campus, those scholars advise more theses and dissertations than do their colleagues who work in traditional areas covered by a larger number of faculty members. A related concern, of course, is that many minority scholars believe an integral part of their work to be community service. Yet in the present elitist academic culture community service is not valued. Rather, publishing is, and the more prestigious the journal or press, the better one's chances of getting tenure or promotion (another way in which the "star" system and the class structure are kept secure). Another concern, and a well-kept secret in academe, is that untenured minority faculty members are expected to do more, to pitch in more than their share during hard times or budget crises. Therefore, it is not unusual to see untenured minority faculty members assume, as part of their "regular" workload, administrative duties as, say, the director of an underfunded, understaffed program. In other words, minority faculty members are exploited, because they are committed and principled and because the larger university community often fails to be. Needless to say, neither advising theses nor doing administrative work is valued in tenure and promotion applications. Not surprisingly, minority faculty members' tenure applications are frequently bitterly fought, controversial processes. In the hard economic times that have befallen the academy, at a time when the number of faculty positions continues to shrink at most universities, every tenure case or vacant position takes on crucial importance. In academe, presence means influence and, for the dominant majority, might.

In short, the tenure and promotion process can be a form of intimidation, a way to dull voices of change and to further interpellate women and people of color into a marginalized subject position. Solutions to this particular problem include increasing minority representation in higher education; re-visioning the tenure and promotion review process, particularly the yardstick used in assessing applications; and re-visioning the economic base of tertiary education and the criteria by which funds are allocated.

Without fundamental changes in attitudes toward the purposes of teaching, community service, publishing, and the very notion of academic merit and reward, structural changes that can bring true democratization to tertiary education cannot occur. An important site for such changes in attitudes lies in the alliances that can be built among various groups committed to effecting meaningful change, between white female academics and women of color, for instance. Presently, most alliances between white women and people of color are problematic ones. Apparently, understanding the ways in which a gendered identity is a means of oppression often does not transfer to the locus of race. White women (and men and people of color, for that matter) in the academy are often engaged in garnering power for themselves and not in challenging or reimagining the nature and function of that power. And to the extent that one's goal is power, then one has been co-opted by the existing hierarchy. To the extent that white women (and men and people of color) publish, teach, and write without seriously questioning what compels them, then they are maintaining and enabling the dominant belief system. The time has come for white female and male academics to give serious thought to their relatively privileged position, to articulate clearly and firmly their commitment to a total program of democratization, consisting not only of their agenda but also of the myriad concerns of people of color. It is time for white academics to rigorously examine the ways in which they buttress prevailing academic attitudes through the decisions they make about every aspect of their academic lives: the topics they decide to write on, the "star" system they help maintain, or the travel grant they voted against. Profound change in higher education will not occur unless strong alliances are cemented between white women and people of color, between white men and people of color. Such alliances, however, must be based on mutual respect and a profound understanding and acknowledgment of one's role in maintaining hegemony. The difficulty that white academics have in launching a truly trenchant critique of the academy is an indication of how deeply embedded most academics are in the present culture and material reality, so much so that we do not question or even recognize the class, race, and gender divisions that alienate us from one another, that constitute academe.

Higher education has a long way to go before meaningful democratization is achieved. Its socioideological and economic structure must be seen not just as a contestatory response to the larger society in which it resides but also as a structure that is itself formed by, that works in conjunction with, and that is ordered by the overall societal hierarchy. Most of us in higher education believe that we have to deal with budget cuts or attacks on affirmative action only when those events impinge directly and harshly on the academy; we ignore the fact that the socioideological and economic forces that drive specific cuts in funding or a xenophobic backlash are themselves inherent in the institution. Unless we are ready to deal with the ways in which academe is itself an exploitative, hierarchical, elitist, and masculinist concern, deeply implicated in the capitalistic reality of the larger society, then we will continue to see the erosion of past gains in a liberal agenda and the growing irrelevance of the thinking that we do and the role of the university in the twenty-first century.

Notes

1. Cary Nelson, writing about the labor crisis at Yale, states, "Whatever happens in the next decade, the stratification of higher education is likely to increase, and the nature of work in academe is likely to change. It is a watershed moment for an enterprise that has so far mostly held on to the expanded mission

it took on after World War II. If we are to resist its degradation, we will have to change not only our practices but ourselves" ("Crisis" 30).

2. Other signs of the marginalized position of women, both white and nonwhite, in academe include the following: Between 1972 and 1995, the number of female faculty members nearly doubled, but the increase occurred mostly in two-year institutions, which have had the lowest salaries and salary increases over the same period (Wechsler 11); male full-time faculty members earned 24% more than female faculty members did in 1993–94 (Wechsler 7); and an important index to professional status is having the wherewithal to conduct research and publish. As Suzanne Lie and others note, "Women's lower participation at the country's most elite institutions, such as research universities, contributes to our disadvantaged status. Faculty at research universities have more opportunities for research and publication, which, in turn, present further opportunities for public recognition, consulting, and overall greater occupational mobility" (188). Job mobility aside, women's exclusion from these elite institutions also means, to a significant degree, our exclusion from the dialogues that shape and develop our disciplines.

3. According to the *Chronicle of Higher Education Almanac*, other states that have either already passed anti–affirmative action laws or are in the process of attempting to do so are Colorado, Maryland, Michigan, and Oregon (12).

4. In the past fifteen years, English faculty teaching loads have continued to increase. In contrast, for some disciplines outside the humanities, particularly the sciences, faculty members typically carry a much lighter teaching load. For those faculty members, the sign of academic prowess is the ability to obtain government or private sector grants for research. The concern here is not simply an unfair distribution of teaching responsibilities but also the ways in which accepting monies from the government (for example, the Pentagon) or private industry compromises college curricula, student recruitment, allocation of funding to various departments, and ultimately, faculty hires for the university.

5. In November 1997, a group of Asian American activists at the University of Maryland who had been working for three years to push the administration to establish an Asian American studies program announced that they had finally got the university to deal with their demands seriously. The chancellor asked the provost to set up a task force that would review the necessity of having an Asian American studies certificate program. This review process, which will take another year to complete, is another example of the continuing opposition by school administrations to demands for more programs in Asian American and other American ethnic studies. The latest struggle for an Asian American studies program is at the University of Texas, Austin.

6. In the words of Cary Nelson, "The time has come when the political meaning of teaching and scholarship can no longer be avoided. Attacks on feminists, minority, multicultural, and theoretical research in the academy are helping to discredit those values and constituencies in the general culture as well" ("Cultural Studies" 285).

7. A more detailed breakdown of the category Asian follows: Chinese 6.2%, Filipino 15.2%, Japanese 22.3%, Korean 2.2%, Vietnamese 0.5%, Samoan 1.4%, other Asian or Pacific Islander 1.5% (U.S. Bureau of the Census, table 3).

8. A more specific breakdown of the Asian–Pacific Islander category at the university is as follows: Japanese 25.8%, Chinese 12.3%, Filipino 9.2%, Hawaiian 7%, Korean 3.4%, East Indian, mixed and other Asian or Pacific Islander 18.7%. The student population also includes 1% Hispanics and 0.8% African Americans (University of Hawai'i Office of Student Equity, Excellence, and Diversity).

9. According to the university's Equal Opportunity and Affirmative Action Office, tenured and tenure-track faculty members in 1994–95 were 69.6% Caucasian; 12.7% Japanese; 10.1% Chinese or Korean; 1.1% Filipino; 1.7% Hawaiian; 3.4% East Indian, mixed, or other Asian and Pacific Islander; 0.8% Hispanic; 0.3% African American; and 0.3% Native American.

Works Cited

Althusser, Louis. "Ideology and Ideological State Apparatuses." *Lenin and Philosophy*. New York: Monthly Review, 1971. 127–86.

Carter, Deborah J., and Reginald Wilson, eds. *Minorities in Higher Education: 1996–1997. Fifteenth Annual Status Report*. Washington: Amer. Council on Educ., 1997.

Chronicle of Higher Education Almanac. 29 Aug. 1997.

During, Simon. "Popular Culture on a Global Scale: A Challenge for Cultural Studies?" *Critical Inquiry* 23.4 (1997): 808–32.

Graff, Gerald. *Professing Literature: An Institutional History*. Chicago: U of Chicago P, 1987.

Hippensteele, Susan. "Toward a Shared Reality of Campus Ethnoviolence: Data as a Tool for Combating Victim Isolation." *Women in Hawai'i: Sites, Identities, and Voices*. Ed. Joyce N. Chinen, Kathleen Kane, and Ida Yoshinage. *Social Process in Hawai'i* 38. Manoa: U of Hawai'i, Dept. of Sociology, 1997. 72–91.

Hune, Shirley, and Kenyon S. Chan. "Special Focus: Asian Pacific American Demographic and Educational Trends." Carter and Wilson 39–63.

Lie, Suzanne, et al., eds. *The Gender Gap in Higher Education*. Philadelphia: Kogan Page, 1994.

Lippard, Lucy. *The Lure of the Local*. New York: New, 1997.

MLA Committee on the Status of Women in the Profession. "CSWP Draft Statement on People of Color in the Modern Languages." *MLA Newsletter* 29.2 (1997): 12.

Nelson, Cary. "Always Already Cultural Studies: Academic Conferences and a Manifesto." *What Is Cultural Studies? A Reader*. Ed. John Storey. London: Arnold, 1996. 273–86.

———. "Between Crisis and Opportunity." *Will Teach for Food* 3–31.

———. ed., *Will Teach for Food: Academic Labor in Crisis*. Minneapolis: U of Minnesota P, 1997.

Tamura, Eileen. *Americanization, Acculturation, and Ethnic Identity: The Nisei Generation in Hawai'i*. Urbana: U of Illinois P, 1994.

United States Bureau of the Census. *1990 Census of Population. General Population Characteristics. Hawai'i*. 1990 CP-1-13. June 1992.

University of Hawai'i. Office of Women's Research. Fact Sheet Series 4. 1995.

Wechsler, Harold. *The NEA 1995 Almanac of Higher Education*. Washington: NEA, 1995.

Characteristics of Full-Time Faculty Members with Teaching Duties, Fall 1992

	Full-time Faculty Members	American Indian		Asian		Black		Hispanic		White	
		Men	Women	Men	Women	Men	Women	Men	Women	Men	Women
Total	526,222	0.3%	0.2%	4.0%	1.3%	2.6%	2.3%	1.7%	0.8%	58.9%	27.9%
Type of Institution											
Public research	108,493	0.1	0.1	5.7	1.3	1.5	1.2	1.4	0.5	68.7	19.7
Private research	32,350	0.2	—	6.7	2.4	2.8	1.9	1.2	0.7	59.2	25.0
Public doctoral *	54,433	0.6	0.2	4.9	1.4	1.6	1.3	1.7	0.6	62.1	25.7
Private doctoral *	25,397	0.1	0.1	5.1	1.4	2.9	1.2	2.3	1.0	66.5	19.4
Public comprehensive	96,350	0.2	0.3	4.1	1.0	4.9	3.9	1.8	0.8	55.5	27.5
Private comprehensive	36,548	—	0.1	2.5	0.9	1.4	1.6	1.0	0.6	60.5	31.3
Private liberal-arts	37,560	0.3	0.1	1.9	0.9	3.7	1.8	0.9	0.5	54.2	35.8
Public 2-year	109,551	0.7	0.3	1.9	1.4	2.5	3.6	2.5	1.6	47.8	37.7
Other †	25,540	0.3	0.2	3.7	0.9	1.6	1.2	0.8	0.4	67.3	23.6
Academic discipline											
Agriculture and home economics	11,466	—	0.7	1.0	1.8	2.2	1.5	1.6	0.2	71.3	19.6
Business	39,848	0.6	0.3	4.0	0.8	1.9	2.0	0.9	0.4	62.3	26.6
Communications	10,344	0.9	0.3	4.3	1.2	2.8	2.8	1.6	—	56.3	29.8
Education	36,851	0.7	0.3	0.5	1.1	3.9	5.1	0.9	2.4	43.9	41.2
Engineering	24,680	0.7	—	15.6	1.3	2.1	0.6	2.8	0.2	73.0	3.8
Fine arts	31,682	0.3	0.2	1.2	1.6	3.8	1.8	2.1	0.3	60.4	28.3
Health sciences	77,996	0.1	0.1	4.0	2.0	2.0	3.2	1.3	0.7	43.1	43.5
Humanities	74,086	0.3	0.1	1.3	1.9	2.1	2.0	2.0	2.0	53.5	34.8
Law	7,337	—	—	0.2	0.7	5.8	2.9	1.3	1.1	57.8	30.0
Natural sciences	101,681	0.2	0.1	7.2	0.9	2.5	0.9	1.5	0.3	69.0	17.4
Social sciences	58,526	0.3	0.2	2.6	0.7	2.9	2.9	1.9	0.8	65.4	22.3
Occupationally specific programs	15,395	0.5	0.2	1.9	0.2	3.5	0.9	3.1	0.3	75.9	13.5
Other	27,466	—	0.1	2.3	0.6	2.8	3.3	2.0	0.7	58.1	30.1
Academic rank											
Full professor	161,252	0.2	0.1	4.5	0.4	2.1	1.1	1.4	0.3	75.7	14.3
Associate professor	123,471	0.3	0.1	3.6	1.0	2.9	2.1	1.3	0.8	63.1	24.7
Assistant professor	123,285	0.2	0.2	5.0	2.1	2.8	3.0	2.0	1.2	47.5	36.0
Instructor	72,986	0.7	0.3	2.2	1.7	3.1	3.8	2.2	1.1	44.1	40.8
Lecturer	11,655	—	1.1	3.9	2.6	2.6	3.7	2.0	1.1	29.6	53.4
Other	16,753	0.2	0.1	4.2	1.7	4.2	4.6	2.2	1.8	41.5	39.5
Not applicable	16,820	0.9	0.3	2.0	1.6	1.2	1.3	1.9	0.9	51.6	38.3

Note: The figures are based on responses to a survey conducted in 1992 and 1993 of 25,780 full- and part-time faculty members and other instructional personnel at 817 colleges and universities. The survey covered employees whose regular assignment included instruction; people with faculty status whose regular assignment did not include instruction; temporary and permanent employees who had any instructional duties; and faculty members and instructional personnel on sabbatical leave. The survey excluded graduate teaching assistants, among others. The sample was weighted to produce national estimates. This table is limited to only those faculty members and other personnel who did at least some teaching. Details may not add to totals because of rounding.

— Too few cases for a reliable estimate
* Includes medical schools
† Includes public liberal-arts, private 2-year, religious, and other specialized colleges and excludes medical schools

SOURCE: U. S. DEPARTMENT OF EDUCATION, "FACULTY AND INSTRUCTIONAL STAFF: WHO ARE THEY AND WHAT DO THEY DO?"

Employees in Colleges and Universities by Racial and Ethnic Group, Fall 1993

		U.S. citizens and resident aliens					Non-resident aliens	Race unknown
	Total	American Indian	Asian	Black	Hispanic	White		
Full-time								
Professional staff								
Faculty	545,706	1,997	25,269	25,658	12,076	468,770	10,829	1,107
Executive, administrative, managerial	137,834	726	2,243	12,232	3,580	118,651	246	156
Non-faculty professionals	355,554	1,723	15,434	33,373	11,044	284,226	9,209	545
Non-professional staff	744,416	4,783	19,088	147,811	47,260	520,664	3,628	1,182
Total	1,783,510	9,229	62,034	219,074	73,960	1,392,311	23,912	2,990
Part-time								
Professional staff								
Faculty	369,768	1,410	10,020	19,514	10,236	310,271	4,049	14,268
Executive, administrative, managerial	5,841	19	152	387	135	5,086	33	29
Instruction and research assistants	202,819	677	14,832	7,487	5,245	131,242	37,751	5,585
Non-faculty professionals	69,765	277	2,568	4,676	1,769	57,693	1,980	802
Non-professional staff	170,909	1,003	6,225	23,417	9,645	125,395	2,634	2,590
Total	819,102	3,386	33,797	55,481	27,030	629,687	46,447	23,274

SOURCE: U. S. DEPARTMENT OF EDUCATION

Apps. A and B reprinted from the 1997 *Chronicle of Higher Education Almanac* (26).

NOTES ON THE CONTRIBUTORS

Carrie Tirado Bramen is a professor of English at the State University of New York, Buffalo.

Johnnella E. Butler is a professor of American ethnic studies at the University of Washington.

C. L. Chua is a professor of English at California State University, Fresno.

Sandra Gunning is a professor of English and American culture at the University of Michigan, Ann Arbor.

María Herrera-Sobek is a professor of Chicano studies and holds the Luis Leal Endowed Chair in Chicano Studies at the University of California, Santa Barbara.

Ruth Y. Hsu is a professor of English at the University of Hawai'i, Manoa.

Sheila Minn Hwang is a graduate student in English at the University of California, Santa Barbara.

Annette Kolodny is a professor in the program in comparative cultural and literary studies at the University of Arizona, Tucson.

Shirley Geok-lin Lim is a professor of English and women's studies at the University of California, Santa Barbara, and chair professor of English at the University of Hong Kong.

Genaro Padilla is a professor of English and vice chancellor of undergraduate affairs at the University of California, Berkeley.

W. S. Penn is a professor of creative writing and literature of the Americas at Michigan State University.

Susana Chávez Silverman is a professor of Spanish at Pomona College.

Robyn Wiegman is a professor of English and women's studies at the University of California, Irvine.

John A. Williams has held distinguished professorships at City University of New York and Rutgers University, Newark.

Index